# Awaken Your Power!

## The Secret of Life Revealed - How Your Thoughts Create Your Reality

### Joe Rapisarda

**BALBOA.**
PRESS

A DIVISION OF HAY HOUSE

Balboa Press books may be ordered through booksellers or by contacting:

Balboa Press
A Division of Hay House
1663 Liberty Drive
Bloomington, IN 47403
www.balboapress.com
1-(877) 407-4847

Because of the dynamic nature of the Internet, any web addresses or links contained in this book may have changed since publication and may no longer be valid. The views expressed in this work are solely those of the author and do not necessarily reflect the views of the publisher, and the publisher hereby disclaims any responsibility for them.

The author of this book does not dispense medical advice or prescribe the use of any technique as a form of treatment for physical, emotional, or medical problems without the advice of a physician, either directly or indirectly. The intent of the author is only to offer information of a general nature to help you in your quest for emotional and spiritual well-being. In the event you use any of the information in this book for yourself, which is your constitutional right, the author and the publisher assume no responsibility for your actions.

Any people depicted in stock imagery provided by Thinkstock are models, and such images are being used for illustrative purposes only.
Certain stock imagery © Thinkstock.

Printed in the United States of America

ISBN: 978-1-4525-3954-6 (sc)
ISBN: 978-1-4525-3955-3 (hbk)
ISBN: 978-1-4525-3952-2 (e)
Library of Congress Control Number: 2011917688

Balboa Press rev. date: 11/23/2011

To my children, Ryan and Alexa, I hope when you grow up you choose to use the information in this book to create the life you want to live. It's a father's dream to see his children happy in life. The information in this book gives you the tools to create any life you desire. Remember that your thoughts are things; dream big positive dreams, believe they will happen, work toward them, and the reality will follow.

The knowledge of this book is also a gift to all of humanity. Anyone who is attracted to this material can learn these principles to achieve whatever they want in life. Your life is yours to create however you want it to be.

Also, I would like to give special thanks to Trevor Carrington of Skyline Designs for creating the cover artwork for this book.[1]

*"The future depends on what you do today."*
*—Mahatma Gandhi*

# Contents

# Preface

In my early thirties, I became interested in how the universe worked and the latent capacities human beings have dormant within themselves. I then decided to set out on a journey to find these secrets.

My journey started one day when I decided to try acupuncture. A nagging martial arts injury that my doctor was unable to fix convinced me to try something new. Something inside of me told me to try acupuncture. I had been told that acupuncture was the art of using little needles to stimulate unseen energy points in the skin. It works on the premise that an unseen energy system flows through our body, and injuries and diseases are caused when there are energy blockages in the body. Since I had never heard of this energy, I was fascinated. I asked Linda Li, the owner of the acupuncture place, what this energy was made of. She told me that the energy was made up of Qi (Chee). She said that Qi is the life force energy that makes up all things, and if I was interested in learning more, I could visit her mother, a Qigong master. I later found that Qigong means "energy work" and is a practice that works to balance the energy of the body.

I decided to visit her mother, Professor Huixian Chen, and then spent the next five years as her student learning about Qi and Qigong.[2] Qigong is similar to the popular practice of Tai Chi and is used to balance the energy with the body. Eastern medicine works under the principle that diseases are caused when a person's energy becomes unbalanced. Qigong works to restore the balance of energy within the body to promote good health and to expand awareness. Professor Chen had learned Qigong twenty years earlier in China when she had terminal cancer. When she was at her deepest despair, a stranger came up to her and told her about Qigong. She decided that she had nothing to lose and began practicing it every day. When she eventually went back to the hospital, the doctors informed her that a miracle had occurred. The cancer was gone! Since then, she has dedicated her life to teaching others about Qigong.

During my time with Professor Chen, I developed an insatiable appetite for knowledge about Qi—and how we might be able to use it to better our lives. I began to read every book on wisdom, spirituality, and holistic medicine I could find. I studied Einstein's theory of relativity and quantum physics to see if our science could show any supporting documentation for the things I was reading. In my search for this wisdom, I did not limit myself to any particular field of study. I allowed my search to take me wherever it was found in life. I began to see the same messages buried in seemingly unrelated texts.

One day, I came across a book that talked about the universal laws that affect life. These laws are based on energy and provide a structure for us to work with this energy in a way that can empower our lives. They teach that this energy is actually part of us—and that we can influence it to create the reality we desire. I felt as if I had discovered the secret to life! I was excited that I had profited from this search, but I wondered how many others would be willing to invest as many years reading the countless number of books I had to read to fully learn this amazing information. I decided that I must write a book that brought all this information together in a way that the reader understood and could immediately use. I felt this information had to be more easily shared with humanity. The universal laws state that you get what you give. This book is my attempt to share this collective information and give back to the world.

As a disclaimer, I would like to note that I am not a physicist or a doctor and that my views and opinions in this book are based on my own personal understanding and experiences with this material.

Before we proceed, I would like to share something that happened to me while I was writing this material. One night, I suddenly awoke with a flurry of creative thoughts running through my mind. As fast as I could, I wrote down the words to a poem that came to me. For the most part, I had never written a poem before. I am not sure if this inspiration was my own creativity or a gift from the unknown. The following poem, I feel, sums up this entire book and illustrates how to successfully use the universal laws—especially the law of attraction. I hope you will do as I have done and memorize this poem and say it to yourself daily. This poem has helped me countless times to remind myself to refocus my thoughts on what I wanted rather than whatever negative things I was experiencing and to use my feelings as a guide to see the direction I was headed. This poem is called "Thoughts are Things."[3]

## Thoughts are Things

Whatever you think, whatever you feel,
It doesn't matter if it's make-believe, or if it is real.
Thoughts are things that go out into the unknown
To bring you back whatever you've sown.
Positive thoughts vibrate high,
While negative thoughts vibrate low.
Just focus on your own thoughts to see how your future will go.
You see, your thoughts are a map of where you are headed,
And your feelings decide if that direction is welcome,
Or if it is dreaded.
So change how you think to change how you feel,
And watch how the universe attracts to you,
That which you have made real.

# Introduction

What if I told you that you could create your reality with your mind? I am not talking about making your dreams a reality through only hard work and action, but you also have the ability to actually affect the chance, coincidence, or lucky events that happen in your life by the way you think. Yes, you can create luck. Luck is defined as a force that brings good fortune or adversity.[4] This force that brings good fortune or adversity is within your control. This book will show you how to master this force and how to use it to create the life you want to live. You were meant to use your mind to influence the reality you experience.

What if I also told you that you already are creating with your mind and always have been? That's right—you have been creating your own reality all your life and probably didn't know it. It is time for humanity to begin consciously using this amazing power to take responsibility for creating their own reality. This book will teach you all the skills you need to be able to do that.

This book also teaches about the universal laws that apply to us all, whether we believe in them or not, and how we can learn to use them to our advantage to create the life we desire. Anything is possible with the universal laws. If you want to be rich, successful, healthy, happy, or find the love of your life, it can all happen by learning to master these laws in your life.

It is a belief of mine that at some point in our distant past mankind understood these laws and how to use them to better their lives. For one reason or another, over the years we must have forgotten about them, or a decision may have been made not to share them with the public. How else can we explain why this empowering information is not accepted and used by everyone on the planet today? It is easy to imagine that this information might have been hidden from the public in the past out of fear that its empowering content would be used for evil. Another possible reason for keeping this information a secret is that the rulers may have felt that empowered people would threaten their control over society. Regardless of the reason why this information has been kept a secret, the truth is that today it is available for anyone to use. Times have changed, and now you have the power to change too!

Not knowing these laws is like trying to play a game without knowing the rules or how they affect us. The truth is that we are playing a game, the game of life, and it is time again for us to relearn how to work with these laws to positively influence our own lives and the lives of those around us.

What if we could prevent or heal any illness? Anything is possible when we learn to use these laws to our advantage. Most of us don't realize that we have the ability to influence the future events that happen in our lives. The truth is that through our thoughts, words, and actions, we can—and do—influence our own lives every day, usually without knowing it.

This book is meant to be a guide to help those who are attracted to its empowering information. Although many people are drawn to this wisdom now, there are still others who are not yet ready for this material. Regardless of when it is needed, the knowledge of this book sits waiting, now and forever, for anyone who is attracted to it.

# How to Use This Book

*Part 1 is about energy, the universal laws, and how they apply to your life.* This explains how you can use these laws to your advantage to create the life you want to live.

*Part 2 shares "The Secrets of the Law of Attraction" and how you can use your thoughts to create your physical reality.* Discover, step-by-step, how to master the law of attraction, and how to overcome the roadblocks to manifestation that many people encounter.

*Part 3 is "Your Thirty-Day Empowerment Program."* Learn how to take the necessary steps in your life to evolve from being someone who has life happen to them into someone that creates their life as they desire it to be. Your thirty-day empowerment program will show you how to think, say, and do things that attract the type of positive energy into your life that allows you to make your dreams become reality.

*Part 4 demonstrates how to use the universal laws in everyday situations of life.* This is meant to be a reference guide on how use the universal laws during different life experiences.

I recommend that you read this book once to get a general understanding of this knowledge. Then go back and reread it; you will find that each time you reread this material, you will learn something new and get a deeper understanding of the material.

# Part 1:
# Energy and the Universal Laws

# Chapter 1: The Universal Laws

What are the universal laws? I first discovered the universal laws in *The Light Shall Set You Free* by Dr. Norma Milanovich and Dr. Shirley McCune.[5] These laws were not created by man or governments—they are universal laws of nature and energy. As we will discuss in this book, science has discovered that everything in our existence is made up of energy. This energy consists of the formless energy we don't see, and the solid matter that we do.

Most of us go through life adapting to life as it happens to us. It appears that we were not meant to live life that way. It appears that we were meant to be much more; we were meant to be powerful creators of our own life experiences. We were meant to create our reality *before* we experienced it. This entire book is about learning how to work with this energy and use it creatively to create the reality we desire. The universal laws are our instruction manual that shows us how to create whatever reality we wish to experience.

When I first learned about these laws, I wondered why I hadn't heard of most of them before—and whether there was any truth to these laws being able to affect my life. Since I am a pretty open-minded person, I decided to look into them further. When I searched online for "universal laws," I found many references to them.[6] My next step was to test them over a period of time to see if they were indeed working in my life. Over the next four years, I was amazed to find that these universal laws were true, accurate, and working in my life. I then went on to learn how to use these laws to my advantage to create the type of life I wanted to live.

It should be noted that I have modified the order that the universal laws were originally listed, and the definitions of the universal laws listed in this book are my interpretations of their meaning based on the definitions listed in *The Light Shall Set You Free* and my own life experiences with these laws. Also, I changed the name of the first law from the law of divine oneness to the law of oneness in an attempt to appeal to all people—even those who are not religious.

# 1. The Law of Oneness

This law states that everything in our existence is made up of the same universal energy.

> Human beings and all living things are a coalescence of energy in a field of energy connected to every other thing in the world. This pulsating energy field is the central engine of our being and our consciousness, the alpha and the omega of our existence.[7]

In physics, the law of conservation of energy states that energy cannot be created or destroyed, but it can change forms. This means that energy can be formless or take the form of anything solid. Everything in our existence is just a different manifestation of the same energy. If this is true, then everything in our existence is also connected to—and is—part of us. Everything is part of us, and we are part of everything. The plants, trees, rocks, animals, and the planet—everything is made up of the same fabric of life, which is energy.

In Eastern religious teachings, Buddha stated that the world is but an illusion. Was he alluding to the fact that he understood that everything in our existence is the temporary physical manifestations of the same universal energy? I believe he was.

In the section on quantum physics, we discuss how Einstein's theory of relativity and formula $E=mc^2$ show that energy is the building block of everything in our existence. We will also discuss how scientists describe the quantum phenomenon called entanglement where two particles that have previously interacted are somehow able to stay invisibly connected to each other regardless of how much time or distance is between them. Both of these principles give scientific support to the claim that our entire existence is made up of connected energy. This is the law of oneness.

All too often, man sees his actions as singular acts with no consequences. The truth is that every thought, emotion, word, or action has a definite impact on the environment, the planet, and the entire universe. If everything and everyone is made up of the same energy, then anything we do to anything else will affect how that energy is affected.

The North American Indians understood this principle and saw everything in nature as a family member. They had respect for the land. They harvested only what they needed. When they hunted and killed an animal, they gave respect and thanks to the animal for providing them with the food they needed to live. They loved Mother Nature and understood the energy within the earth.

An excellent example of the balance of nature as an ecosystem is *Avatar*. The earthlike planet in this movie shows how all life is interconnected and interdependent on each other. Whether we realize it or not, earth is a very similar planet where each system within it is codependent on the other for the overall health of the planet. When these systems get out of balance, the planet gets sick. Ironically this is the same reason our own bodies get sick. Whenever we get out of balance through abuse or neglect, our bodies begin to break down and diseases manifest.

Unfortunately, modern man has not been as respectful as the Indians were. Today we are seeing signs of man's negligent actions toward our planet. Years of selfish actions have led to pollution, deforestation, and abuse of our planet. Man has failed to understand that the entire planet is an ecosystem that relies on the balance of nature to flourish. Our neglectful actions have made our planet become out of balance, and we see the effects of this destabilization in melting polar ice caps, massive earthquakes, and ever-increasing tsunamis around the world. The good news is that society seems to be becoming aware of this situation and is making attempts to rebalance the planet by taking such measures as reducing pollution and reforestation. Even so, it will take a concerted effort to correct this balance for our planet and ourselves.

The law of oneness also applies to us as individuals. How we treat each other—and the things around us—has a definite impact on everything in our existence, especially ourselves. Think about it—when you are nice to people, aren't most people nice back to you? When you are friendly to a dog, doesn't the dog usually respond in a friendly manner? In most cases, the answer is yes. Our actions toward others directly affect our experiences with those we interact with. So the next time you see nature, try appreciating it as part of yourself. Respect it, and it may respect you. Create a better life by choosing to be more friendly and open to those you meet and watch how they will be more open with you. The law of oneness says that everything is connected—your actions with others will have the same effect on you.

# 2. The Law of Vibration

The law of vibration states that everything in the universe is made of vibrating energy. The form of an object is a result of its vibration. This energy can take the form of non-physical energy, or it can take the form of physical matter. In *The Light Shall Set You Free,* the law of vibration is described as:

> Everything in the universe is in motion, whether solid, liquid, or gas. All things move, vibrate, and travel in circular patterns. Each thing that exists is identified by its own unique vibrational frequency. Frequency is defined as the number of periodic oscillations, vibrations, or waves per unit of time. No two things in the universe are truly identical, because each has its unique vibrational pattern. The differences between matter and energy are explained primarily by the differences in these vibratory motions. Phenomena, such as light, heat, magnetism, electricity, and sound are forms of vibratory motion, just as trees, desks, flowers, and animals are.[8]

Let's review that again. What makes one thing different from another is how this energy takes form. Energy takes different forms by vibrating at different frequencies. Each different thing you experience has its own unique vibrational frequency or signature.[9] "Vibrational frequency is defined as the rate at which the atoms and subatomic particles of a being or object vibrate. The higher this vibrational frequency is, the closer it is to the frequency of light."[10]

The law of vibration is a key fundamental basis for understanding that energy can manifest into different things based on the vibration of the subatomic particles. Everything in our physical world is just energy taking physical form by vibrating at different vibrational frequencies. In *The Hidden Messages in Water,* Masaru Emoto states:

> Existence is vibration. The entire universe is in a state of vibration and each thing generates its own frequency, which is unique.[11]

Let's imagine that you could reduce your body to microscopic size, and that you set off on an exploration to discover the secrets of this universe called you. You would soon see that each thing consists of nothing more than atoms, each atom being a nucleus with electrons rotating around it. The number and shape of these electrons and their orbits give each substance a particular set of vibrational frequencies. You would discover that whatever the substance, nothing is solid. Instead there is only a nucleus surrounded by an endlessly rotating wave. Everything is eternally moving and vibrating—on and off, at an incredible speed.[12]

> Human beings are also vibrating, and each individual vibrates at a unique frequency. Each one of us has the sensory skills necessary to feel the vibrations of others.[13]
> All things vibrate, and they vibrate at their own frequencies.[14]

Once we accept that everything is energy, we can begin to understand how to positively affect the energy in our world.

We can also control our own vibrational frequency based on the thoughts, words, and actions that we choose. In *Frequency,* Penny Peirce states:

> Your personal vibration—the frequency of energy you hold moment by moment in your body, emotions, and mind—is the most important tool you have for creating and living your ideal life. If your frequency is high, fast, and clear, life unfolds effortlessly and in alignment with your destiny, while a lower, slower, more distorted frequency begets a life of snags and disappointments.[15]

Here are a few more detailed working terms that physicists use to describe frequency:

> *Wavelength* is the distance between successive peaks or successive troughs of the waves. The *frequency* refers to the number of up-and-down cycles of oscillation that a wave completes every second. It turns out that the frequency is determined by the wavelength and vice versa: longer wavelengths imply lower frequency; shorter wavelengths imply higher frequency. Finally, physicists use the term

*amplitude* to describe the maximum height or depth of a wave.[16]

If you're not a physicist, then these terms may seem overwhelming. This next section on resonance should help to make the concept of vibrational frequency a little easier to understand.

## Resonance

What is resonance? Resonance is when one vibrational frequency aligns with and acts on another like-type frequency. It has been called "sympathetic vibration" because when one frequency is vibrating, it causes other like-type frequencies to vibrate along with it.[17] Masaru Emoto gives a wonderfully simple definition of resonance in *The Miracle of Water*:

> Resonance is simply the act of vibration resulting in more vibration. It requires the interaction of two complementary objects or energies.[18]
>
> Perhaps when you were a child, you conducted an experiment using two tuning forks. When one tuning fork is struck to make a vibrating sound, the other tuning fork placed nearby starts to make the same sound. This is resonance, and in order for it to work, the two objects need to have the same number of vibrations; they need to be on the same frequency. If the two tuning forks are of different frequencies, no matter how hard you strike one, it won't have any effect on the other.
>
> It's not hard to see why something vibrates when you strike it, but it takes some thinking to understand why one object vibrates when you strike a completely separate object. It's a simple experiment, but it is eloquent in expressing the fundamental characteristics of energy.
>
> Let me explain this more thoroughly. If vibration is energy, then resonance is the reverberation of energy, and resonance is thus capable of relaying energy.[19]

There are many types of resonance, but let's use an example of acoustical resonance. If you take two guitars both tuned the same and place them side by side, when you pluck the C string on one guitar, you will see the C string on the other guitar start to vibrate as well.[20]

I believe the principle of resonance gives us scientific support of how the law of attraction and other universal laws work in our lives. When the energy of one frequency is emitted, it aligns with and interacts with other like-type vibrational frequencies. I would dare to say that alignment and attraction are meant to be the same thing. Because both terms mean the joining of two frequencies. With the law of attraction, you are aligning your vibrational frequency, through your thoughts, words, and actions, with the vibrational frequency of whatever you desire. This is what I believe is meant when the law of attraction states that you attract what you think about. I think it means that you align with the frequency of whatever you desire, which, of course, has the same effect as attracting it to you. Let's take a look at how this might apply to everyday life.

Have you ever talked to someone that you had just met, and the entire conversation just felt right? You were comfortable listening to her; what she said corresponded to your beliefs; and everything just seemed to flow for the both of you. You were both on the same vibrational frequency. You were aligned. This is where the saying, "What she said really *resonated* with me," comes from. This means you related to what she was saying because it *felt* right to you.

Resonance happens to you when someone or something's energy matches your vibrational frequency. This can be good or bad—depending on what energy you are attracting. Being human with a consciousness, you have the ability to choose your thoughts, words, and actions. You get to choose the energy (vibrational frequency) that you want to emit to the world. The law of attraction says that other like-type energies will be attracted to you in the same way the plucked C on one guitar makes the same C vibrate on another guitar in the same room. I feel that resonance gives us an understandable example of how energy attracts to us, and also acts as a reminder for us to be conscious of our thoughts and the energy that we attract to ourselves. The simplest way to always attract positive energy is to always think and do positive things.

## Morphic Resonance

Morphic resonance is the idea that the thoughts, words, or actions of one person are added to the universal consciousness in a morphic field that is able be absorbed and used by others with the same vibrational frequency—regardless of time or distance between the parties, or even if they know of each other.

> The British biologist Rupert Sheldrake gives us an example of how written spoken words can have an effect on other unrelated people all over the world. According to his theory of "morphic resonance," when a person begins something new, if it's good and wholesome then the words of that person will go to other people who have similar consciousnesses.[21]

Sheldrake then listed an experiment where he divided fans of the *London Times* crossword puzzle into two groups. One group did the crossword puzzle the day they got the paper. The other group waited a least a day before doing the crossword puzzle. He found that the people who waited until later to do the crossword puzzle did significantly better than those who did it right away. Sheldrake credited morphic resonance for this improved difference in results. He felt the knowledge of the first group discovering the answers helped the second group to do even better—even though the second group was not consciously aware of the first group, or the answers they found.

The effects of morphic resonance are far reaching. This could be considered by some as scientific support for the power of prayer, meditation, and psychic skills like ESP. There have been stories of groups of people going to cities and praying for peace for a month straight. After the group left each city, statistics showed that the crime rates had decreased.

Morphic resonance applies the law of vibration to the law of oneness. It supports that everything is connected, and that every thought, word, and action affects the universe as a whole. Think of the impact of this knowledge. If our good deeds add energy to a collective consciousness, then one good deed could indirectly help many others through this energy. A prayer of hope could be received by countless others who are seeking hope. An act of kindness can influence others on the other side of the world to show compassion. A technological breakthrough by one scientist can help other scientists on the other side of the world make a similar or even better breakthrough. Conversely, an act of hate or revenge can affect others the same way. The law of oneness says we are all one. Morphic resonance appears to show us how our personal vibration affects the concept of oneness.

In summary, the law of vibration is a key element to understanding that we are vibrational beings. We can choose the thoughts we want to think, which determines how we vibrate. Our ability to choose what we think—rather than just acting on instinct—is what sets us apart from most, if not all, of the other life forms on our planet. This ability to choose energy allows us to create what we desire by resonating or aligning with the energy we desire. Once we start to understand that the vibration we choose determines the life we attract, we are able to stop living life as it happens to us and can start living life by our own design. Each day when you wake up, ask yourself, "How do I feel today? Am I feeling positive and optimistic, or am I feeling negative in some way." Your feelings are a direct indicator of your vibrational frequency. If you are feeling positive emotions, then your vibration is resonating with—and attracting—positive energy. If you are feeling negative emotions, then your vibration is resonating with—and attracting—negative energy. It's that simple. If you are feeling negative, stop and take a few minutes to focus on some positive aspect of your life or on the positive things you want to have. Once you feel the good feeling, then you will know your vibration is in the right place.

## 3. The Law of Attraction

The law of attraction is often touted as the most important and powerful of the universal laws. It is arguably the most popular of the universal laws. If you only learn one thing from this book, I would suggest that you learn about the law of attraction. It has the power to completely change your life.

The law of attraction states that energy attracts other like-type energy. This means that positive energy will attract more positive energy, and negative energy will attract more negative energy. The law of oneness states that everything—including thoughts, words, and actions—is energy. Since we can control our thoughts, which create our words and actions, we can also control the type of energy we attract to ourselves. We have the power to create with our minds; the thoughts we think create the life we live.

Many people live life as it happens to them rather than creating it to be the way they desire. When negative events happen to them, they often blame others. This book is about teaching humanity that we all have a direct input in the creative aspect of our own lives. We can influence how things "happen" in our lives. When we think positive thoughts long enough, positive things begin to happen to us. When we think negative thoughts long enough, negative things begin to happen to us. Nothing in our existence is there without our vibrational input.

So the next time you are having a bad day and the world seems to be against you at every turn, stop and think, "Could I be attracting these events in my life?" The solution may be as simple as no longer focusing on what is negative—focus on and appreciate the positive things. Conversely, the next time you're having a great day, stop and appreciate it by giving yourself a pat on the back for having been in a positive vibrational frequency to attract this positive day into your life. The events you experience today were created by your past vibration and tomorrow's events are being created right now by your current vibration——whether you realize it or not.

If you are happy with your life, take a minute to appreciate it, and keep thinking happy thoughts to attract new positive energy into your life, which will allow your happiness to continue. If you want your life to change for the better, stop thinking about negative things you are experiencing, and start thinking about what you want your life to be like. The universe feels your vibration and responds by sending you the same type of energy—so focus on how you feel. When you feel good, you are in a state of positive vibration. When you feel negative feelings such as fear, anger, or worry, you are in a state of negative vibration, and therefore are not attracting positive things into your life. The law of attraction sees your focus as your desire or request, and your feelings are your indicator of what type of energy you are attracting. The following is an example of how I first learned about the law of attraction.

## A Back Injury Introduces the Law of Attraction

I had my first conscious experience with the law of attraction when I hurt my back years ago doing Jiu-Jitsu (the martial art of submission grappling). Jiu-Jitsu is like a wrestling chess match where each person attempts to physically outwit the other, and lure them into a position where they can be defeated with a specific submission technique. I was grappling a younger, stronger opponent who was trying to use his strength rather than technique to win. This forced me to use more effort than I normally did. My opponent was on top of me while I was on my back facing up. In order to counter this position, I arched my back while pulling him up and over me so that we both rolled over and reversed our positions. When I did this move, I felt something twinge in my lower back. I brushed it off and finished the match. My back felt funny, but I felt okay at the time. When I got out of bed the next morning, my back was very sore. Foolishly, I did some stretching exercises and applied heat to it. This inflamed the joints of my lower back, and began one of the most debilitating injuries of my life. As the swelling increased, any movement of my lower body sent lightning streaks of pain shooting down my legs. On a scale of one to ten, the pain streaks were a level ten. For the next month, I was limited to the fetal position in what I called a "pocket of peace" because it didn't hurt as bad in that position. If I turned over or adjusted my position, I experienced the shooting pains all over again. I had to sleep on the floor because the bed wasn't firm enough and caused the sharp pains to happen regularly.

I was unable to work—and was limited to moving around on my hands and knees because I could not stand up or walk upright. During this time off, my mother bought me two books that changed my life forever. *The Secret* and Lance Armstrong's *It's Not About the Bike: My Journey Back to Life* held examples of people using their minds to heal from incurable diseases or impairments with little explanation from modern medicine on how they were able to be healed. Since I was in so much pain, I was initially reluctant to read the books. However, as the days went by, I often had nothing to do but read or watch TV. Before long, I began to read these books and was amazed at the miracles that had happened. I figured that if these people could use their minds to heal themselves, I could too. This was my introduction to the law of attraction. I decided right then and there that I was going to mentally commit myself to getting better. From that point on, I refused to let any doubt, worry, or fear enter my mind. Believe me—this was not easy. I just focused on my back getting better. I didn't know how it was going to happen, but I was going to do my part mentally to heal it.

My only focus or desire was to become healthy again. I had to be honest with myself based on how I was feeling. I was in constant pain. I couldn't tell if the nerves in my back were permanently injured, or if they were just being temporarily squeezed or pinched by the inflammation and swelling. I knew that it was no way for anyone to live. I became determined to do whatever I could to get better—and fast! I wondered how it would be possible for me to be healed. I had my doubts at first because at that time I believed that I had to know exactly how it was possible to be healed for it to actually be a possibility in my life. After reading *The Secret* again, I understood and trusted that I didn't need to know how it was possible to be healed. I only needed to focus on being healed. The universe would do the rest.

I also read about Emil Coue, a mental pioneer at the beginning of the twentieth century, who felt that most illnesses were caused by our thinking. Over the next few weeks, I repeated his daily affirmation—"Every day, in every way, I'm getting better and better!"—thousands of times in my head until I eventually started feeling better. I believe that I mentally willed myself to get better.

When I did the affirmations, I saw myself as fully healed with a strong back and as able to bend forward, backward, and side to side. I developed tunnel vision, and envisioned my back getting better each day. I added passion of thinking about how good it felt to have my back healed. This was an added challenge since I was still experiencing a lot of pain in reality. It took a lot of willpower to focus on the good feeling that I desired rather than the pain I was experiencing. In my mind, I saw the finished product of my healed back—and was just waiting for it to show up in my reality. I had erased the doubt, and believed my back would somehow be healed.

It took longer than I expected to see results. I had expected to see immediate results. I didn't know at the time that there is often a delay between the time you desire something and when it shows up.[22] I expected to see gains each day from crawling, to kneeling, to walking, to finally running. In reality, it took a while to see any results—but the results did finally come. There were many days that I saw little or no gains at all. It was difficult to stay focused and not let doubt creep in. However, I knew I could not live the rest of my life in such horrible pain. I had no choice but to believe a miraculous healing was possible. During this process, I developed a sincere empathy and compassion for anyone who suffers from a chronic illness or deals with daily pain. I never appreciated my good health as much as when it was gone. Fortunately, I was motivated and passionate about finding a way out of my situation. I realized that doubt, frustration, or worry about the fact that my health had not yet recovered would mentally sabotage my recovery. Even without results, I continued to imagine seeing and feeling my healed back. I expected it to show up in my life and, like an expectant family dog, I was willing to mentally sit by the door, and wait for it to come home to me.

Slowly but surely, I began to see results. First, I was able to get a better range of movement on the ground without great pain. Then I was able to get to my knees—and then to my feet—but bent over to protect my back the way an old man would walk with a cane. With the help of crutches, I was able to hobble to my doctor's appointments. I visited the doctor, chiropractor, acupuncturist, and physical therapist. I was open-minded and motivated to get better. I was in a frame of mind where I would try anything if I thought it would help.

When I first visited the physical therapist, I was in a wheelchair. He was very understanding and helpful. He gave me some really simple back exercises. When I went home, I did the exercises, and tried to push my body as much as I could without overdoing it and reinjuring myself. This is the action part of my manifestation. Each day I wanted to do a little bit better than before. Believe it or not, I started getting better quickly! I could feel the healing momentum building.

Amazingly, two weeks later, I was able to walk to my next appointment. The physical therapist's face could not hide his surprised look. After going through some movement exercises, he said that I didn't need to see him anymore. He asked what I had been doing to heal so fast. I told him about the law of attraction. He said, "Well, whatever you are doing, keep it up because you healed in record time."

After that visit, I was able to go back to work and live a normal life again. It took another year for my back to regain its normal strength, but I just felt grateful that it healed at all because I know how injured it was.

In life, we can choose what we desire, but we can't always choose how that desire will manifest in our lives. Was this just a temporary injury that healed itself—or had I successfully used the law of attraction to heal myself? I choose to believe I was able to use the law of attraction to help heal myself. Since then, I have successfully used the law of attraction in every other aspect of my life. This experience taught me about the law of attraction, and how to use it in my daily life.

# 4. The Law of Action

> *"Opportunities multiply as they are seized."*
> —*Sun Tzu*

The law of action gives the law of attraction an opportunity to manifest. Once you decide what you desire, it can help to apply action to your desires because the energy that you are attracting will come to you in the path of least resistance. If you are actively working toward your desires, then you are giving the law of attraction a way to manifest in your life.

When working toward your goal, it can be tricky deciding exactly how to apply action. You can "will" things to happen by applying action to your goal in the way you see fit. This is how I have always done things in the past. I have always been goal-oriented, and felt that if something was going to happen for me, it would be because of my actions. This approach works—but it is also forceful and is not always the best way to manifest things. This method uses the power of the will. This simply means that you take action to make your goal a reality rather than waiting for any other force to assist with the creation.

A better way to use the law of attraction is to ask for your desire, and then allow it to happen. By doing nothing, you *allow* ideas to pop into your head or opportunities to arise in your life. Once you see opportunities and intuitively *feel* the time is right, you can then apply *action* to make them grow. When you try to impose your will on a manifestation, you only give it one way (your way) to manifest for you; however, when you sit back and allow it to happen, you give the universe an infinite number of ways to manifest your desire for you. In the second part of this book, we discuss the three minds and how they relate to the law of attraction. We discuss how the universe (the superconscious mind) knows everything, including which is the best way for your desire to come to you. So relax and let it come to you.

I want to be clear here—I am not saying that you shouldn't work toward your goals. On the contrary, work or action is almost always necessary in seeing your goals succeed. Be more patient about when and how to act. Keep an open mind and let your intuition tell you when to act. If you grow impatient waiting for it, you can definitely start working on it yourself, but it would be wise of you to be open-minded about how and when your desire might manifest in your life.

Action gives focus to your desire. Focus is alignment. Alignment is what makes the desire manifest. We have control over our thoughts, words, and actions; when we use all of them together toward achieving our desires, we add extra focus and energy toward our goal of manifesting our desires. This added focus helps our desires to manifest sooner.

When using the law of attraction, how you feel inside is even more important than the action you put forth. If you are not in a good emotional state, your actions are unlikely to produce the results you want because your personal vibration will not be a vibrational match to your desire. When your mind is feeling positive emotions, such as anticipation and happiness, your actions can work miracles. When your mind is not in the right place by feeling doubt or fear, no amount of action can overcome this misalignment to your desire. Actions can be good or bad—depending on your mind frame and personal vibration. The bottom line is you must be aligned with your desire. Only then can your actions help you achieve your goal.

The law of action also helps to build momentum in your life. Good momentum is a powerful force that allows you to realize your dreams rapidly. Momentum happens when you experience a success, then another success follows, and then another, and another, and still more until you can look back on where you started and see great growth and progress. The following is an example of the law of action.

## A Fitness Program Uses Action to Build Momentum

I experienced the momentum of the law of action when I did the "Body for Life" fitness program in 2003. I wasn't badly out of shape, but I wanted to lose a few pounds to look and feel better. The "Body for Life" is a twelve-week program that includes weights, cardio training, and diet. The program is a good one, but it is difficult in the beginning. The hardest part was the first few weeks when I was sore and adjusting to a new way of life. During the first stage, I was excited at the prospect of a positive change in my fitness.

The first results I noticed were not in how I looked—it was how I felt. I felt changes in my body. I was feeling healthier, stronger, and more fit. Although I was bit sore and tired, it also felt good that my whole body felt like it was improving. This was puzzling because I could not see any change in the way I looked. I just felt good on the inside. My confidence was beginning to brim with expectation of what my body was going to look like when I was done. Each day I felt better about what I was doing for myself. I noticed that I had cut out the unhealthy food from my diet and ate correctly six out of seven days. As part of the program, I gave myself a cheat day to enjoy whatever I wanted with a dose of moderation. The cheat day was a great way to have a day off, but still stay on track with the program.

Before long, I could feel that momentum was starting to build. I was on a streak. I was feeling great and starting to see results in my muscles. It felt good to be working toward a goal. During the first seven weeks, I felt great, but I only saw minimal results. After the seventh week, I saw a dramatic change in the way I looked too. In what seemed like overnight, I started to lose the unwanted fat and replaced it with firm, toned muscle. I loved how this made me feel. The momentum was firmly in place. At first, I felt good, but now I was looking good too!

It's funny how feeling good can change your life. Once I felt good about how I looked, I felt better about myself as a whole. I have always been confident in myself, but this change was evident to everyone around me. I could feel the momentum working in my life—and I felt like there was nothing I couldn't do. I felt like Superman! Consequently, this momentum carried over to my personal life, my social life, and my career. It seemed to attract others who wanted to know what I had done to get the results I had experienced. Being fit is an amazing feeling that everyone should be able to experience. I remember thinking that this is how wonderful life should feel all the time.

At the end of my program, although I didn't win any awards, I was very pleased with the results—not only in my fitness, but in my life as a whole.

Momentum is a wonderful thing to experience, but I have noticed that many of us, including myself, sometimes do things that prevent momentum from happening for us. What do I mean? We start a diet, but we give up after a week and binge at the nearest fast food restaurant. When you focus on a desire, do yourself a favor and—once you get momentum going—don't let it slip away by choosing actions that don't complement your goal.

The law of action builds momentum. Momentum is like a surfer trying to catch a wave. You can feel the wave building beneath you—as it swells up, you have the opportunity to jump on it and ride it to your goal or you can just sit there and let the wave gently roll by. The choice is always yours.

The next time you feel momentum in your life—from hard work or by coincidence—ride it for what it is worth.

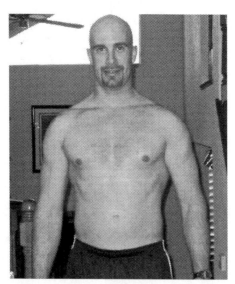

**Figure 1: In 2003, at the completion of the three-month fitness program. It felt great to be in shape!**

# 5. The Law of Cause and Effect (Karma)

The law of cause and effect states that the energy you give out will always return to you. This law is also known as karma. In simple terms, this law states that your actions will eventually come back to you in one way or another. If you are positive and do good deeds for others, you will attract that type of positive energy back to yourself, which will create more pleasant experiences. If you think or do negative things, you will attract that type of negative energy and those negative experiences.

This law is perfect because it attracts to a person the same type of energy they give out. It rewards good deeds and, when necessary, seeks justice for negative actions. In reality, there is no justice or punishment. The universe is simply seeking to restore the balance of energy by attracting to you the same type of energy you give out. Each person is in control of how their life will play out based on the thoughts, words, and actions they produce.

People often think they have to correct the behavior of others who act differently than they feel is appropriate. When we seek to control or correct someone else's actions, we are choosing thoughts, words, and actions that determine the energy that we attract to ourselves. For example, if we try to tell someone that they are doing something wrong, and they in turn disagree and start a fight with us, we have just chosen to align our energy with their negativity.

Do we really want to attract this type of negative energy? Knowing that our actions attract the same energy, why would we choose to interfere with someone else's actions? Obviously there are times—such as with family or loved ones—when it is necessary for you to get involved with their actions, but for the most part in life, it is better to stay out of other people's affairs. Whatever they are doing is their business and their actions—good or bad—will eventually return to them in the energy they gave out. There is no need for our interference because the law is perfect in restoring balance to nature.

Let's look at an example of how the cause-and-effect nature of someone's actions affects their life.

## Bad Luck Chuck

I knew a man who I will call Chuck. Chuck always seemed to be fighting the world. He had experienced a tough childhood, and his family life growing up was less than desired. These early experiences made Chuck angry at the world—he felt that he had to fight for everything he wanted. This taught Chuck to be combative with others. Chuck felt that the world owed him. He felt that he was entitled to things without working for them. He was bitter and angry that he hadn't had a better childhood. He was angry he didn't have someone to love him. He was angry he didn't have more money. Whenever Chuck didn't have something, he blamed others for why he didn't have it in his life. In fact, Chuck felt that others were to blame for all his misfortunes in life. Never once did he consider that he might be creating his own reality with the thoughts, words, and actions that he was choosing.

One day Chuck went to the doctor's office and was forced, like many people, to wait for what seemed like a long time before being seen. After a half hour passed, he went up to the receptionist, and demanded in a loud voice that he be seen immediately. When the receptionist was not able to help him, Chuck insisted on talking to her supervisor. When the supervisor came to talk to him, Chuck began to yell at her, insisting he be seen immediately. The supervisor asked Chuck to return to his seat and to calm down. She informed him the doctor was running behind schedule; there were others who had been waiting longer than he had who needed to be seen first. In a rage, he stated that he wouldn't tolerate being treated that way and walked out of the office. The problem was that Chuck had an ear infection that desperately required medical attention. At the time, Chuck did not realize how his impatience would affect his health. Chuck went home angry, and his ear infection got worse. Days later, Chuck, out of necessity, called for another doctor's appointment. By the time Chuck was finally able to be seen by the doctor, his health had deteriorated to the point where he had to be admitted to the hospital. Chuck ended up spending a few days in the hospital before his health began to return to normal. He blamed his stay in the hospital on the doctor who had originally made him wait.

Another time, Chuck checked into a hotel while on vacation. He had made reservations online before his trip, but the receptionist informed him that the room he had booked was not available—but another one just like it was open if he wanted it. Instead of agreeing with the situation, Chuck went into offensive mode. Throughout his life, he had learned that he could often get his way if he made a scene by yelling and making others uncomfortable. His antics often made others feel it was easier to give him what he wanted than to continue to deal with him. Chuck raised his voice to the receptionist and insisted on the exact room he had booked. When that didn't work, he asked to speak to her supervisor. He asked the supervisor for his room to be upgraded at no additional cost. The supervisor informed Chuck that it was not possible, but he would give him a twenty-five-dollar voucher for dinner at the hotel restaurant. Chuck dismissed the offer, and told the supervisor that he would take his business elsewhere. He left and went to find another hotel. What Chuck didn't realize was that this was a busy time of year, and all the other hotels were booked. After unsuccessfully trying to book another hotel, Chuck ended up settling for a lesser *motel* on the edge of town where he continued to brood about the miserable experience he was having on this trip. He wondered how such bad luck could always seem to follow him around.

What happened to Chuck? His life has been one bad experience after another. He blames the world for his problems when, in reality, he is the one who is creating every experience he has. He does not realize that his thoughts lead to the words and actions that he chooses to use. Those thoughts, words, and actions work to co-create the events he experience in his life.

If Chuck had chosen to be patient at the doctor's office, he would have been seen that day, and gotten the necessary medication. He would have avoided the painful and costly hospital stay—and he would have avoided the fight with the staff and the jaded feeling that the doctors were all incompetent. If he had chosen to be patient and understanding and wait like the other patients, he could have controlled his outcome, which would have allowed him to be happier. The law of cause and effect says that you get the energy you give. When Chuck chose to respond negatively and with anger, it attracted more of the same energy back to him, which led to an unwanted hospital visit.

When he tried to check into the first hotel, he had the option to be understanding and agreeable with the hotel receptionist, but he chose to use negative energy to argue and fight with her and her supervisor. The law of cause and effect brought back more of that negative energy to Chuck and he found that his hotel experience continued to be negative. Had Chuck been more easygoing and agreeable, he would have been able to stay in the hotel he wanted—and he would have gotten the dinner voucher! Chuck would be wise to learn one simple lesson: Those who do not learn from their mistakes are destined to relive them until they do.

Do you know anyone like Chuck? Most of us do. People like Chuck always seem to be looking to others for their happiness. They never consider that they may be creating their own problems by the way they interact with others and how they choose their thoughts, words, and actions.

The law of cause and effect is simple. It is like a mirror—it reflects the same type of energy you give out. It is important to realize that we are, in fact, in control of how our lives are played out. We have the choice of creating positive or negative energy with our thoughts, words, and actions. Be good to yourself and follow the Golden Rule: "Do unto others as you would have them do to you."

It is hard to deny that our actions play a part in how our lives are experienced. Just ask Chuck. As I said earlier, these laws work with or without your belief in them. Whether you choose to believe in them or not, you should realize that your actions determine the reality of your experience. By taking responsibility for yourself and your actions, you are taking responsibility for your own happiness.

## 6. The Law of Compensation

*If you are always in the giving state of mind, you will always be in the receiving state of mind.*

The law of compensation is about giving and receiving. It states that when we give, we receive that same energy ten times greater. Energy moves in a circular motion and the energy you give always comes back to you. Are you starting to see a trend with energy about giving and receiving? The law of compensation is about gaining abundance in our lives and having success.

If you want to have abundance, you can have it. So can everyone else who desires it. The law of compensation says that there is never a shortage of energy; therefore, there is never a shortage of whatever you desire.

You may be wondering if there is so much abundance, then why are there so many shortages in our world? We have shortages of food, oil, love, money, and just about everything else. The reason why there is still so much shortage and suffering in this world is because the world does not yet realize that they have the power to create with their minds. They have experienced so much shortage in life because their reality has taught them that there is a limited supply of what they want. This creates a focus on the lack or shortage of what they want. This focus turns into a vibration that the law of attraction sees as what they want and it brings more of that to them.

I have great compassion for anyone who suffers from a lack of anything. We should all live abundant lives. Once a shortage of anything becomes a reality in our lives, it takes a strong will to focus on the future we desire instead of the lack of whatever we are currently experiencing.

If you want financial riches, they can be yours. Any type of abundance can be yours. You just need to learn how to use the law of compensation correctly. All you need to do is create a belief about what you want.

Abraham of Abraham-Hicks teaches that a belief is just a practiced thought. This means a belief is a thought that is repeated. You can create your own belief by just repeating whatever it is you want to create and expecting it to happen. If you want to be wealthy, repeat, "I am abundantly wealthy now." To add the power of the law of attraction to this, you must feel the positive feeling of what it feels like to have that money.

The secret to an abundant life is believing it is possible—and then learning to give back to yourself and others so that you can continue receiving abundance. Giving attracts and resonates with the same energy you wish to get. Giving can be money, love, attention, support, understanding, or anything else that helps you or any other living being.

Develop a feeling of appreciation for the things you already have and the good feeling inside that you get when you give to others and to yourself. The good feeling that comes from giving allows you to know that you are in alignment with your desires and ready to receive this same energy. This step is important because if you give—but are giving in a feeling of fear, sorrow, resentment, or any other negative energy state—the law of compensation will not bring you what you desire because you will not be a vibrational match to it. Just allow good things to come to you. When your desire arrives, make sure to give an acknowledgement for its manifestations—and then continue giving to continue receiving.

Giving doesn't necessarily mean giving money. Giving comes from the heart. It means helping others when the opportunity arises by doing any action that helps any other living thing. You don't need a plan to do certain actions. In fact, it usually works better if you give as the situation presents itself. Because energy is circular in nature, if you are always in the giving state of mind, you will always be in the receiving state of mind. Just make sure to give to yourself as well. Love must come from within. Not giving to yourself shows that you don't have enough love for yourself. To give endless amounts of love, you must already have that within yourself. There is definitely a fine balance with regard to giving to yourself and others. If you desire something, the best way to get it is to start giving whatever it is you want.

# 7. The Law of Perpetual Transmutation of Energy

*"Only love can conquer hate."*
*—Marvin Gaye*

This law states that the energy of a higher vibration will always consume and transmute the energy of a lower vibration into a higher vibration, or the lower vibration will be forced away. This can be applied to the emotional vibration we choose for ourselves based on how we feel. When we feel love, we resonate with the higher vibrational frequency of love. When we hate, we resonate with the lower vibrational frequency of hate.

This law works only one way—meaning a lower vibrational frequency, such as hate, can never consume a higher vibrational energy, such as love, and change it into a lower vibrational frequency. The only way a higher vibrational frequency can be changed is if a person chooses to vibrate at a lower frequency by choosing to express emotions such as hate, anger, and revenge.

The higher vibrational energies are love, forgiveness, understanding, openness, compassion, and other positive emotions. The lower vibrational energies are hate, anger, fear, worry, doubt, jealousy, envy, and other negative emotions. When the vibration of love meets the vibration of hate, love transmutes (transforms) hate into love every time, or the hateful energy must leave the presence of love. The story of Gandhi is the perfect example to illustrate this point.

## Gandhi—An Example of Love Transmuting Hate

My favorite example of someone using the law of perpetual transmutation successfully is Gandhi. Mohandas Karamchand Gandhi was famous for applying passive resistance to the British rule of India. During the first half of the twentieth century, the British government had complete military and governmental control of India, and the Indian citizens desperately desired their independence. Gandhi had become a leader of the people of India in their resistance to British rule.

**Figure 2: Mohandas Karamchand Gandhi**

When Gandhi started to implement change, he chose to change with love rather than hate. He understood the law of perpetual energy transmutation. He instinctively understood the flow of energy and knew that violence only creates more violence. He instructed the people of India to protest, but not to physically fight back against the British oppression. If the Indian people were physically hit, they were instructed to turn the other cheek and let the British hit them again. It was Gandhi's hope and mission that eventually the British government would see that they were persecuting innocent people—and that these people did not want to be ruled any longer. During this period, many innocent Indian people were killed or abused by the British. Amazingly the entire country rallied around Gandhi's passive vision of a land freed from British rule. In time, the British realized that their overwhelming military force could not change the will of the people into making them obey the British laws. Since the people of India would not fight back, the British did not have an enemy to fight. They only had people to persecute. Eventually the British decided to pull out of India and give the people their freedom back. Gandhi's vision became a reality.

Gandhi's passive resistance, which used love rather than violence, allowed the law of perpetual transmutation of energy to work for the people of India. Gandhi knew that if the people of India fought back using the lower vibrational action of hate and violence, the British would use their military might to defeat them. Instead, he chose to use the higher vibrational actions of love and compassion. In time, the British decided to pull out of India and give the people of India their independence back. The higher vibration of love had successfully forced away the lower vibration of the British occupation.

# 8. The Law of Relativity

*Your perception is your reality.*

The law of relativity states that a person's perceived reality of an object or event is relative (dependent) on their point of view. This is meant both literally and figuratively.

> There are no absolutes—everything is relative, for the speed of light. That alone is always constant. Measurements of speed, mass, space, and time are all dependent on who is measuring them and what they are doing at the time.[23]

This law of relativity in *The Light Shall Set You Free* may or may not be meant to be the same law of relativity that Einstein created, but ironically they both have the same premise: your point of view in relation to an object or event affects how you see or experience it. Your reality is relative to your point of view.

The law of relativity applies not only to the actions and events of our reality but also to our emotions. How we think and feel about the events that happen in our lives affects how we experience that reality. Perceived reality seems to be a difficult thing to define because it can be different for each person. The law of relativity states that your perception of reality is your reality. In life, many things happen to us. Sometimes these things are good and sometimes they are bad. How we perceive these events determines how they affect us.

Two people who experience the same event but have different outlooks on life can experience two different realities. Let's take a look at the following example of a house fire in two homes next to each other.

## House Fire: Two Different Relative Perspectives

Let's take the example of neighbor A and neighbor B. Both neighbors have families. One night, a fire blows through and burns down both houses. Both families escape without anyone being hurt.

Neighbor A is devastated by the total loss of his house and all his possessions inside—even though he is covered by homeowners insurance. Months later, he is still focused on this tragic event. It has negatively affected his life. Since the fire, he has been constantly depressed, and his life has been riddled with one negative event after another. He feels like there is a cloud of bad luck over his head that is making everything in his life go wrong.

Neighbor B is also affected by the loss of his house, but as soon as he learns that his entire family is safe, he is thankful and appreciative that he still has his family. He realizes he could have lost them all to the fire. He knows that a house is replaceable while his family is not. His positive outlook helps him to move on emotionally and rebuild faster than his neighbor.

The law of relativity states that our view of reality is relative to what we are comparing it to now. Neighbor B was able to handle the loss better than neighbor A because neighbor B was focused on appreciating that he still had his family, while neighbor A was focused on the loss of his house. Both men had the same circumstances, but their relative points of view affected how they viewed the reality of the events that happened.

A trick to using the law of relativity in any situation is to try to seek out the most positive aspect of whatever event you are experiencing. I realize that during times of trauma or personal grief that seeing the positive can be extremely challenging. It is okay to feel negative emotions, such as anger, frustration, or worry for short periods of time, but it becomes a problem when these emotions become a long-term habit. This is because the law of attraction interprets your focus as your desire. The more you focus on something, the more the law of attraction thinks that you want it. A friend of mine once said that it is okay to fall into a ditch, but make sure you don't decorate it and plan to stay there. This applies with life too. It's okay to occasionally experience down times, but as soon as you can, start thinking positive thoughts and start mentally creating a better future for yourself.

An excellent example of the law of relativity is when I was hit by a car as a young boy. The experience was sure to forever change my life. How the experience would change me depended on how I perceived it and reacted to it.

## Hit by a Car: A Lesson in Relativity

I had an experience with this law when I was twelve years old. I was playing with my friend, Curt Schmitke, at the racquetball club. We were playing a game to see who could collect the most tennis balls around the tennis court. We had about the same amount of tennis balls when we looked through the chain link fence and spotted a ball on the other side of the street. Without thinking, we unlocked a side gate and ran across the street. I decided to run after it first. The area where we crossed was at the bottom of hill that was a blind spot to oncoming drivers. I got about halfway across the street when I saw a car coming right at me. Like a deer in headlights, I was too startled to jump out of the way, and the seventeen-year-old driver, who had just recently received her driver's license, was unable to stop in time. I turned to shield myself the way a person turns away when trying not to get hit when a ball is thrown at them. The car hit me going an estimated sixty miles an hour, launching me up and over the car.[24] I landed in a ditch twenty-five yards away with my broken leg in a contorted position behind my head. I had a compound fracture of my right femur. I woke up to the view of the inside of a fireman's helmet. The helmet was being held over my head to keep the sun out of my eyes and to keep me from seeing the horrific sight that the paramedics saw. My father unfortunately had to see it all. I think it was tougher on him to see that happen to his son than it was for me to go through the experience. As soon as I regained consciousness, I could feel the hot summer asphalt sizzling into my bare back. When the paramedic straightened out my leg, the pain I felt was indescribable. To this day, I cannot comprehend that level of pain. I just remember squeezing my father's hand so hard it must have hurt him.

Inside the ambulance, I was able to feel every pebble the tires went over. The severed nerves in my leg were like downed power lines after a storm with electricity shooting out of the wires. It was excruciating. The whole thing just felt like a bad dream. As soon as I realized it wasn't a dream, I accepted my situation and began to instinctively focus on recovering. I never doubted that it would happen. I didn't know it at the time, but I was using the law of relativity to get better—without knowing what that law was or how it worked.

When we got to the hospital, I was given some morphine. I had seen war movies where wounded soldiers would get morphine to dull the pain, but I had never before experienced what that was like. Let me tell you—that stuff was a miracle for me. The pain was unbearable, but after getting the morphine, a sense of peace came over me and allowed the pain to fade away.

I learned later that I could have easily cut my femoral artery in my leg and quickly bled to death. The doctors told me that if I had been hit a few centimeters higher I would have hit my growth plate in the bone, which would have stopped the growth and eventually have caused me to have one leg much longer than the other. They also said that if I had hit much higher up on my leg, I could have been hit under the car and killed. When I heard that information, I thought of how lucky I was to be alive. The funny thing is that death never crossed my mind. As soon as I awoke, my only focus was on getting better. I didn't know about any of these laws or that the mind could heal, but they worked for me nonetheless.

After emergency surgery, I was put in traction and a pin was drilled through my lower leg and attached to a weighted pulley system that kept the broken bones close to each other so they could mend. I was in the hospital for a month this way. Due to the traction device, I was unable to turn over. Imagine being in bed for month without being able to turn on your side or turn over. I had to get powder put on my back to keep bedsores from developing. I shared an open hospital ward room with many other sick or injured children. This proved to be quite a learning experience for me. At all hours of the day and night, someone was crying, vomiting, screaming, or just talking. This experience taught me tolerance and patience. I realized that my recovery was going to teach me lessons that would help define who I would become. After a month, I could go home, but the next stage of my recovery required a cast from my chest down to my legs. I had a small section cut out between my legs for my bathroom needs. That became part of my lesson because I was reliant on my family any time I had to go to the bathroom. This was a lesson in humility.

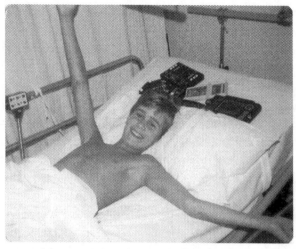

**Figure 3: Happy to be alive. I believe a positive attitude helped me to heal so quickly.**

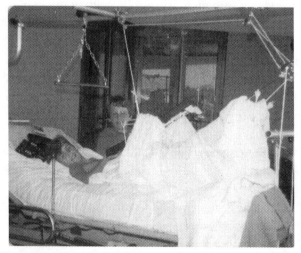

**Figure 4: This is the traction device on my bed that helped mend my broken leg. (Pictured: my childhood friend, John Carr, and I.)**

I made it a point to never complain. Not once did I blame God or wonder why this had happened to me. Something inside told me that none of that mattered. What mattered was how I handled the situation. I knew that the important thing was to deal with where I was and to find a way to get to where I wanted to be. I learned that a crisis doesn't just build character—it reveals it. Some people choose to act like victims while others choose to act like survivors. I chose to act like a survivor.

When I got home, I had a hero's welcome from the entire neighborhood. In an effort to help me fit in with my friends, my parents had gotten me a large contraption that was basically a twelve-inch board that was about five feet long and had wheels. I was given a helmet and some gloves and told to go play. At first, I felt a little self-conscious about being handicapped, but that feeling soon passed as the neighborhood kids adapted and played with me.

**Figure 5: I was welcomed home by this great sign our friends, the Gallagher family, had made for me. (Pictured left to right: Jill, Matt, and Gayle Gallagher)**

During my recovery, my grandfather gave me a kitten. I loved the kitten, but she had fleas and they went down into my cast. The itching was unbearable. I did everything the doctor told me not to do. I used a wire hanger to scratch inside the cast and even sprayed flea killer into the edges of the cast. Luckily, I didn't experience any complications from the scratching, the flea spray, or the fleas themselves. In time, the flea problem was over and I was okay. I just wrote the whole experience off as part of tempering my character to endure life's challenges. It made me tougher.

A month later, the cast was cut off, and I was allowed to use crutches. I felt so light, naked, and completely vulnerable without my plastered armor. It took a while for me to get comfortable on crutches. I had not been upright on my feet in almost three months. I could feel the nerves mending inside my leg. I really didn't understand at the time that a miracle was happening inside my body for it to heal the way it did. Unfortunately, this miracle was not a pleasant experience. When I would stand, the blood in my body would drain down to the bottom of my feet. My healing leg would throb and go numb the way your hand does when it falls asleep, or when you hit your funny bone. It was excruciating. This went on for weeks. Eventually the normal feeling came back to my leg. The muscles in both legs had completely atrophied. I was amazed by how quickly muscle could vanish. After a month on crutches, I was finally given the okay by the doctor to walk on my own.

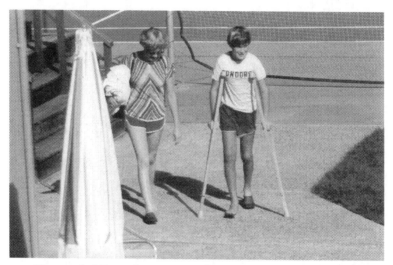

**Figure 6: Mom shares one of her sandals with me as I walk on crutches to our daily physical therapy sessions. We didn't have an actual physical therapist, but my mom acted as one to help me make a full recovery.**

Being able to walk again was the greatest miracle of all. I was so thankful for a second chance to walk. Since the accident, I have always considered myself as someone who was supposed to be crippled, but somehow found a way out or was given a second chance. When I see a handicapped person, my heart goes out to them as a brother or sister. I know their struggle and commend them for being strong enough to make the best of their situation because perception is reality. I believe I too would have made the best of whatever situation I was eventually dealt had I not healed the way I did.

A few weeks after I started walking, my friends noticed that I had a limp. The doctor informed me that I would always have that limp, and I would never be able to play contact sports. My mother enjoys telling me that something inside of her told her what she needed to do for me. She immediately signed me up for the swimming team. Before the accident, I had been playing football, basketball, soccer, and baseball year around. I gave up all those sports and for a year all I did was swim. I swam many hours a day. After a year of swimming, another miracle happened. My limp had vanished! The year of constant swimming had strengthened my leg to the point where it was as healthy as the other leg. An added benefit was that the constant swimming trained me to become a strong swimmer and feel comfortable in the water. I went on to high school to play all types of sports—baseball, basketball, football, and rugby—never did my leg give me trouble again.

I did not have a choice in how I experienced my injury, but I did have a choice in how I perceived and reacted to the event. Instead of feeling sorry for myself and wondering why it had happened to me, I chose to accept the circumstances and make the best of what I could. The experience taught me how to focus on a goal and how to have the patience and persistence to see it through. While I was in the hospital, I learned compassion and tolerance of others. Ultimately, I learned that any experience is what you make it. My experience helped make me into the person I am today and—although I would not choose to go through it again—it was a very positive influence in my life.

More than twenty years after the accident, I went to get lunch at local restaurant. I had gotten to know the lady who worked there. One day she came up to me with tears in her eyes and said, "You don't know who I am, do you?" I said, "Of course I do." She said, "I am the girl who hit you with my car when you were a boy." She broke down in front of me, saying she was sorry, and that she never visited me because she was so scared. She asked for my forgiveness. I smiled and told her that there was nothing to forgive. I was thankful for the lessons I learned and had not carried any resentment toward her or anyone else associated with that part of my life. I totally understood how she must have felt. I told her that she could buy me lunch and we could call it even if it made her feel better. Then we laughed together. It felt good to see her release the guilt and negative energy that she had been carrying around with her for so many years. That conversation made both of us feel better.

Life *is* about perception. I could have held a grudge toward her for having to go through all that suffering and pain, but I would have been affecting my own happiness. I would have let those events make me feel negative and angry toward the world. I am glad I didn't do that. I have my parents to thank for that because they have always instilled in me to focus on the positive parts of life. During my recovery and throughout my life, my parents have always been there to offer encouragement and support. This has made a huge difference in my life!

I have a saying that I love to share with others who ask me about this law. It defines that our perception of reality is what makes our reality real for us. It goes like this: The experiences in life make us who we are, but we make the experiences what they are. This means that our outlook affects the experience as much as the experience affects us. Remember that the law of relativity says that our view of reality is relative to our outlook, so it is in our own best interest to be as positive as we can about life because we are the ones who create our own reality.

# 9. The Law of Polarity

The law of polarity states that everything has an opposite, and that our reality resides between the two polar opposites of anything we experience. This rule can apply to anything in our existence—from physical locations, to emotions, or to character traits. Let's explore this concept further.

Opposites are everywhere. Our planet has a north pole and a south pole that are opposites of each other. The opposite of positive is negative. The opposite of light is dark. The opposite of hard is soft, and so on. The law of polarity shows us that both opposites are needed to make up the whole. A sunrise is needed in order to appreciate having a sunset. Both are part of the same process. If we didn't have darkness, wouldn't it always be light? If we only knew light, how would we know what it really is? It takes an opposite for us to be able to compare or appreciate the value of anything. In other words, polar opposites are necessary for us to really know that anything exists. This law is very useful to keep nature in balance.

The law of polarity also applies to our emotions and is useful in making changes in our lives. Let's take the example of happiness and sadness as polar opposites. Both are needed for either happiness or sadness to be understood, right? If you only knew happiness, would you be able to appreciate being happy? Most likely, you would be happy, but you wouldn't know it. It is only when happiness is compared to sadness that happiness is truly appreciated.

Where does sadness end and happiness start? If we drew a line, we would have happiness on one end of the continuum and sadness on the other. The emotions in between are the secret to manageable change. If we feel sadness from a breakup, we might experience worry, anger, fear, and hopelessness on our way back to happiness. Later, we might reach a point where we feel indifferent about the whole situation. At this point, we are ready to start feeling hope and anticipation, which can eventually lead to us feeling joy again. When we are happy, we feel great, but when something happens to us where we experience a negative emotion like anger, fear, worry, or sadness, we are no longer feeling positive emotions. We usually desperately wish to feel happy again, but are at a loss for how to get back to happiness. The reason why we can't become happy again immediately is because when we are experiencing negative emotions, we are vibrating at a frequency that is at the opposite end of the spectrum from happiness. It is usually not possible for us to make a quantum leap along the emotional scale from being angry, worried, fearful, or sad to feeling immediately happy.

Luckily, there is a way to become happy again. You can move from sadness to a slightly better emotion, and then another better emotion, and continue to make small moves until you have moved to the polar opposite emotion, which is happiness. This way, you can make the transition from sadness to happiness one emotion at a time.[25]

## The Breakup: An Example in Emotional Traveling

A long time ago, I had a relationship with a girlfriend that was passionate and intoxicating. I was young and I thought I was in love. I was so happy from these exhilarating feelings of what I thought was love that they dominated my thoughts every second of the day.

As many relationships do, after a period of time, it ended. She had found someone else. I went from the high feelings of happiness and excitement to the low feelings of sadness, worry, fearfulness, and hopelessness. All I wanted was to feel good again, but as the days went by, I felt powerless to change how I felt inside.

When I saw her with her new boyfriend, I felt envious. As the days passed, the envy turned to being upset and then to judging her. I thought that she had done something wrong to me. I eventually realized that this is a free world and that we are all free to make our own choices. She had chosen to go in another direction away from me. I had to accept her choice. At some point, I became aware that I was no longer upset. I just felt emotionally helpless because the weight of the situation dominated my thoughts. During that time, I was disappointed and doubtful that I would find anyone like her again. After a while, I finally got tired of feeling this way and decided to focus on my future and not my past. I started working on myself to be the best I could be. I got into really good physical shape. Once I started to see results in the gym, I began to feel better about myself. I noticed that I again felt fortunate and hopeful about what great surprises the future would bring. Through the power of positive momentum, one good thing after another happened to me. Before I knew it, I had regained my passion for life and I was happy and felt empowered that I could do whatever I set out to do. I was proud because I had achieved this feeling by myself instead of feeling like I had to find someone new to replace the void that my ex-girlfriend had left. Once I regained my confidence and zest for life, it attracted many wonderful new women to my life. Looking back, it showed me how to recover from any setback.

I was able to move from one emotion to the next. Each time I looked for a slightly better emotion. It was okay, normal, and even healthy for me to experience and vent negative emotions by choosing other less negative emotions on my way to finding better emotions. The trick was not to stay focused on any negative emotion too long. I realized that each emotion was a stepping stone to the ultimate emotion that I desired, which was happiness. I was traveling from one end of the spectrum to the other. In my example, I was unable to jump immediately from sadness to happiness so I used the other emotions to slowly move toward happiness.

In summary, the law of polarity is there for us to manage our journey from one range of emotions to another. So the next time you feel down and out, decide which emotion you want to get to and start moving your way toward it—one emotion at a time.

## 10. The Law of Rhythm

This law could have easily been named the law of balance. The law of rhythm states that energy will always seek to restore balance to itself. Looking around, we can see signs of this law in effect everywhere. There is the rhythm of the day and night. Day gives way to night, and then night again gives way to day. Each year has four seasons, and the oceans have cycles of high tide followed by low tide. We even have the cycle of life where we are born, grow up, mature, grow old, and eventually die. There are cycles of life happening everywhere all of the time.

The law of rhythm uses these cycles to keep balance in the world. Whenever life gets out of balance, the law of rhythm will eventually work to restore this balance. We can see the effects of the law of rhythm seeking to restore balance in all aspects of our lives. This balancing effect doesn't just apply in nature. It also applies to us as human beings. We have the free will to do whatever we want in life. The choices we make in life determine how this law applies to us. If we live a balanced life—avoiding extreme mental and emotional highs and lows—we will enjoy a smoother life filled with less surprising corrections from the law of rhythm. If we choose to live life to extremes, we can expect this law to eventually bring corrections to restore balance in our lives.

It is not uncommon these days for people to be constantly stressed. Stress in the short term is okay and even normal, but exposure to constant stress over a period of years can cause the body to live out of balance and eventually manifest an illness.[26] In cases such as these, the law of rhythm seeks to restore balance, usually through some type of physical illness. Is it a coincidence that cancer, strokes, and heart attacks are common among people who experience high levels of stress over long periods of time? Physical diseases and ailments are often the manifestation of a stressor or emotional imbalance within the body. These imbalances can be caused by any type of stressors, such as excessive lifestyle, stress, diet, emotions, environment, and many other causes. The bottom line is that when we live out of balance, sooner or later, nature will seek to restore balance in our lives. A disease is usually a wakeup call for us to change our ways and restore balance to life before things get worse.

We cannot control the law of rhythm, but we can control our thoughts and our actions. If we choose thoughts, words, and actions that are in balance, we have less of a chance of this law affecting us in a negative way.

Unfortunately, there are times when everyone is affected by the law of rhythm regardless of their actions. During these times, those who decide to accept change, rather than resist it, will have an easier time adjusting, and may even find ways to capitalize on the opportunities that this change creates.

## Crash after Life in the Fast Lane

I know from experience that this law is real. I fondly remember the period during my late twenties to mid-thirties in which I was enjoying a very active social life. I was young, had a good-paying job, and loved to have fun. I worked hard and I played hard. It was normal to go out to socialize and have cocktails at least three nights a week. Each night out was followed with a morning hangover. Often my lifestyle didn't allow me to get enough sleep. My motto was, "If you're going to play, you've got to pay." I would not allow myself to miss work if I was hung-over or tired from the night before. Those were some of the best times of my life, although I knew, even then, that my lifestyle was tough on my body. It seemed like almost every weekend I was traveling to Sacramento, San Francisco, Los Angeles, San Diego, Las Vegas, or Cabo San Lucas to have fun. My lifestyle was burning the candle at both ends, and I kept up this pace for many fun-filled years until things suddenly changed for me.

Eventually the law of rhythm came knocking on my door. After another amazing but exhausting weekend in Las Vegas, I boarded my flight home. About ten minutes after takeoff, I physically felt something break inside my body. It felt like machinery that had broken. I know we don't have machinery inside us, but that is how it felt. I started having chest pains and shortness of breath. I also noticed my left arm began to go numb. I couldn't help but notice my symptoms were eerily similar to the definition of a heart attack. I tried to keep from panicking, but I knew I was in trouble. I thought, *Oh God, I've killed myself with my lifestyle!*

If it wasn't stressful enough to think I was quite possibly having a heart attack, I had to contend with that fact that I was on a plane at 30,000 feet with no real medical help nearby. I went to the back of the plane to have the flight attendant look after me to make sure I didn't get any worse. Luckily, things did not get worse and by the time we landed, I was feeling okay again. Still, to be safe, I went to the hospital to make sure I was okay. The test results showed I did not have a heart attack, but I didn't need lab tests to know something was wrong with me.

Over the next couple of months, I noticed that my heart was beating faster all the time. My heart was beating up to 110 beats a minute even while I was sleeping. A normal heart beats between 60–70 beats a minute. I went to the doctor's office to do some tests and was diagnosed with Graves' disease. My body had been out of balance for a long time and it had manifested a disease! Graves' disease is an autoimmune disease where the thyroid is overactive, producing an excessive amount of thyroid hormones. Most people, if they don't have a problem with their thyroid gland, probably don't even know where their thyroid gland is or what it does. Those who do have a problem with it know it can cause wreak havoc on the body. The thyroid controls how quickly the body uses energy, makes proteins, and controls how sensitive the body should be to other hormones.

Graves' disease causes hyperthyroidism, which is when the body is producing too many hormones at once. This caused my metabolism to work faster and faster. At first, I didn't mind this effect as it had increased my metabolism enough where I could eat whatever I wanted and still stay lean and trim. The doctor told me not to get used to it because if I kept it like that for too long without medical treatment, it would eventually endanger my life.

After weighing my options, I decided to follow the doctor's advice to have my thyroid medically "destroyed" by swallowing a radioactive iodine pill (RAI). I was told that one of the functions of the thyroid is to process all the iodine in the body. Since the pill was iodine, I swallowed it and my thyroid gland attracted it from my stomach directly to itself. The doctors made me stay home away from people for two weeks because of the radiation. That was a unique experience being self-quarantined. I enjoyed the time, but it was also scary to think I could be harmful to someone else if I got too close to them during those two weeks. It also made me wonder how safe it was for the rest of my body. All in all, other than a sore throat, I felt fine.

Two weeks later, the doctors said I was safe to go back to work and be around people. *Wow, that was easy*, I thought. A few days later, I started getting really tired and felt lethargic. A week later, I noticed I had put on seven pounds. A month later, I still felt sluggish, generally unhealthy, and had put on a total of thirty pounds—and I didn't eat any more than I normally did. In fact, I doubled my efforts in the gym doing about an hour of fast-paced cardio each day. Nothing was able to slow the weight gain.

Almost overnight, I went from being fit and in shape to overweight and unhealthy. When I went in for my next doctor's visit, I was informed that my thyroid was either underactive or completely destroyed and was no longer producing enough hormones for my body. The radiation procedure had changed the thyroidism from hyperthyroidism (fast metabolism) to having hypothyroidism (slow metabolism). My metabolism had slowed almost to a stop. The doctor told me that no matter what I did I wouldn't be able to prevent the weight gain until I started hormone replacement therapy. For the first time in my life, I felt helpless to control how my body looked and felt. It made me wonder how many others have the same challenge with controlling their weight.

I've always been kind and considerate to others, but in our society, overweight people are often judged for how they look. I learned firsthand that sometimes people just can't help how they look. Some people's metabolism or genetics may be different than the majority of society. This taught me additional compassion and understanding for others and that we should never judge another based on appearance because we don't know their circumstances.

The next step in my treatment was when the doctors started me on synthetic hormone replacement therapy. They calmly informed me that I only needed to take one pill every day for the rest of my life, and I would be fine. I thought, *That doesn't sound too hard.*

To make a long story a little shorter, it wasn't fine. Over the next ten years, I struggled with this disease. I went from 6'1" and 195 pounds at the beginning of this process to 225 pounds at my highest point. No matter how much exercise I did, I couldn't lose the weight. I eventually found a balance where I wasn't gaining any more weight. Since the human body is constantly changing metabolically, my medication also had to be adjusted every six weeks. This led to constantly feeling "not right" inside. I was constantly feeling sick, tired, cold, hot, moody, or all of my energy would be gone. Other times, I would feel fine and then would suddenly crash with hypoglycemia sugar lows like diabetics have. What an awful experience! It was hell on earth.

I felt helpless and wondered why modern medicine didn't know more about how to properly handle this disease. Finally, I came to the conclusion that I had to educate myself and become a thyroidism expert. I went on a mission to learn everything there was to know about this disease. If I was going to beat the thyroidism, I had to know how it worked. Luckily, through the law of attraction, I stumbled across a doctor in my local area that was both an MD and a holistic doctor. She was open to treating me in different ways than the other doctors did. This made a big difference.

The worst side effects of the thyroidism were the heart palpitations. Either the medicine or adrenal fatigue caused my heart to beat irregularly for periods of minutes or more. These bouts would come on randomly or whenever I would experience stress. Sometimes I wouldn't have them for months, but other times, they would happen every day. I went to a cardiologist and he gave me a clean bill of cardiovascular health, but I didn't need the doctor's approval to know there was something wrong with me. It's a scary feeling to know there is something really wrong with you and the doctors can't find the cause.

If you have ever had heart palpations or anything wrong with your heart, you know what true stark terror is. It's the feeling that you could drop dead at any moment. The panicked feeling of the unknown is what the fear is really about. I had lived with this fear for years. My initial doctors wouldn't acknowledge that the thyroidism was causing the heart palpations so they just wanted to prescribe me anxiety medicine. I choose not to do that. I had been doing meditation for a few years and had learned to control the fear in my mind. I could control the anxiety, but I felt helpless to control what was happening inside my body.

What really set me free was when I finally accepted the situation. In order to get control of my current reality, I had to accept the worst-case scenario. I decided to accept that I may just drop dead at any moment. I also decided that for as long as I lived, I would focus my life on being the best person I could be. If I died before I could make that a reality, then that was okay with me. I was not going to be a prisoner to fear any longer. I chose to only focus on what I could control. Once I accepted my situation and stopped focusing on my fear of death, I started to feel better. I learned about the law of attraction, and I only saw myself as 100 percent healthy. When I would feel heart palpations come on, I would focus and say, "I know I don't feel well right now, but I know my body knows how to heal itself and all I need to do is allow it to do that. I know in time I will be healthy again." I would tell myself that I was relaxed and safe. I would chant this to myself over and over again until I could feel myself relax. After saying the chant enough times, the palpitations usually went away. This helped change my vibration from one of fear to one of being relaxed and a feeling of wellness.

The palpitations would often come back when I became fatigued, stressed, or if I stopped focusing on what I wanted. Eventually, through trial and error and research, I learned that I had adrenal fatigue as well as thyroidism. My body had been under different types of stress for so long that it was now hypersensitive to all types of stress. In hindsight, I believe that the adrenal fatigue was the cause of my chest pains and palpitations. Avoiding stress was a way to prevent those symptoms. My positive thinking about accepting my situation and manifesting better health really worked. I was able to relax my stressed body to a point where the symptoms significantly lessened. Thankfully, in time, I was able to make a full recovery and go on to live a normal life again.

My point is to illustrate how nature restores balance. When you live life out of balance the way I did when I was younger, you can expect some type of correction. Was my lifestyle the real cause of the ailments

I experienced? I don't know for sure, but I do know that my excessive lifestyle activated them in my life. If I had it to do over again, I would still live life the way I lived it before because those were some of the best days of my life. However, I would be more moderate about it so that I could have fun but not suffer the consequences of living out of balance.

I've learned the hard way that moderation is the key, but I do think some good did come from this experience. In my search to get better, I learned about the universal laws, especially the law of attraction, and I discovered the importance of treating my body better. Looking back on this experience, I am now able to see that this health challenge was a blessing in disguise because it allowed me to grow in ways that were not previously possible.

# 11.  The Law of Gender

This law could have easily been named the law of opposites. The law of gender states that everything has an opposite. Some examples of this law are masculine and feminine, light and dark, up and down, light and dark, good and evil. As you may have noticed, all of the universal laws are a part of each other. The law of gender differs from the law of polarity in that the law of gender says that everything in our existence has an opposite characteristic, while the law of polarity shows us how to use the points between these opposites to live our lives.

The Chinese often refer to this law as yin and yang. They use yin (feminine) and yang (masculine) to describe the two sides to everything in life. Yang is light and masculine, while yin is dark and feminine.

The Chinese do not view one side as better than the other because both sides are necessary for the other to have meaning. It is up to each individual person to choose which parts they want for themselves at any particular point in time.

**Figure 7: Yin and Yang Symbol**

When I first learned these laws, I wondered why we didn't just get rid of the negative stuff we don't want and keep the stuff we do want. I believe that we can and should choose for ourselves what we want in life, but trying to eradicate the negative part of the whole is often not possible or desired in our existence. Opposites in life are inevitable and a natural part of our existence. The trick is to no longer see good and bad as opposites, but to see them as two parts to the whole. Each half gives us a diversity of choices to make. We alone have the power to choose which parts of the whole we wish to experience. Whatever choices we make, the universal laws will react accordingly to affect the reality we experience.

Each person has both yin and yang traits within them. When a person is aggressive, outgoing, competitive, ego-driven, and enthusiastic, they are considered to be yang. When a person is a good listener, humble, patient, relaxed, and easygoing, they are consider to be yin. Yang is strong and forceful. Yin is calm and relaxed. The trick is to balance these traits. Balance is found by using yin and yang traits evenly rather than favoring just one side. When a balance of these traits is achieved, a person lives a more pleasant and enjoyable life. While the law of rhythm is about cycles and finding balance, the law of gender is about understanding and accepting that both yin and yang qualities are necessary in life.

How do we know when to choose to be yang and when to be yin? The answer is to listen to your intuition. Your intuition, or gut instinct, once developed, will tell you how you feel about any subject.

This law reminds me of a great Cherokee wisdom story of the "Two Wolves."

## The Cherokee Wisdom Story of "The Two Wolves"

An old Cherokee man told his grandson about a battle that goes on inside people. He said, "My son, the battle is between two wolves inside us all. One is evil. It is anger, envy, jealousy, sorrow, regret, greed, arrogance, self-pity, guilt, resentment, inferiority, lies, false pride, superiority, and ego. The other is good. It is joy, peace, love, hope, serenity, humility, kindness, benevolence, empathy, generosity, truth, compassion, and faith."

The grandson thought for a minute and then asked, "Which wolf wins?"

The old Cherokee simply replied, "The one you feed."

**Figure 8: The two wolves inside us all.
Which one will you feed?**

I love this story because it is a perfect example that shows us that we all have good and bad within us, but it is up to us to decide which traits we wish to develop.

In summary, by working with the law of gender, we understand that all things in life—good and bad—are necessary in order for us to have the diversity in our experiences to make the choices that will allow us to create our own reality. We can then choose which traits we wish to use for ourselves. Those traits become who we are.

# 12. The Law of Correspondence

The law of correspondence holds the law of oneness together. The law of oneness states that everything in our existence is part of the same universal energy source. The law of correspondence states that all of the other universal laws act together in harmony with each other. They all correspond and relate to each other. As you may have noticed, it is often difficult to know where one law ends and another begins. These laws apply throughout the universe.

The saying, "As above, so below" means that these laws work everywhere because everything is made up of this same energy. The law of correspondence works because we live in a holographic universe. Each part of the universe contains the entire blueprint of the entire universe as a whole within it. Our DNA does the same thing. Each cell has a complete blueprint of our body. Why is this? It is because everything is connected through same universal energy that makes up our existence. Everything is connected, which means that everything corresponds to everything else.

# The Universal Laws Summarized

### The Law of Oneness

Everything is made up of the same energy source. Everything is connected. There is no separation from oneness. Anything separate from oneness is an impermanent illusion.

### The Law of Vibration

Each thought, emotion, word, action, or thing has its own unique energy signature or vibrational frequency.

### The Law of Attraction

This law states that like-type energy is attracted to itself. Positive energy attracts more positive energy, and negative energy attracts more negative energy. Being human, we are able to choose our own energy and the energy we want to attract through the thoughts, words, and actions we choose for ourselves.

### The Law of Action

You can help things to manifest in your life by adding actions that complement your desires.

### The Law of Cause and Effect (Karma)

Energy is circular and attracts itself. Our choices attract back to us the same energy we give out. "What goes around, comes around."

### The Law of Compensation

The law of compensation says that the energy of our thoughts, words, and actions will come back to us ten times stronger in the future. This can be a positive or negative thing, depending on what we choose for ourselves and others.

## The Law of Perpetual Transmutation of Energy

Higher vibrational frequencies will always consume and transform lower vibrational frequencies into higher ones, or the lower frequencies will be forced to leave.

## The Law of Relativity

Our reality is relative to our point of view. We are the ones who determine how the events of our lives affect us.

## The Law of Polarity

Everything has two poles or opposites. There are many different points of reference along the continuum from one polar-opposite to the other. These points are instrumental in making small manageable changes to move from one place or emotion to another.

## The Law of Rhythm

This law states that everything in our existence has its own season or flow, and that nature is always seeking to find balance or equilibrium. We can minimize the re-balancing effects of this law by living a balanced life that avoids extreme thoughts, words, or actions.

## The Law of Gender

Everything has an opposite. Light must have dark in order for us to realize that either exists. This is also called yin and yang by the Chinese. It is up to us to appreciate the need for both sides of everything in our world because we need the contrast of the two sides to understand the meaning of either side. We can use our free will to choose which sides we wish to have in our lives.

## The Law of Correspondence

All of the universal laws correspond to each other. In reality, it is impossible to use one law by itself because they are all part of each other.

# Chapter 2: Does Quantum Physics Give Us Proof?

In this chapter, we discuss how science appears to have given us information that supports that our minds can control the energy that creates matter. Quantum physics, also known as quantum theory or quantum mechanics, is the mathematical study of the interactions between energy and matter through wave-particle duality.

The premise of this book is that everything in our universe is made up of the same source energy. That means all things—living and non-living—are made up of, and connected by, this same energy. Some of this information can be a little confusing at first, but it doesn't have to be. In this chapter, we will go over some of the quantum physic principles to allow you to draw your own conclusions about what is possible. Don't worry—we won't get too heavy into this subject as we will be covering mostly theory without a lot of mathematics. You don't have to be a physicist to understand this chapter. In each example, I will give the actual and more complicated definition first, and then follow it up with a more easy to understand definition.

Note: Although this chapter is important to show how science appears to support the universal laws, I understand that not everyone is able to relate to the subject of quantum physics. So, if you find this material to be too complicated or uninteresting feel free to skip ahead to Chapter 3: How the Law of Attraction Works.

# Theory of Mass-Energy Equivalence ($E=mc^2$)

**Figure 9: Einstein's Theory of Mass-Energy Equivalence ($E=mc^2$)**

In 1905, Albert Einstein's famous $E=mc^2$ formula proved that energy and matter are not only equivalent, they are one in the same. Einstein's theory of relativity beautifully illustrates how energy manifests into matter and matter into energy.[27]

Let's first discuss the formal definition. The theory of mass-energy equivalence ($E=mc^2$) is the concept that the mass of a body is a measure of its energy content. Einstein said, "The mass of an object represents the amount of energy locked up inside it."[28]

Everyone knows about $E=mc^2$, but few people in the general public know what it means or how it works. In this formula, the "E" represents energy, "m" represents mass or matter, and "$c^2$" represents the speed of light multiplied by itself."[29]

Let's break this down into an easier-to-understand model. If energy is matter vibrating at a frequency of the speed of light times itself, or in more simple terms, energy is mass or matter vibrating very fast, then the opposite must also be true. That would mean that matter is simply energy vibrating more slowly.[30]

Using simple algebra, we can rework the formula of $E=mc^2$ into $M=e/c^2$ to find out how matter is made. $M=e/c^2$ means that matter is energy vibrating at a frequency of energy divided by the speed of light times itself. In simple terms, this means matter is energy that is vibrating at a much slower vibrational frequency. Did you get that? If energy is matter moving very fast, then matter is energy moving very slowly. Based on this information one could easily deduct that energy and matter are not two separate things—they are two different manifestations of the same thing:

energy. If this is true, it supports the claim of the law of oneness that everything is made of energy, and that everything is connected.

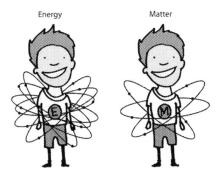

**Figure 10. Energy and Matter: The Same Thing, Just in Different Forms.**

> The Einstein equation was simply a recipe for the amount of energy necessary to create the appearance of mass. It means that there aren't two fundamental physical entities—something material and another immaterial—but only one: energy.[31]

*The Dancing Wu Li Masters: An Overview of the New Physics* states, "The special theory of relativity also tells us that space and time are not two separate things, but that together they form space-time, *and that energy and mass are actually different forms of the same thing, mass-energy*" (italics added).[32]

Again, because we can feel matter and since energy is formless, we often think of them as two separate things, but in reality everything in our universe is just energy manifested in different ways: solid and formless.[33]

Let's review what we learned in this section.

## Theory of Mass-Energy Equivalence ($E=mc^2$) Summary

- Energy is everything.
- Energy is matter vibrating at a faster speed.
- Matter is energy vibrating at a slower speed.
- Energy and matter are the same thing only in different forms.

So what does this suggest exactly? It supports the law of oneness by showing that everything is connected to each other through the same source energy.

# Entanglement

Quantum entanglement, or non-locality as it is often called, happens when subatomic particles that have previously interacted with each other are able to affect each other even if they are separated by space and time. This gives support to the law of oneness, which states that everything in our existence is connected.

> Mathematical proof for the existence of non-local interaction among subatomic particles surfaced in 1964 when John Stewart Bell showed how two different particles separated by distance and time remained unified and interconnected. The technology available to Bell at the time wasn't sufficiently advanced to allow him to prove his hypothesis in a laboratory. In 1982, physicists Alain Aspect, Jean Dalibard and Gerard Roger of the University of Paris validated Bell's work experimentally.[34]

## Entanglement Quotes

Gregg Braden, in *The Spontaneous Healing of Belief,* says, "A quantum particle can be in one place at a time, two places at a time, or even many places simultaneously. The interesting thing, however, is that no matter how far apart these locations appear to be physically, the particle acts as if it's still connected."[35]

Einstein said nothing can travel faster than the speed of light "but actually, in quantum physics there does seem to be something that happens faster than the light: communication between what are considered entangled particles."[36]

Einstein called this entangled communication between separated particles "spooky action at a distance."[37]

"These entangled particles are pairs of particles emitted when one particle decays (either naturally, or because a physicist smashed it) into two particles, so that if one has spin of up, the other has spin of down. But quantum physics also says those particle have no definite spin at all until that spin is measured."[38]

"So it seems that, once the spin of one particle is measured, it immediately communicates to its twin what the spin should be."[39]

"Experiments have shown that communication between entangled particles happens at speeds millions of times faster than the speed of light."[40]

A simplified definition of this theory is when two or more subatomic particles—electrons, protons, or neutrons—interact and then are separated by distance and time, they both react the same way. This implies that the separated particles were communicating with each other. This shouldn't have been possible unless they were somehow connected. If everything is made of the same energy field, then isn't it conceivable that two separated particles could somehow communicate to each other?

Have you ever had a thought about someone that you haven't talked to in a long time and then got a call from them that same day? Married couples or family members are often able to finish each other's sentences. Twins are often able to feel what is happening to the other even if they are separated by time and distance. Could this phenomenon be a sign of quantum entanglement or non-locality at work in our own lives?

Entanglement suggests that everything is connected—regardless of distance or time. This is another concept that gives credibility to the law of oneness.

Dr. Stuart Hameroff appears to support this statement.

> With entanglement, nonlocal interactions among living beings and physical events can in principle occur (the "law of attraction"). Shaping one's reality, psychic phenomena/ESP, influence by Platonic values (or "following the way of the Tao," or "divine guidance") and even life-after-death become plausible. This is not to say that they do occur but that they are not at all impossible.[41]

Let's review what we learned in this section.

---

## Entanglement Summary

- Particles separated by space and time are connected and able to communicate with each other.
- The speed of communication is faster than the speed of light.
- This evidence supports that claim that everything in our universe is connected.

---

# Wave-Particle Duality (Double-Slit Experiment)

This experiment shows that energy can travel both as a particle (subatomic physical mass of matter) and as a wave (non-physical energy), but also implies that energy manifests differently depending on the expectations of any observers. The double-slit experiment, which is often referred to as Young's double slit experiment, demonstrates the inseparability of the wave and particle natures of light and other quantum particles.[42] This experiment can be difficult to understand at first. I had to review it quite a few times before I was able to understand and grasp the magnitude of these findings.[43]

The double slit experiment was originally performed by Thomas Young in the beginning of the nineteenth century by letting sunlight (photons) pass through a slit on a screen and landing on a screen behind it. The experiment showed that light travels both as a wave of energy and as a particle of matter.

Years later, scientists again did the double slit experiment, but instead of sunlight, they used a machine that was able to shoot subatomic particles, like electrons, through a slit on one screen. The vertical slit was so small that not all of the electrons went through the slit. Some of the electrons hit the screen and bounced back. The electrons that did go through the slit ended up hitting the second screen, which was behind the first screen, and left a pattern in the form of one vertical pillar. This pattern is a signature of when energy behaves (travels) as particles of matter.

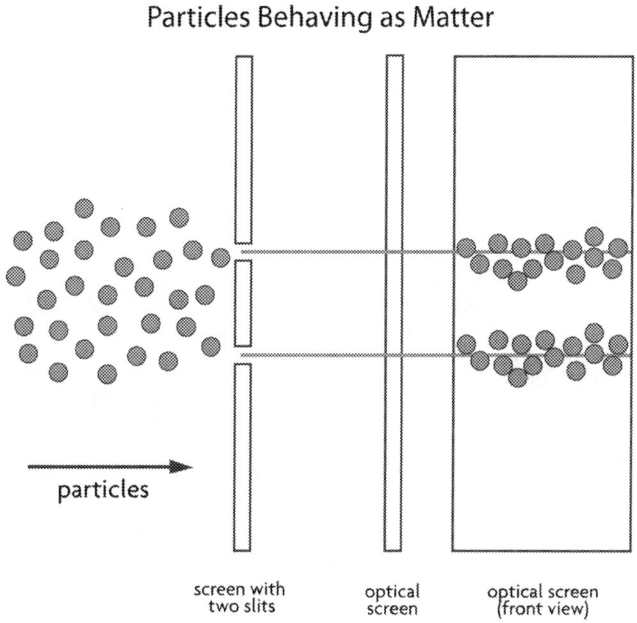

## Particles Behaving as Matter

screen with
two slits

optical
screen

optical screen
(front view)

**Figure 11. Particles Behaving as Matter**

Scientists decided to add a second slit to the first screen. When they fired electrons at the screen, now with two slits, they expected the markings on the second screen to be in the pattern of two vertical pillars, which would represent particles going through the two slits. But this was not what they found. The particles left a pattern of wave-like bands of light and dark pillars. These bands are the signature of waves of energy rather than particles of matter.

The particles were traveling as waves of formless energy and then landing as solid particles. This was a revolutionary find because it showed that particles of matter were behaving like waves of energy. Before this experiment, scientists had thought that particles and waves were two different things, not the same thing. This experiment showed that particles can behave like particles of matter or formless waves of probability. The wavelike bands of light and dark marks are what happen when particles behave as waves of energy.

## Particles Behaving as Waves of Matter

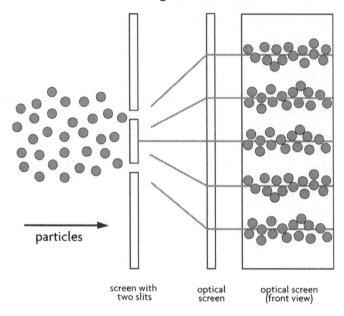

particles

| screen with | optical | optical screen |
| two slits | screen | (front view) |

**Figure 12. Particles Behaving as Waves of Energy.**

Scientists were confused and thought maybe the electrons were bouncing off each other and were causing the interference pattern that waves make so they decided to make another special device that would shoot only one electron at a time through only one slit while both slits were open. Since the particles were only being shot through one slit, they expected to see a pattern of just one vertical pillar on the screen behind the slit, but what they found baffled them. They again found the same alternating light and dark bands that waves produce. They wondered how this could still be happening when they were only firing one electron at a time through only one slit. Logic would say that since only one electron was being fired at a time through only one slit there shouldn't be any interference with other electrons that would cause the wave-like pattern of a band of light and dark pillars. They deduced that this had to mean that each electron was being shot out as a particle of matter and then became a wave of potentials going through both slits simultaneously and then was interfering with itself before landing again as a particle of matter to make the same wavelike patterns on the screen. The electrons were traveling both as particles and waves. "Quantum Energy can exist in two very different forms: As visible particles or invisible waves. The energy is still there either way, just making itself known in different ways."[44]

Then something even more bizarre happened. Scientists decided to put a measuring device by one of the slits and what they discovered astonished them. This time the electrons had stopped making the alternating light and dark bands that waves make and started making the pattern of vertical pillars that particles make. *The particles had changed how they were acting based on the observation of this device.*

It seems that whenever there are two or more choices, subatomic particles travel as an energy wave of potentials experiencing all possible outcomes, but not choosing any of them until influenced by an observer. Once an observer is present, the wave collapses into a particle of matter as just one outcome is chosen.

So what does all this really mean? It means that subatomic particles, like electrons, can move both as particles and waves, and it appears that they are also conscious and aware of when they are being watched. They seem to somehow be able to change their behavior based on who is watching and what their expectations are!

How this energy travels appears to depend on whether an observer is focused on it and what he or she expects of it.

> Very simply stated, it says there is no meaning to the objective existence of an electron at a specific point in time—for example, at one of the two holes in the double slit experiment—independent of observation.[45]

The double slit experiment appears to suggest that electrons or energy are just un-manifested possibilities of reality until they are influenced by the focus of a conscious mind into manifesting in a certain way. In other words, this information suggests that we can and do influence this energy with our minds. Could this be the secret behind the power of the law of attraction?

# Wave-Particle Duality Quotes

In *The Field*, Lynne McTaggart states, "The quantum pioneers had discovered that our involvement with matter was crucial. Subatomic particles existed in all possible states until disturbed by us—by observing or measuring—at which point, they'd settled down, at long last, into something real. Our observation—our human consciousness—was utterly central to this process of subatomic flux actually becoming some set thing, but we weren't in any of the mathematics of Heisenberg or Schrodinger."[46]

In *The Hidden Messages in Water*, Masaru Emoto states, "But now the science of quantum mechanics generally acknowledges that substance is nothing more than vibration. When we separate something into its smallest parts, we always enter a strange world where all that exists is particles and waves."[47]

"According to the Hanyashingyo, the Buddhist Wisdom and Heart Sutra, 'That which can be seen has no form, and that which cannot be seen has form.' We can now say that this strange contradiction, spoken ages ago by Buddha, has been proved true by modern science."[48] The wave-particle duality as described in the Buddhist Wisdom and Heart Sutra suggests that the physical things in our existence are really formless energy vibrating a certain way to make them solid. It also suggests that formless energy can become matter depending on how it vibrates. This is because formless energy and matter are both just the same energy in different forms. This supports the law of oneness, which says that everything is a part of the same connected energy.

Critics argue that quantum physics do not apply to the larger world that we live in, but I disagree. Quantum physics as a whole suggests that energy is everything and, through our focus as the observer, we can affect how this energy manifests. Think about it. If this energy is everything in our existence, and if this energy reacts to our focus and our expectations, and if we have control over our expectations, isn't it logical to think that we should be able to control how this energy forms in our lives? After all, doesn't this energy consist of subatomic particles, which make up the atoms that are the building blocks of every physical thing in our existence?

The answer is yes. So it's not much of a mental stretch for us to see how our thoughts, through the observation and expectation of this energy, are able to affect how this energy forms into reality. (The light bulb goes on!) This information gives scientific support to the claim that thoughts create reality.

In *The Science Behind The Secret: Decoding The Law of Attraction*, physicist Travis S. Taylor, PhD states that our brains are quantum computers, and we live in a quantum universe.[49] He ties in quantum wave functions with our larger reality by saying, "But no matter what the reality is at any given instant, when you have a new thought, you are setting up a new quantum state. With each new thought, a new qwiff [quantum wave interference function] is generated that begins interacting throughout the universe. Your new thought continues to interact with the universe and other qwiffs in the universe that are similar to it until a new entangled and common qwiff 'coheres' and becomes the next instant's reality.[50] This *is* the essence and the heart of *The Secret*."[51]

He also states, "It is, perhaps, this communication to the outside environment that causes the law of attraction to take place. These turned quantum oscillations, these turned thoughts, are oscillated to the universe whereby the next instant in reality is cohered, creating each individual experience."[52]

He sums this all up by stating, "You really are creating your very own 'conscious experience' and your own reality. Your thought oscillations superimpose upon the 'noisy' quantum environment of the universe and cohere with something generating your next instant, your next real experience."[53]

Let's review what we learned in this section.

## Wave-Particle Duality (Double Slit Experiment) Summary

- Subatomic particles can travel both as particles of matter and as waves of energy.
- Particles are the things that make solid matter.
- Waves are the formless possibilities of every possible outcome.
- This energy is somehow aware of when it is being watched.
- The act of observing this energy affects how the energy manifests.

- Whenever there are two or more options, and the particles are not being observed, the particles behave as waves.
- The wave (many choices) collapses into a particle of matter (one choice) once it encounters an observer.
- This information supports the claim that our thoughts can and do influence and create the reality we experience.

## String Theory

Albert Einstein's theory of general relativity gives us the working framework to understand how big things, such as planets, stars, and galaxies work in nature. Quantum mechanics gives us a framework to understand very small things, such as atoms, and subatomic particles like electrons, and quarks work in nature. The problem with these two theories is that they don't work together. Einstein tried to solve this challenge by coming up with what he called a unified field theory that would unite both the theories of big and small under one unified theory that worked together seamlessly. Unfortunately Einstein was unable to discover this unified field theory during the last thirty years of his life.[54]

In recent years, a new theory has gained popularity as possibly being the unified field theory or "theory of everything" (T.O.E.) that Einstein sought. This theory is called superstring theory, or string theory as it is commonly known. In order to understand string theory, we must first break down the atom. The atom is composed of subatomic particles, such as electrons, protons, and neutrons. Electrons are elemental particles in that they cannot be divided into smaller particles. The protons and neutrons in the atom's nucleus are broken down into quarks. "According to string theory, both quarks and electrons, at their most basic level, are composed of vibrating strings. These strings make up the atoms that are the building blocks for everything in our existence."[55] In *The Elegant Universe,* Brian Greene says the following about string theory:

> From one principle—that everything at its most microscopic level consists of combinations of vibrating strands—string theory provides a single explanatory framework capable of encompassing all forces and all matter.

String theory proclaims, for example, that the observed particle's properties are a reflection of the various ways in which strings can vibrate. Just as strings on a violin or piano have resonate frequencies at which they prefer to vibrate—patterns that our ears sense as various musical notes and their higher harmonics—the same holds true for the loops of string theory. But we will see that, rather than producing musical notes, each of the preferred patterns of vibration of a string in string theory appears as particles whose mass and force charges are determined by the string's oscillatory pattern. The electron string is vibrating one way; the up-quark is vibrating another way; and so on. Far from being a collection of chaotic experimental facts, particle properties in string theory are the manifestation of one and the same physical feature: the resonant patterns of vibration—the music, so to speak—of fundamental loops of string. The same idea applies to the forces of nature. We will see that force particles are also associated with particular patterns of string vibrations and hence everything, all matter and all forces, is unified under the same rubric of microscopic string oscillations—the "notes" that strings play.[56]

String theory and this statement by Greene seem to support the premise of this book that the vibrational frequency of anything determines what is created.

Let's review what we learned in this section:

## String Theory Summary

- Sting theory says that, at their most basic level, every atom is composed of vibrating strings that work to create the matter we experience in our reality.
- These vibrating strings act like a DNA code that tells energy how to manifest into reality.
- This information supports the claim of the law of vibration that each individual thing has its own unique vibrational signature.
- This theory provides a possible explanation of how the very small world of quantum mechanics can—and does—affect the larger world in which we live.

# Overall Review of Quantum Physics

Here is a list what we have learned in this
chapter about quantum physics:

- *Einstein's formula E=mc²* shows that energy and matter are equivalent to each other. This supports the theory that everything in our existence, including matter, is made of energy. This supports the law of oneness.

- *Non-locality (Entanglement)* states that once two or more particles interact with each other, they become connected or entangled and instantly react to each other regardless of the space or time between them. This supports the idea that everything in our existence is made up of the same fabric of energy and that everything is connected. This supports the law of oneness.

- *Wave-Particle Duality (Double Slit Experiment)* shows that subatomic particles of matter travel both as particles of matter and as waves of energy. This again supports the idea that everything, even matter, is made up of energy. This experiment, through the impact of the observer, also supports the idea that our thoughts affect how energy manifests into matter.

- *String Theory* states that in every atom there are elemental particles, such as electrons and quarks and in these subatomic particles there exists vibrating strings that are the building blocks of our reality. This theory suggests that how strings vibrate determines what they create. This theory has been suggested as being the unified field theory that unites quantum mechanics and Einstein's theory of relativity. This theory supports the law of vibration showing that each thing in our existence has its own unique vibration.

In summary, I feel that this chapter helps to support that claim that quantum physics does apply to the larger world we live in and that our thoughts really do create our reality. Look at all of the evidence of the energy ($E=mc^2$), how everything is connected (entanglement), how matter and energy have been shown to be the same thing (wave-particle duality in the double slit experiment), and how vibrating strings of energy are the building blocks of matter (string theory). All of these individual aspects of quantum mechanics seem to come together to paint a picture that everything in our existence is energy; everything is connected; and that this energy is alive and reactive to the effect of an observer. This suggests that our conscious minds can influence how this energy manifests to make everything we experience in our reality.

# Part 2:
# Secrets of the Law of Attraction

# Chapter 3: How the Law of Attraction Works

*"In a malleable world where everything from atoms to cells is changing to match our beliefs, we are limited only by the way we think of ourselves in that world."*
*-Gregg Braden, The Spontaneous Healing of Belief*

This chapter will show you how to specifically use the energy of your mind to create anything in life that you desire. We have learned that everything is made up of the same energy, and that we are also part of this energy. We've also learned from Einstein and quantum physics that energy can be in the form of waves of energy (non-physical) or particles of matter (physical form).

Let's take a minute to review a little bit from Part 1 of this book. Since we are made up of energy, we are all vibrational energy beings in physical bodies. Each living and non-living thing has its own vibrational frequency or energy signature that makes it unique. It's like an energy DNA code that tells the subatomic particles to spin in a certain way and speed to manifest into specific forms of energy or matter.

If everything in our universe is made up of the same energy, then our thoughts, words, and actions are also made up of this same energy. If we can control our thoughts, words, and actions, then we should also be able to control how this energy manifests in our lives.

Since this book is about using the mind to influence the manifestation of energy, we will depart from discussing scientific theory and make the assumption that we can and do use our minds to influence the manifestation of this energy in our lives.

When we focus our thoughts, we are able to influence how energy manifests in our lives. This is the power behind *The Secret, Ask and It is Given,* and *Think and Grow Rich,* as well as many other wonderful books that teach the law of attraction. The power of the mind is so much more than just positive thinking and belief. It's about changing future events. When you think a certain way, you change the way the energy reacts and influence how energy manifests into the events, situations, and things in your life.

Let's say you wanted to become rich and learned how to properly use the law of attraction to manifest an abundance of money. If you use the law of attraction correctly, you will eventually start to experience strange coincidences or occurrences that will help you achieve your desire. A coincidence is defined as the occurrence of events that happen at the same time by accident but seem to have some connection.[57] Could this connection be the alignment of our thoughts with the vibrational frequency of our desires? Could it be the law of oneness at work through the effects of quantum entanglement (non-locality)? Could both of these explanations be the same thing? The answer appears to be yes.

Creating with your mind is both easier and harder than you think. You have already been doing it your whole life and probably didn't even know it. It is simple to learn but difficult to train yourself to do consistently.

When we focus and believe something will happen, it will almost always eventually come to us. If we want money we can focus on it and it will come to us. Unfortunately the opposite also works. If we are worried about not enough money, we are tapping into the vibration of lack of money, which keeps money from coming to us.

When I first started learning about the law of attraction, I thought these rules seemed simple enough. I thought I would just focus on what I wanted and it would appear, but I found out that it was very difficult to focus on what I wanted when I constantly had to view the reality of the situation that I was currently experiencing, especially if that situation was unpleasant or negative. After years of studying the law of attraction and practicing it in my own life, I was able to become more successful in making it consistently work in my life. I would like to help you learn from my mistakes so that you can learn to manifest what you want faster.

# The Conscious, Subconscious, and Superconscious Minds

Before we discuss how to use the powers of the mind, we should discuss what those powers are and how they affect us. The mind is much more than just a complicated thinking machine. It is also a sender and a receiver of information to everything in our existence. Let's discuss the three levels of the mind.

It has been said that each of us has three minds or selves. Max Freedom Long interpreted the Hawaiian Huna belief system by stating each person has three minds: the middle self, the lower self, and the higher self.[58] The famous pioneering psychologist Carl Jung created his own theory of a three-part mind, consisting of the ego, the personal unconscious, and a collective unconscious.[59] Let's take a closer look at how the Huna belief system defines these three minds.

## The Conscious Mind (Middle Self)

The conscious mind is the mind we use to think with each day. It is our consciousness. It is the mind that most of us associate with who we are. *The conscious mind is in charge of thinking and logic.*[60] *It is the consciously awake part of you that makes conscious decisions.* The conscious mind sends orders to the subconscious mind (lower self) through its thoughts and feelings.

## The Subconscious Mind (Lower Self)

The subconscious mind lives beneath our conscious awareness. It is able to remember everything that we have ever experienced. It can read a page by merely glancing at it for a split second, and can remember things that the conscious mind misses. *The subconscious mind is in charge of physically manifesting the desires of the conscious mind. It deals with our feelings and emotions.*[61] The subconscious mind, unlike the conscious mind, does not think for itself. It is like a soldier that blindly follows orders without ever questioning the validity or accuracy of the requests that are given to it. It assumes the instructions it gets from the conscious mind are exactly what the conscious mind wanted.

The subconscious mind acts as an intermediary between the conscious mind and the superconscious mind by taking instructions from the conscious mind in the form of focused thoughts and feelings and relaying them to the superconscious mind to create that physical reality.

In *Think and Grow Rich*, Napoleon Hill discussed the subconscious mind:

> The subconscious mind works day and night. It draws upon the force of Infinite Intelligence for the power with which it voluntarily transmutes desires into their physical equivalent. You cannot entirely control your subconscious mind, but you can voluntarily hand over to it any plan, desire, or purpose you wish to be transformed into concrete form.[62]

He seems to be describing how the subconscious mind draws upon the source of infinite intelligence, the superconscious mind, to manifest desires into reality.

## The Superconscious Mind (Higher Self)

This third mind has many names: the superconscious mind, the universal mind, the collective unconscious, the higher self.

The Huna belief system believes that the superconscious mind is the universal mind or higher self that is comprised of everything in our existence and beyond. It is the oneness in the law of oneness. This mind or self is the energy that connects everything and has the power to create miracles.[63] Carl Jung called this mind the collective unconscious. Jung describes the collective unconscious as follows:

In addition to our immediate consciousness, which is of a thoroughly personal nature and which we believe to be the only empirical psyche (even if we tack on the personal unconscious as an appendix), there exists a second psychic system of a collective, universal, and impersonal nature which is identical in all individuals. This collective unconscious does not develop individually but is inherited.[64]

In *Creative Visualization: Use the Power of Your Imagination to Create What You Want in Your Life*, Shakti Gawain explained the higher self:

Your spiritual source is the supply of infinite love, wisdom, and energy in the universe. For you, *source* may mean God, Goddess, universal intelligence, the Great Spirit, the higher power, or your true essence. However we conceptualize it, it can be found here and now within each of us, in our inner beings. You can think of contacting your source as connecting with your higher self, the wise being who dwells within you.[65]

The superconscious mind is our connection to everything. Do you remember the section on quantum entanglement earlier in this book? This is where two particles, which had interacted with each other, were separated by space and time and yet were able to act as if they were somehow connected or communicating. Since everything in our existence consists of the same energy—based on this principle—we all should be connected to it as well. This is the law of oneness. This is the superconscious mind.

The superconscious mind is everything that is manifested in our existence and everything that has the potential to ever be manifested. It is both everything and nothing. It is the God-force in us that religion teaches. It doesn't matter if you believe in religion or not—the superconscious mind exists and works just the same with or without belief in it. The superconscious mind is also known as the higher self. This self has the power to create anything. It can allow you to heal from any sickness, create wealth, find true love, and do anything else you can desire. It can also send you valuable insight and wisdom. The higher self communicates to us through the heart center in the form of intuition.

I have included these examples of the three minds of the Huna belief system and Carl Jung's teachings because they give us telling support of an infinite power source within us that is capable of manifesting miracles.

Most people would agree that we have a conscious mind along with a subconscious mind. Not as many people know about the universal mind—or collective unconscious as Jung called it. That is unfortunate because it appears that this often unknown mind is what connects us to our infinite power. It connects us to everyone and everything, including the source that some call God. This superconscious mind, the universal mind, the higher self, the spiritual self, or whatever you want to call it appears to be the secret energy source that allows the law of attraction to work and lets us manifest our desires into reality.

## Using the Three Minds to Create

When you desire something, your conscious mind chooses thoughts that communicate mentally what you wish to create. The subconscious mind is then waiting for any thoughts that come from the conscious mind. It listens to your thoughts and mindlessly thinks that you want whatever you are thinking about at that time. The subconscious mind then connects with the universal mind to create and manifest the thought into the physical reality.

Let's say you wanted to get a new job that pays more money. Your conscious mind thinks the thought that you want a better-paying job. Your subconscious mind takes that thought as a request that you want a better-paying job. It then sends a request to the superconscious mind to make that request a reality. The new job that you desire will manifest through the path of least resistance. This means you may get promoted at your current job and get a raise, or a competitor may notice your work and offer you a better-paying position.

## How and When Your Desire Will Manifest

How your desire manifests and when it happens are not your responsibilities. That is the job of the superconscious mind. The superconscious mind, which is much wiser than your conscious mind, will send your request to you in the most efficient and beneficial way possible. Sometimes you may not initially agree with how or when your desire manifests, but you will look back on the experience and see the wisdom of it.

You can help your desire to manifest sooner by staying open to ways it can come to you and by constantly feeding your mind positive thoughts that reinforce your desire. This helps you to vibrationally align with your desire which will bring you to it.

## Time Delay

Luckily for us, all there is a time delay between when we focus on or ask for something and when it manifests in our lives. This gives us ample time to change our minds about what we really want or to decide if we desire something else. Imagine what our lives would be like if every thought we had manifested immediately before our eyes. Our lives would be chaotic with us endlessly running around trying to correct the messes we didn't mean to create. This time delay requires that we stay focused on what we want for a period of time before our desire will manifest in our life.

The law of attraction likes repetition, not in asking, but in feeling the result of what we desire as if it has already happened. It likes to receive, over and over again, the positive thoughts and feelings of you already having enjoying that manifestation even if it hasn't manifested for you yet. When you think good thoughts, you are able to avoid thinking any negative thoughts that contradict your initial desire.

When the subconscious mind gets a desire of good health from you in one thought and then a little later gets a worried or fearful thought of sickness, it doesn't know which one to give you. The thoughts often cancel each other out. So you will either become more ill or will stay the same. You need to monitor your thoughts and be consistent with the way you think if you want your desire to manifest.

## You Are the Master of Your Fate

One of my favorite books about using the law of attraction, especially with money, is *Think and Grow Rich* by Napoleon Hill. Napoleon Hill (1883–1970) spent much of his life uncovering the secrets of the law of attraction. Hill talks about English Poet W.C. Henley's prophetic lines, "I am the Master of my Fate, I am the Captain of My Soul."

> He (W.C. Henley) should have informed us that the reason we are the Masters of our Fate, the Captains of our Souls is because we have the power to control our thoughts.
>
> He should have told us that the ether in which this little planet floats, in which we move and have our being, is a form of energy moving at an inconceivable high rate of vibration, and that the ether is filled with a form of universal power which *adapts* itself to the nature of the thoughts we hold in our minds; and *influences* us, in natural ways, to transmute our thoughts in the their physical equivalent.[66]

When I first read this line, I wondered how it was possible for a man over a hundred years ago to know about this empowering knowledge when even today it is considered cutting edge information. When I read the book, I discovered that he initially learned this magical information from Andrew Carnegie, who claimed to have used this power to build his steel empire many years ago.

I found myself wondering why the law of attraction wasn't household knowledge by now. Why hadn't the world understood and embraced this amazing discovery that our thoughts create reality? Instead, it is still widely considered to be *The Secret*. I hope books like this one and others like it will help the world to understand that we are so much more than just human beings; we are the empowered co-creators of our own reality.

Let's learn how to specifically use the law of attraction to create what we want in life.

In this section, I share two different ways to use the law of attraction. The first way is the simple way. I call it the Focus, Feel, and Expect Process. This way is perfect if you can focus your thoughts long enough to make it work. The second way is called the Nine A's to Acing the Law of Attraction Checklist. This slightly longer process is a checklist that will help you go step-by-step to make sure you are doing the right things to make your desire manifest.

## The Focus, Feel, and Expect Process:

Step 1 is to ask for whatever it is that you desire. Your *focus* on something is the same as asking for it because the law of attraction interprets your focus as your desire.

Step 2 is to align vibrationally with the energy of your desire by thinking, feeling, saying, and doing things that support your desire. It is important to *feel* the good feeling of your desire *before* it manifests into your life. Use your imagination to feel what it is going to feel like when that desire shows up in your life. This is necessary because you must align vibrationally with your desire in order for it to show up in your life. Your feeling is an indicator of your vibrational alignment. When you are focused and feeling your desire, you are aligned with it. This allows it to manifest in your life. Let's discuss the concept of vibrational alignment a little more.

Step 3 is to *expect* your desire to show up in your life. We are unable to stay focused on fear and hope at the same time. This means when you are constantly focused on your desire showing up in your life, you are unable focus on the fearful or doubtful thoughts that prevent your desire from manifesting. Believing your desire will manifest is a key ingredient in making it a reality.

## The Focus, Feel, and Expect Process

Step 1:  *Focus* on what you desire.
Step 2:  *Feel* the good feeling of having that desire in your life right now.
Step 3:  *Expect* your desire to show up in your life.

## Align with Your Desire by Feeling It

As we learned earlier, energy aligns with other like-type energy. When we mentally create a desire, we must align with the energy of that desire by becoming a vibrational match to it. Our feelings are our indicator of our alignment, or lack of alignment, with our focus or desire. You may be asking yourself why you need to align with your desire. The reason is because you need to become a vibrational match to your desire in order for it to manifest into your life.

Once you ask for your desire through your thoughts or focus, it is created and awaits you at a specific vibrational frequency. In this instance, a vibrational frequency is very much like a radio dial. For example, if you want to listen to rock music, you would tune into the rock station on 98.5 FM. If you want country music, you would tune into the country radio station on 105.1 FM. You could do this same thing for any type of music you wanted to hear. You wouldn't expect to hear rap music on a country station or vice versa so it is important to tune into the correct station. Tuning into your desires is no different.

You need to go to the frequency to where your desire is waiting for you.[67] Once you do that, you will be aligned with it and it will be able to start showing up. You are probably asking, "How will I know what is the frequency of my desire?" The answer is simple. In order to go to the frequency of your desire, you don't need to know a specific number or frequency—you just need to believe in your desire and feel good about it happening. Your emotions and feelings are your guide to your frequency. When you feel positive and expectant about your desire, you are aligned with it. When you feel negative, fearful, or doubtful about your desire manifesting, you are not aligned with it—and are keeping it from manifesting into your life. You must be aligned for your desires to manifest. You must first be it before you can receive it.

The law of attraction is really that easy to use, but before you get too excited, you must know that life is often complicated with emotional ups and downs. It can often be difficult for us to stay aligned with our desire by being consistent with our thoughts and feelings.

Initially, for what seemed like the longest time, I had trouble making the law of attraction work in my life. I felt like I was doing everything right, but my desires were not manifesting for me. This led me to do exhaustive research on the law of attraction to see what I could possibly be doing wrong. Then through trial and error with my own life experiences, I eventually found a more consistent way to make the law of attraction work in my life. These experiences with the law of attraction led me to create the Nine A's to Acing the Law of Attraction Checklist. I hope that this checklist will allow you to successfully manifest the law of attraction in your life much easier than I was able to do when I was first learning it.

# The Nine A's to Acing the Law of Attraction Checklist

## Step 1. Accept your current situation.

Whatever negativity is currently happening to you has already been created. Your current reality was created by your thoughts in the past. There is nothing you can do to change the past, but you can start right now in the present moment to create your future by accepting the present situation. When you accept the present situation, you remove resistance to it. When you remove resistance to it, you allow yourself the space to create something else in its place.

When you are experiencing challenging times, you have two choices. Your first choice is to resist what is happening to you by denying that it is happening, fighting it, or suppressing it. If you resist, then you will be focusing on whatever you are resisting. The bottom line is if you are focusing on something, you are attracting more of that same energy to yourself.

The other choice you have is to accept what has already happened. By accepting your present reality, you release all resistance and negativity, which allows you to be able to focus on creating the positive future you desire.

Know that it takes a strong person to be able to ignore the pain and suffering that is happening when they are sick, and instead choose to focus on mentally creating the well being they desire. Your mind is a creative tool whether you realize it or not. You can create what you want only when you start thinking and feeling on purpose rather than in reaction to the events that happen to you. You must accept your reality to remove resistance.

## Step 2. Ask for what you want.

When you are ready to start the creation process, decide what you want to create. Most people go through life experiencing it as it happens to them rather than creating the way they desire it. When you see something that you want to have, all you have to do is ask for it. Often we have to experience something we don't want, like sickness, to really see what we do want, which in this instance would be wellness. The highs and lows of life allow us to experience the contrast in life. It is up to us to decide what we want in our lives; sometimes the only way we can know what we want is by experiencing what we don't want in our lives. This is because the more we experience what we don't want, the more we will know what we do want in our lives.

The law of attraction will allow you to ask for what you want in a number of ways. The most common way to ask the law of attraction is to merely place your mental focus on something. When you think of something, you are focused on it. The longer you stay focused on it, the more energy is focused around your desire. When you add emotions to your thoughts, they become supercharged with energy, which intensifies the law of attraction. Using emotionally charged repetitive thoughts is a powerful way to manifest your desires, but it is also a powerful way to manifest what you don't want if you are continually focused on negative things like worry or fear.

## Step 3. Align with positivity.

Once you have decided what you want, your desire is created and waits for you at a specific vibrational frequency. Your energy of aligning is different from your energy of asking. This is an important step to note because many people simply never stop asking. You create your desire by asking; however, to manifest your desire, you must align with it vibrationally. Most people neglect this difficult step and therefore never see their desires manifested in their life. So how do you align with your desires? It's both easy and difficult to do. You can match your frequency to that of your desire by mentally seeing, feeling, and believing that it has already happened. Positive thoughts about your desire are aligned with it. Stay focused on your desire—seeing and feeling what your life will be like until it manifests for you. That's the simple part. The difficult part is that in order for you to stay focused on the positive expectation of your desire already being in your life, you will have to consciously choose to remove all negative thoughts.

## Step 4. Avoid negative thoughts and feelings.

This step is very important if you wish to see your desire manifest. This is also the hardest part about mastering the law of attraction. When life is raining on you and you are feeling pain, sorrow, fear, or worry, it is hard to focus on the happy things you wish to create. However, the fact remains that the law of attraction works by attracting more of the energy we send out. If we are thinking, saying, or doing something negative, we are effectively telling the law of attraction that we don't want something positive in our life because our energy is negative. If we ask for something positive like good health, and then a few minutes later we start worrying about our health, we are sending the law of attraction mixed messages. The person is not able to stay positively focused on their desire long enough for it to manifest in their life. This is a big reason why many desires never get manifested.

Instead of monitoring all of your thoughts, an easier method is to just monitor your feelings. If your thoughts make you feel good, then you are thinking in a way that is aligning with positive energy. If your thoughts make you feel negative emotions, then your thoughts are aligning with negative energy. As we've already learned, we attract the same energy we choose for ourselves. If you are feeling negative, you may want to change how you think so you change how you feel. If you are sick, you can still feel sick and imagine feeling good emotionally with thoughts of hope at the same time. Remember that once you align with positivity, it is only a matter of time before your desire manifests for you. It is your responsibility to stay positively focused on your desire until it manifests.

## Step 5. Acknowledge what you are willing to give.

The law of compensation states that when you give energy, you get it back ten times greater. You must be willing to give something to get something.

The greatest thing you can give yourself is your commitment to making your desire become a reality. You can commit to being faithful and diligent by thinking, saying, and doing positive things that complement your desire. You can also give to others.

If you are on a diet, you may commit to eating right and exercising regularly. If you are sick, you may commit to getting lots of rest and taking better care of yourself. If you're struggling financially, you may commit to cutting costs to save money. You could also give some of your money to the poor. It is always best to give what you want to receive. If you want to run a marathon, you might commit to running so many miles a week in training. If you give effort out, it will come back to you in result. Just be sure to be consistent with your effort.

## Step 6. Allow yourself to be open-minded.

Allowing is a key part of the law of attraction. All too often, we want to dictate how our desire will come to us. This is because most of us are used to "willing" things to happen in our lives through our actions. Willing things into reality is one way of using the law of attraction and it sometimes works. However, sometimes the things we will into reality are not the best things for us. A better way is to be open-minded about how the universe brings your desire to you. The universal mind is ultimately wiser than your conscious mind and will always bring you your desire in the way that benefits you the most. You may not agree with how it comes to you, but the wisdom of it is usually understood in the future when you are able to look back on the past. When using the law of attraction, it is best to allow your desire to come to you through an opportunity that presents itself. Then it is up to you to act on that opportunity to bring your desire into reality.

An example of this is that you may desire to be a millionaire today by winning the lottery but the universe has other plans. Unless your karma or life plan prevents it, the universe will manifest your desire of becoming a millionaire, but instead of winning it, you may have to earn it through an ingenious idea that you market, or through running your own business. The point is to be open and ready for signs that the law of attraction is trying to manifest your desire for you.

## Step 7. Agree to be patient and persistent.

Staying focused on your goal until it manifests is very important. As stated before, it is easy to get distracted by negative things, doubt, or worry. Agree to stay focused and persistent with your positive thoughts and actions until your desire manifests.

When using the law of attraction, you are in charge of what you want to create. The universe is in charge of how and when it comes to you. Sometimes desires manifest immediately; sometimes they take years. Your job is to stay focused on what you want until it shows up.

## Step 8. Act when opportunities arise.

When your desire begins to materialize in your life, it will most likely manifest for you in an unexpected or coincidental opportunity. It is up to you to be open-minded and aware enough to recognize this opportunity and to act on it when it happens. This opportunity is like a door to your desire that is open for a very short period of time. It has been my experience that these opportunities come at unexpected times and often hide themselves in a crisis. You may get in a fender bender and, through exchanging information with the other driver, meet your future husband or wife. You may have lost your job and were forced to wait tables at a local restaurant to make ends meet, but your excellent service catches the eye of an executive of the company you wanted to work for and he offers you a job. You never know when or how the opportunities will happen, but they will—so keep your eyes open and be ready to act when they do.

## Step 9. Appreciate when your desire manifests.

When your desire finally manifests, make sure to appreciate it because the law of compensation states that when you give appreciation for something, you are sending out positive energy into the world that will come back to you ten times greater. Gratitude is very important in keeping the positive momentum going in your life.

Many people make the mistake of not believing that the law of attraction was responsible for their desire coming true. They often say it was coincidence, or that it was luck, but the bottom line is that they asked for it and it came true in their life. However it came true is irrelevant. When your desire somehow manifests, be sure to keep the positivity coming by recognizing and appreciating it.

## The Nine A's to Acing the Law of Attraction Checklist:

Step 1.   *Accept* your current situation.
Step 2.   *Ask* for what you want.
Step 3.   *Align* with positivity.
Step 4.   *Avoid* negative thoughts and feelings.
Step 5.   *Acknowledge* what you are willing to give.
Step 6.   *Allow* yourself to be open-minded.
Step 7.   *Agree* to be patient and persistent.
Step 8.   *Act* when opportunities arise.
Step 9.   *Appreciate* when your desire manifests.

## Manifestation Exercise

It is time to use the Nine A's to Acing the Law of Attraction Checklist to create the reality you desire. Remember you can always use the Focus, Feel, and Expect Process of simply asking for what you want and then aligning with it. For people who have trouble staying aligned, I suggest using the Nine A's to Acing the Law of Attraction Checklist.

Here is an example of how to use this process. In this example, I will act out the role of someone who is struggling financially but who wishes to become rich.

1. *Accept* your current situation. I am currently feeling fearful and worried about money, but I know that by thinking, feeling, and acting positively, I will create a new brighter future for myself. I accept that I am currently struggling financially, but trust and believe better times are on the way.

2. *Ask* for what you want. I ask for financial abundance. I desire to become a millionaire.

3. *Align* with positivity. I align with my desires by thinking positive thoughts. I tell myself every day that it is only a matter of time before I achieve my goals of becoming a millionaire and having financial security. It is a certainty in my mind even though it has not happened yet. I don't know how long it will take, but I know I will eventually achieve my goal.

4. *Avoid* negative thoughts and feelings. I agree to avoid all negative thoughts because I realize that negative thoughts attract more negativity. The only way to align with my desires is through positive thinking. I will no longer think about my financial problem and instead will think about my abundant financial future.

5. *Acknowledge* what you are willing to give. I acknowledge that I am willing to give my complete mental and emotional dedication to being positive—regardless of how I feel or what happens to me. My actions and words will complement my goals. I am also willing to work hard to make my dream of becoming a millionaire a reality.

6. *Allow* yourself to be open-minded. I allow my desires to come to me by being open to however they manifest in my life. It could be a great idea that I bring to the market, or it could be an inheritance from a relative I didn't know I had. I may

have to work three jobs for the foreseeable future to save enough money to invest. I am open to the many ways I can achieve my goal.

7. *Agree* to be patient and persistent. I agree to be patient in waiting for my desires to manifest and persistent with my thoughts and actions. I realize it can take time for my desires to manifest. I agree to stay focused on my goal until it arrives in my life.

8. *Act* when opportunities arise. I will act when opportunities arise, or when I feel it is time to act. This can mean working extra hours or extra jobs so that there is enough money to survive today and enough money to save in order to achieve wealth tomorrow. I will do whatever the situation dictates I need to do as long as it is within my ethical boundaries.

9. *Appreciate* when your desire manifests. I will appreciate it when my desire manifests in my life. I understand that appreciation brings more of the same energy back to me.

Now it is your turn to use this process to create your future reality. In the spaces below or in your journal, fill in each step of the process.

Step 1. *Accept* your current situation.

_____

_____

_____

Step 2. *Ask* for what you want.

_____

_____

_____

Step 3. *Align* with positivity.

_____

_____

_____

Step 4. *Avoid* negative thoughts and feelings.

_____

_____

_____

Step 5. Acknowledge what you are willing to give.

_____

_____

_____

Step 6. *Allow* yourself to be open-minded.

_____

_____

_____

Step 7. *Agree* to be patient and persistent.

_____

_____

_____

Step 8. *Act* when opportunities arise.

_____

_____

_____

Step 9. *Appreciate* when your desire manifests.

_____

_____

_____

# Chapter 4: Tricks to Using the Law of Attraction

## Positive Makes Perfect

The law of attraction doesn't understand negatives in sentences. If you say, "I do not want to be sick anymore," the law of attraction translates that as, "I want to be sick." It does not hear or understand the "do not" part of the sentence.

A better way to phrase that desire is, "I am healthy and feel great." Think, feel, say, and do positive things even if you currently are sick and don't feel well. The trick is to think and feel things that you can actually believe in that moment. You probably can't convince yourself that you feel fine in that same moment that you are suffering in pain, but you can use the law of polarity to ease from one emotion to a better feeling emotion, then later to another one, and another one until you do feel better. Maybe you can say something like, "I know I am in pain now, but I have felt better before, and I believe I can influence my future with my thoughts. I know in time I will feel better again." This phrasing of the sentence helps you to acknowledge the reality you are currently experiencing while reaching for a better feeling future.

If you desire money, but say to yourself, "I want money so I will not be poor anymore," the law of attraction interprets this as saying you want only enough money to be poor. A better way to reword this desire is to say something like, "I have the money I need now, and I love the way it feels. Money comes to me effortlessly and abundantly. I deserve it and appreciate it." Using positive words ensures that the law of attraction attracts you to your desires and not the opposite of what you desire.

### Perfect Your Desires Exercise

Okay, you try it. List your desires and check them for any negative wording. Use present tense wording as if your desires have already manifested.

Negative Wording: I am fat. I need to lose some weight.

Positive Wording: I am lean and in shape. I feel amazing!

Write down your desire. Check for negative wording. If you see negative writing, then use the second line to correct the sentence. Is every word in your sentence positive? Every word needs to be positive for you to benefit from the sentence.

List Your Desire:

_____

_____

List Your Perfected Desire (Check for Negative Wording):

_____

_____

# Emotions: Your Feelings are Your Guidance System

This is an extremely important part of the book because it teaches you how to use the law of attraction to your advantage.

We have so many thoughts running through our heads that it is often difficult to monitor each and every thought to make sure we are thinking the correct way. A better way is to focus on how you feel. Your thoughts are an indication of the direction in which you are headed, but your feelings will tell you if that is the direction you want to go. If you feel good about your thoughts, then you are heading in the direction you want to go. If you feel negative emotions, then you are heading in the wrong direction and toward attracting energy that you probably don't want in your life.

Below is my poem, "Thoughts are Things." It was listed in the preface of this book, but I feel it is pertinent to include it again. It shows how our thoughts create our reality and how we can use our emotions as a guide to show us where we are heading. This poem is an excellent learning tool to use with the law of attraction. It tells you everything you need to know to make the law of attraction work in your life. Memorize this poem and say it daily and you will never have to remember anything else about the law of attraction.

## Thoughts are Things

Whatever you think, whatever you feel,
It doesn't matter if it's make-believe, or if it is real.
Thoughts are things that go out into the unknown
To bring you back whatever you've sown.
Positive thoughts vibrate high,
While negative thoughts vibrate low.
Just focus on your own thoughts to see how your future will go.
You see, your thoughts are map of where you are headed,
And your feelings decide if that direction is welcome,
Or if it is dreaded.
So change how you think to change how you feel,
And watch how the universe attracts to you,
That which you have made real.

The point of this poem is that you create what you think about. Your thoughts are a map of where you are headed and your feelings decide if that direction is welcome or dreaded. If you want good things in your life, you need to think good, happy thoughts. If you don't feel happy, you need to change how you think to change how you feel.

I recite this poem daily to help me stay focused on creating the life I want to create. I also say it silently anytime I am not feeling as well as I would like to feel. It assists me in refocusing my attention on what I want rather than whatever negative situation I am experiencing at that moment. I hope you will allow it to do the same thing for you.

Now that we have learned about our emotions, let's look at an example to see how this method works in real life when something happens that causes us to get upset.

## Road Rage: How Do I Want to Feel?

Let's say someone just cut you off on the highway. You're angry and want to catch up and yell at them. At this time, you are thinking, "Hey this guy just almost ran me off the road, and he needs to know that his behavior is not acceptable. He deserves to have someone set him straight." Then you search your feelings to see how this thinking feels to you. You decide that you feel angry, mad, vengeful, and upset! You think, "Is this really how I want to feel? Will confronting this guy make me feel better or worse?" You decide that it may feel better in the short term to confront this person, but more than likely the conflict with him will make you feel upset for the rest of the day. A better way of controlling your thoughts and emotions is to feel what is right for you and then act accordingly. You might say to yourself, "I want to feel good. Confronting this guy is not going to accomplish that. Yes, his behavior deserves to be corrected, but I don't have to be the person to do that. I know the law of cause and effect is perfect and restores balance to all actions. I am going to choose to let this go and forget about it. I will not let his behavior affect how I feel in my body. I can only be mad if I allow myself to be mad."

When you choose to control your thoughts and actions, you begin to control what energy is attracted to you and how it affects you. What kind of energy do you think you would have been attracting to yourself if you confronted that person and got into a fight with him? It doesn't take a genius to see it wouldn't be positive for you or him. What someone else is doing is their business; how you react is yours.

When we choose to listen to our emotions and seek the best feeling emotion, we are able to control the types of energy we attract to ourselves and live a better life.

## How Do I Feel Exercise

One way we can be mindful of our thinking is to stop at least three times a day to become present and focused in the moment and ask ourselves one question. "How do I feel?" If you feel good, then you are thinking in a way that is attracting positive energy to yourself. If you are feeling angry, irritated, sad, worried, depressed, or any other negative emotion, it is time to take a few minutes to see why you feel the way you do. Use the law of polarity to help you move in the right emotional direction. You can change how you feel by changing how you think.

If you use the law of relativity, you can change your perception of your reality by choosing to find the good in the situation rather than the bad, and therefore transform your own energy from negative to positive. This is called personal or spiritual alchemy. Alchemy is defined as a medieval chemical science and speculative philosophy aiming to achieve the transmutation of the base metals into gold, the discovery of a universal cure for disease, and the discovery of a means of indefinitely prolonging life.[68] Alchemy in the past was the art of transmuting or transforming lead or other base metals into gold. Today you can change negative energy into positive energy through the law of perpetual transmutation of energy and the law of relativity by choosing to change how you think.

Remember that you are in control of you. You don't need to monitor every thought in your head—just monitor how you feel. You can only be upset if you allow yourself to be upset; use your feelings to guide you through life and, when necessary, change how you think to change how you feel.

## The Power of Belief/Faith

When you ask for something, you are requesting it from the universe. When you align with it, you are matching your vibration to the vibration of your desire. This is what allows your desire to manifest in your reality. One of the most powerful and easiest ways to align with your desire is to use belief or faith. A belief is a state or habit of mind in which trust or confidence is placed in some person or thing.[69] Faith is the confident belief or trust in the truth or trustworthiness of a person, concept, or thing.[70] When you believe or have faith in something, you are adding emotion, confidence, and conviction that your belief is true—regardless of whether you know how or why it is true. When you believe in something, you are sending out the strongest emotionally charged thoughts possible. Belief and faith are what make miracles possible. A few verses in the Bible appear to support the power of belief or faith when using the law of attraction. Jesus said:

Have faith in God. I tell you this: If anyone says to this mountain, "Be lifted from your place and hurled into the sea," *and has no inward doubts, but believes that what he says is happening*, it will be done for him. I tell you, then whatever you ask for in prayer, *believe that you have received* and it will be yours [italics added].[71]

Did you notice how Jesus included "no inward doubts and belief"? Let me ask you something. If prayer was just asking for help from God, then why didn't Jesus just say, "Ask for it and it will be yours?" Instead he tells us to ask for it, but also to remove all doubts and believe that it will happen.

Jesus also said, "For the man who *has* will be given more, till he has enough and to spare; and the man who *has not* will forfeit even what he has" (italics added)."[72]

I interpret this as a law of attraction parable where Jesus is saying that those who have something will continue to have more of it because *having* is a part of their focus and their vibrational frequency. Those who do not have enough of something will have even less than they have now because *lack* is a part of their vibration frequency. Their reality is reflective of their thoughts.

Don't these quotes from the Bible sound a lot like the law of attraction? Could Jesus have been trying to show us how to use the law of attraction by using belief and faith?

When most people pray, they *ask for help* instead of *asking for what they desire*. Both ways work fine. The difference is that in one way, you ask God or the universe to do it for you. In the other way, you ask God or the universe for what you desire and then you become an active participant in co-creating the desire by becoming a vibrational match to the desire through belief and faith. This may be where the saying, "God helps those who help themselves" comes from.

I feel that Jesus was trying to show us how to be co-creators of our reality rather than just being dependant on him/her. He wants us to grow. Jesus is like a big brother that is trying to show us how we can better our lives by using faith and belief to create our own reality. He said, "The kingdom of God is within you."[73] We already have everything we need inside ourselves. Our minds are so much more powerful than we realize. Most of us don't realize that we have the power to create whatever we want in our lives. So the next time you desire something, make sure to add belief or faith that it will eventually happen for you, and you will be empowering yourself to make your desire a reality by aligning yourself with the vibration of your desire. As I stated before, the universal laws work the same for everyone regardless of their religious beliefs. It is not necessary to believe in God or Jesus for the law of attraction to work in your life, but you do need to believe and have faith in yourself and your desires.

It is important to note that beliefs empower you to do amazing things, but they can also set limits on your creative abilities if you believe in something that is limiting or close-minded. Your beliefs set the boundaries of what is possible in your life. Since you decide what you believe in, you are the one who sets your own creative boundaries. If you believe you can only earn $50,000 a year, then that is probably as much as you will ever earn. However, if you believe you will be a millionaire, then a way will likely present itself to allow you to make that desire a reality. If you believe you have an *incurable* illness, then you will likely never heal from this ailment. Conversely, if you desire to be well and believe that anything is possible, then you open the door for miracles to happen in your life. The point here is that beliefs are tools that set the limits of what is possible in our lives. If your belief is not working for you or if it is limiting you, then it is up to you to discard it and create a new more empowering belief. You create your reality so remember to dream big!

## The Power of Now

Once you learn to use the law of attraction to create your desires, you understand that this present moment is all that matters.[74] The past has already been created and cannot be changed. The future has not come yet. The power of right now means that your power to create the future is right now in this moment. You can only create in the present. You cannot create the future from the future, but you can create your future today! Today was created yesterday (in the past) from your thoughts, words, and actions, and tomorrow is being created today the same way by the thoughts, words, and actions you choose in this moment. Each moment presents a new opportunity to create whatever you desire. Will you waste this moment by focusing on negative thoughts—doubt, fear, worry, or anger—or will you choose to focus your thoughts on more positive thoughts that help to create a better tomorrow for yourself. The choice in how you think and what you choose to think about is yours alone. Remember that the perfect—and only—time to create your future is right now. The question you should constantly be asking yourself is, "What do you want to create right now with your thoughts?"

## The Power of Positivity

Think positive thoughts and you will live a positive life. The more you focus on the positive things in life, the more positive energy you will attract to yourself. I like to play a game with myself to try to find something positive in every situation and every person I meet. As you can imagine, this can be difficult at times, but after a short period of time, I was able to train my mind to consistently think positively. Before long, I started noticing that the people I met were nicer to me than before—and good luck or random fortunate occurrences were beginning to happen to me on a consistent basis. When you are positive, you are able to be happy. When you are happy, you are at a vibrational frequency that is attractive to others. Others see your happiness and are drawn to it because they want it in their lives. This is often seen in people who are charismatic, gregarious, charming, or enthusiastic about life.

Being positive also helps you to be a vibrational match to your desires. Once this happens, you can begin to see your desires manifest in your life. Remember that we don't have control over exactly how and when our desires will manifest in our lives, but one thing is for sure, they won't manifest for us at all until we become a vibrational match to them. Try to be positive all the time—it's for your own good. Be positive while waiting as long as it takes for your desire to show up in your life. This has a positive side effect in that your life will become better and more enjoyable while you wait for your desire to arrive in your life because you will be focused on positive things. Perception is reality. Positive perception brings a positive reality.

## The Power of Words

The common theme throughout this book is that our thoughts, words, and actions determine our reality. Words are just another form of energy. Words have the power to do good or inflict harm. This is not just in an emotional sense; recent studies have shown that words have a physical impact on us and our environment.

In *The Hidden Messages in Water*, Masaru Emoto has discovered that frozen water crystals show the effects of human words and concentrated thought.[75] Emoto shows what water crystals look like when words, such as love or hate are written on the bottle holding the water. The resulting water crystals show that higher frequency words like love formed beautiful crystals and hateful words with lower frequencies formed ugly water crystals. The effect was the same when words were verbally said to water or when different types of music were played next to the water. The underlying premise is that water appears to have a consciousness. The type of crystals it formed depended on the message given to it. What if water is no different than us?

As the book points out, if the human body is composed mostly of water, what does that say about the effects of words or thoughts on our bodies and the environment around us? Here is another piece of documentation that seems to support the claim that everything in our world is alive and connected. This water experiment shows us how our thoughts and words actually affect the environment around us. What if water is not the only thing in our environment that is affected by our thoughts and words? What if everything is affected by the energy we give out? What if we are affected by the environment we helped to create with our thoughts and words? This is why it pays to be happy, loving, and compassionate as much as possible. You may be helping others, but you are also populating your own body and environment with positive energy. You never know the full impact of a kind word—think of that the next time you drink a glass of water.

## The Power of Affirmations

Affirmations are emotionally charged written statements of what you wish to achieve in your life. They are used to help program the subconscious mind with the desire. If you want to find the love of your life, you might write an affirmation that states, "I am in a wonderfully loving and mutually beneficial relationship with the person of my dreams." Then you would repeat this to yourself over and over again every day until it became a reality.

At the time of this writing, twenty-two-year-old professional golfer Rory McIlroy bounced back from blowing a four-shot lead at the Masters to go on to win the US Open by a large margin. He had earlier posted to his Twitter account a quote from famous boxer Muhammad Ali that said, "It's repetition of affirmations that leads to belief—and once that belief becomes a deep conviction, things begin to happen."[76] It appears that Rory McIlroy has realized the power of the law of attraction using affirmations.

### How to Write an Emotional Affirmation

1. List your **Desire.**
2. **Why?** (Find the underlying emotion of you desire.)
3. Write your **Completed Affirmation.**

**Step one** is to list your desire. An example of this is my desire to be a successful self-help author.

**Step two** is finding the underlying emotion tied to the desire. This is important because our emotions are supercharged thoughts that help our desires to manifest in our lives. A great way to find the underlying emotion of your desire is to ask yourself why until you can't answer the question any longer. In my case, I wanted to be an author because I like to write. Why? Writing allows me to feel fulfilled and to help people. Why? I feel happiness when I help people through my writing. So I've discovered that my own happiness is the real reason I write, and I'm happy when I helping others.

**Step three** is writing a completed affirmation that embodies your true intent and includes your emotion. It is best to start with the words "I feel" because it forces you to state your emotion. You don't have to always start with these words as long as you are able to include the emotion of your desire in your affirmation. The affirmation will be in positive wording and in the present tense as if it has already happened. In my example, a completed affirmation would be something like, I feel accomplished and proud that I am a successful self-help author.

Here is how a completed affirmation would look:

1. **Desire:** I am a successful self-help author.
2. **Why?** I feel happy and fulfilled doing what I love while helping others.
3. **Completed Affirmation:** I feel happy and fulfilled being a successful self-help author.

Other teachers of affirmations leave out the emotions and instead teach to write affirmations in the present tense. An example of this is, "I am a successful self-help author." Either way is fine, but I feel emotions add power and energy to your words. Notice how everything in the affirmation is positive and in the present tense? This is very important.

Now it's your turn, list up to three desires in your journal or in the space below. It's good to limit the number of your affirmations at first because you need to be able to focus on them and allow them to become a belief. If you get too many going at once, it is hard to focus on them enough to make them manifest in your life.

## List Your Desires Exercise

| Desire: |
| --- |
| Why? |
| Completed Affirmation: |
|  |

| Desire: |
| --- |
| Why? |
| Completed Affirmation: |
|  |

| Desire: |
| --- |
| Why? |
| Completed Affirmation: |
|  |

# The Power of Momentum

Momentum is a type of secret leverage that the law of attraction uses to make great things happen in our lives. When you desire something and believe it will happen, you become a vibrational match to it. This allows you to eventually see the manifestation of your desire happening in your life. When this happens, it is your golden opportunity to use the law of action to take advantage of any manifestations to build momentum. If you take advantage of the opportunity, you can allow another manifestation to happen and then another and another. Before you know it, you have real momentum going and things are going your way! Since this momentum can take you as far as you want to go, appreciate it when it comes—and take advantage of every opportunity it gives you.

### Momentum in Sports

We've all seen momentum in action when watching sporting events. For example, in football, one team may be beating another team handily when one particular play acts as a catalyst that changes the energy of the game. This catalyst could be an event, such as an interception, a fumble, or a blocked kick, that changes the momentum of the game where the team that was losing begins to gain energy and starts to play better and experience amazing fortunate breaks that go their way.

Momentum in life is no different. When opportunities or lucky breaks come your way, act on them; you will give yourself an opportunity to gain momentum toward manifesting your desires. Let's take a look at an example of building momentum through fitness.

## Momentum Doesn't Take Breaks

When momentum happens, be careful not to sabotage it by taking a rest or not appreciating your manifestations. Let's say you want to lose twenty pounds to get into shape along with mentally using the law of attraction to align with your desire of getting into shape. You also apply the law of action by going regularly to the gym and eating right. After a week, although you are sore, you also feel healthier. You know that is a good sign because with the law of attraction you always feel the results before you see them. After two weeks, you have lost five pounds. You are really starting to see some good momentum being built up and you feel great inside and out! Your confidence is brimming and you are excited to lose the rest of the weight. The good fitness feeling is a great sign that you are close to seeing it manifest in your life.

Then one night your best friend calls and wants you to come out bar-hopping with your friends for his birthday. You feel obligated because it is his birthday. You decide to give yourself a day off, and go out and have a night on the town with your friends. You drink beers all night and then hit the fast food restaurant on the way home. The next morning, you wake up feeling badly. You have a hangover. You decide not to work out that day. Later that day, you have another greasy meal to help you get over your hangover. You go to bed that night without following your fitness program at all that day. The following morning, you wake up and notice that you don't feel like working out again. Something is different. What is it? You realize that your own actions have sabotaged your momentum. That great feeling of positive things happening inside you is gone. You have two choices: start over from scratch and regain momentum or give up. Most people just give up. The only limits of your potential are the limits you place on yourself and the actions that you take to nourish it or throw it away. The moral of this story is to stay focused on your goal until you have achieved whatever it is you are seeking to have in your life. This is because focus, dedication, patience, and consistent action towards your goals are the key components that breed success.

# The Power of Love

The highest of all frequencies is love. In *The Light Shall Set Us Free,* love is defined as "an electromagnetic force which encompasses the totality of the All. Energy emanating from God that creates life."[77] When we are able to think and feel loving thoughts about the things and events in our lives, we are able to become the strongest possible vibrational match to our desires. Through the law of compensation, when we give love to others, we know that we are actually giving love and power to our own creative abilities because the love we give comes back to us and allows us to vibrate at a frequency that empowers us to make our desires come true. Love can have many different forms and meanings. In all forms, love is the caring and thoughtful feeling in your heart for someone or something. Love is so unique that any definition fails to completely describe its feeling and its effect on our lives.

Love is felt in the heart region. When you love with your heart, you love with your entire essence. The heart is an area of our being that is very powerful. It does much more than pump blood. It is one of seven extremely powerful energy centers of the body called chakras. These centers are unseen, but real nonetheless. Our higher self communicates to us through the heart region with feelings of intuition. It is time for all of us to stop thinking so much with our logical minds and start making decisions based on the feelings of our hearts because our higher self knows what is best for us and will never lie to us. When we make decisions based on how we feel, we can be assured it will be the best choice for us and those around us. Remember that logic can be deceiving, but intuition is always true. An easy way to handle this balance between logic and intuition is to think with your mind but act with your heart.

When you love yourself and others, you are able to become a vibrational match to your superconsious mind (higher self). The higher self has the ability to create miracles and manifest the reality you desire. When you merge with your higher self, you will also have this same power. We will further discuss merging with the higher self in the section on meditation.

# The Power of Subconscious Thoughts

Once we become aware of the law of attraction, we must become mindful of our thoughts and feelings. Our thoughts are creating our reality all the time—whether we are aware of them or not. Whatever we focus on with emotion, and for any period of time, we begin to create by attracting that energy to our lives.

Dr. L. Wilson once shared with me that with the law of attraction, it is usually the thoughts that we are not aware of that are causing us most of our problems.[78] It is important for us to pay attention to what we are thinking about to ensure that we are constantly feeding our subconscious mind positive thoughts. If we are consistently worried, stressed, or fearful about something in our lives, we are attracting energy that we don't want in our lives because we are feeding our subconscious mind this energy. Our subconscious mind then interprets this negative focus as being what we want in our life. That is why it's important to stay aware of our thoughts and to be mindful of what we are thinking and feeling.

## The Power of Patience

It is imperative that you have patience with the law of attraction. Most people cannot stay focused on their desires long enough to have them manifest in their lives. Remember that you don't have control over exactly how or when your desires will manifest, but if you focus on them long enough with positive emotions, your desires will show up in your life—unless your karma or life plan prevents this manifestation. We will further discuss these occasional instances when manifestations do not happen in *When the Law of Attraction Doesn't Work* chapter.

So how long should you wait for your desires to manifest? You should stay focused on your desires until they arrive. You will find that some things you desire will manifest almost immediately while others seem to take much longer. Let's take a look at a few examples of patience.

### Waiting for a Sub: A Lesson in Patience

The lesson of patience reminds me of a scene in the movie *Navy SEALs*.[79] At the end of their mission, the SEAL team was treading water in the open ocean waiting for their submarine to pick them up. The submarine was nowhere to be seen and things were beginning to look dire. If they didn't get picked up, they would eventually die in the open seas. The SEAL team, bloodied and exhausted, was quietly huddled together when Charlie Sheen's character says something like, "How long do you think we should wait?" At hearing this, everyone broke into laughter. It was ironic that Charlie Sheen's character would use the world "wait" when there was no other option other than to wait for the submarine. By the way, the submarine showed up shortly thereafter.

This story shows the irony of mankind. Believe it or not, most of us often behave the same way. If we are sick and want to be well, we often ask how long we should wait before we get well. The answer is to wait and stay focused until we *are* well. What other choice do we have? Whenever I have been sick in the past, I often had the same thoughts. I thought, "How long can I stay focused on what I want if it doesn't come to me?"

I often thought that if it didn't come to me, then maybe the law of attraction wasn't real or I wasn't doing it right. What finally saved me was when I got to the point where I had no other choice than to believe it would work for me. I had been focusing on the pain and the sickness I was going through. Eventually there came a point when I got tired of feeling sick and wanted something better. This is when I said to myself, "For better or worse, I am going to be committed to the law of attraction." I had no other choice. This acceptance of my situation and my surrender to the law of attraction is what made the difference that allowed my good health to eventually manifest. Once I stopped thinking about what I didn't want (poor health) and starting thinking about what I did want (my perfect health), things started to improve. I realized that it was not my responsibility to determine how or when my health would arrive. My only job was to ask for what I wanted and to make sure to add positive feelings to allow it to come to me.

Sometimes allowing my desires simply meant me not allowing myself to think any negative thoughts. This could be as simple as watching a funny movie or thinking of some other distracting subjecting that was positive. Even meditating on nothing was better than thinking the repetitive negative thoughts of fear and worry that I had been thinking. When I removed the resistance of my negative thinking, the law of attraction was able to do its work because by removing my own resistance, I was able to align with the desires I wanted in my life. My own negative thoughts had been the proverbial monkey wrench fouling up my own law of attraction machinery. I thought I was focusing on the good health that I wanted, but my feelings of fear and worry told me that I was actually focusing on the opposite of what I wanted, which was the sickness I was experiencing. Things changed for me when I started imagining myself as I wanted to be: physically fit, healthy, and full of energy. I imagined this perfected version of myself enjoying a perfect hot summer day on my boat at the lake. The vision brought a smile to my face. I realized I was feeling good at that very moment. I was feeling good in the *right now* moment. I was no longer focusing on what I didn't want. I was aligned and focusing on what I did want, which was good health and happiness.

## Black Belt in Patience

All my life, I have been fascinated with martial arts. One of my lifelong goals was to earn a black belt in karate. Because I played sports year-round growing up, I didn't have time for karate in my life until I was older. When I was in my mid-thirties, I had stopped playing competitive sports and decided it was time to take up martial arts. I found a place that taught Kenpo Jiu-Jitsu Karate. When I asked how long it would take to get a black belt, the instructor said I would have to earn it, and it would take as long as it took. I then asked him what percentage of the school's students achieved the rank of black belt. The answer I got was numbing. He said less than 1 percent. At this school, it appeared the rank of black belt was a very special and rare thing. He said there were people who had been there ten years that were still working toward the rank of black belt. I would be lying if I said I didn't find this news discouraging. Ten years is a long time to wait for anything, but I could see from watching other students practice that this school taught very valuable and applicable self-defense techniques. I decided that this school was where I wanted to investing my time and effort in earning a black belt.

I set a lofty goal of earning my black belt in five years. The task of earning a black belt with this school seemed overwhelming. In order to make the task more manageable, I decided to break it down into manageable goals of earning each individual belt within a certain time frame. I constantly thought of the saying, "The way you eat an elephant is one bite at a time." Instead of focusing on the huge amount of time and work I would have to put in, I would plod along one day at a time knowing that I would eventually reach my goal by the deadline I had set for myself. The trick for me would be staying on schedule with regard to earning the belts.

The belt system at this school was as follows: white, yellow, orange, purple, blue, green, third brown, second brown, first brown, and black.

I planned to give myself two years to go from white to third brown, then another two years to earn the first brown rank, and finally another year to earn the rank of black belt.

Everything went as planned until about the end of the second year. I noticed that the amount of karate moves and katas was starting to add up.[80] My weekly half-hour lessons were no longer enough time to practice all my moves and still have time to learn new moves too. I decided to make a change to my plan. I decided to increase my lessons from half an hour a week to two hours a week. This wasn't part of my original plan, but I was dedicated to obtaining my black belt by a certain deadline. If that meant having to make corrections along the way, I was willing to do that. This increase in lessons helped me to stay on schedule.

I was able to make my goal of earning my third brown belt in two years. I then was able to earn my second and first brown belt by the end of the fourth year. I was still on schedule to make my five-year goal! My plan was to learn the additional black belt material in six months, and then fine tune all my previously learned material in the final six months to get ready for my black belt test. I did learn the black belt material in the next six months, but I vastly underestimated the amount of time it would take before I was considered ready by my instructors to test for the rank of black belt. The school was very particular about its black belt students, and didn't give the rank of black belt out until they felt the student has reached his or her maximum potential doing the moves to their best ability. I had learned over 280 moves with multiple variation and sixteen katas. All-in-all with katas and variations included, I would have to demonstrate around six hundred moves during my two-hour test.

It took another two years for me to "format" or prepare for the black belt test. During this time, each move was deconstructed and relearned with agonizing attention to detail. This was a trying time for me, as I wanted to keep on schedule to achieve my goal. As the five-year mark came and went, I got very frustrated. I thought, "Do I quit because I am getting frustrated that the preparation is taking so long, or do I stay dedicated and focused to see it through no matter how long it takes?" I decided to reflect on my feelings. Something inside of me told me that this quest was about much more than earning a black belt. It was about finishing a monumental task that was started many years before. I realized that whatever decision I made would forever affect who I was to become. Success or failure was going to have a definite impact on my self-esteem. If I quit, I would become someone who started something but didn't finish it. If the goal was never reached, I would be left wondering whether I was a quitter in other parts of my life as well. If I stayed with the program, eventually my hard work would be rewarded and the black belt rank would become part of who I was. I would become someone who, no matter what, succeeds at what he sets out to do.

I finally decided that I would forget about the time frame and stay with my training until I earned the rank of black belt. I had to surrender to the fact that my desire was not going to come to me in the time frame I had allocated for it to manifest in my life.

Each day, I would look in the mirror and imagine myself wearing my black belt with pride. I would say to myself, "I am already a black belt. All I have to do is stay focused and patient and it will eventually become a reality in my life. If I am patient and persistent, it will happen."

Finally, after what seemed like an eternity to me, I was pronounced ready to test. On April 8, 2009, I tested for my black belt. I was nervous all day. Six years of hard work had come down to a two-hour test. My family and many of my friends came to see my test. Once the test began, it was not long before I began to sweat all the way through my heavy cotton karate gi.[81] The test was a rapid-fire demonstration of all the techniques and their multiple variations as well as all the katas. After a physically exhausting test, I was done. I had done it! I had earned the rank of black belt. Many years of hard work, sweat, and patience had finally paid off. It was an all-or-nothing moment—either I was a black belt or I was not. Now I was one. No one could ever take that achievement away from me. It was truly one of the greatest moments of my life!

Looking back on that event, I see that it was a pivotal growing experience in my life. I realize that my black belt experience taught me how to be both patient, persistent, and focused long enough to attain any goal. It also taught me that I am not a quitter. I have proven to myself that I am someone who can finish whatever I set out to do.

If you want to succeed at something or build up your self-confidence, all you need to do is set goals, act when necessary, and be patient in seeing your goals through. Every successful goal adds to your confidence. Start with small goals to build momentum and then work your way up to larger ones.

Since I earned my black belt, I have been faced with many situations where I wanted to quit something that I was doing. Each time, I have been able to lean on my experience to know that I can accomplish anything I set my mind to do. In fact, writing this book was a much bigger challenge than I had originally anticipated. The successful experience of earning my black belt allowed me to be patient and focused long enough to realize my dream of becoming an author. I hope you will dream big dreams, work hard when necessary to achieve them, and stay focused long enough to see them become a reality.

**Figure 13: Earning my black belt made me feel both a great sense of pride and accomplishment.**

**Figure 14: My black belt plaque. Goal accomplished!**

# When the Law of Attraction Doesn't Work

This sub-chapter deals with the idea that we plan certain events in our life *before* we were born. These claims about pre-life planning come from sources that channel non-physical entities, such as extraterrestrials, spirit guides, and angels for documentation.[82] Channeling is the process of telepathically receiving input or messages from one or more beings. Since there is not currently a way to prove the validity of these claims, we must instead choose to evaluate the truth of the words that are spoken through these channelings based on how they feel to us.

It is important to note that I strongly considered taking this information out of the book because not everyone believes in these entities, or life before or after death, but I thought this information too important to leave out because it gives us some good possible explanations as to why bad things sometimes happen to good people. If correct, this unique input gives us a viewpoint behind the veil of our current reality to provide us with some very valuable insight into the unexplained happenings of our own lives.

Are there ever times when the law of attraction doesn't work? Ironically, the answer appears to sometimes be yes. These rare instances where the law of attraction is prevented from working in our life appear to happen when the choices our human personality makes are not aligned with the choices our soul makes.

*Your Soul's Plan* talks about how we, in the form of our soul, plan our life before we are born. In this pre-birth planning, "we choose our parents (and they choose us), when and where we will incarnate, the schools we will attend, the homes in which we will live, the people we will meet, and the relationships we will have."[83] You, in the form of your soul, which is your non-physical essence, decide at least some of the events that you will experience in this life. These preplanned events can be positive or negative experiences, and are meant to rebalance our energy (karma) to allow us to grow. "The Universe does not punish us by making 'bad' things happen. Like gravity, karma is a neutral, impersonal law by which the world operates."[84] Many life experiences are meant to rebalance our energy and allow us to grow and learn new things.

> Life Challenges give us the opportunity to express and thus know more deeply as love in all its many facets: empathy, forgiveness, patience, non-judgment, courage, balance, acceptance, and trust. Our earthly experience of ourselves as love may also take the form of understanding, serenity,

faith, willingness, gratitude, and humility, among other virtues. Love is the primary theme of pre-birth planning and, therefore, the primary theme of this book.[85]

So this basically means that we may experience some preplanned events in life that we did not create in this life with our thoughts, words, and actions. These events are meant to rebalance our energy and allow us to learn the lessons our soul wishes us to learn.

Things get interesting when our personalities resist the path that our soul wants us to take.

> The personality has free will. Life challenges may therefore be accepted or resisted. Earth is a stage on which the personality enacts or deviates from the script written before birth. We choose how we respond—with anger and bitterness or with love and compassion.[86]

The law of attraction always works from the perspective of your soul. Where things can break down is when you—as a human personality—decide to use your free will to do something that is not aligned with the plan of your soul. This break in alignment causes a separation between the soul and the human personality. This can cause challenges or fate to enter our lives for the purpose of learning whatever it is we are meant to learn.[87] Critics may argue that if this is true then our own free will has a downside. I believe that there is a preplanned "rough draft" version of our life before we are born where certain events are planned to happen to us—but how these events impact our lives is up to us. We can use our free will to do whatever we want to do. We can use the law of relativity to create our own viewpoint of any event. How we react to these events determines how these events affect the reality of our life.

Whenever you experience these life events, they are either a direct result of your thoughts using the law of attraction, or they are your soul's way of trying to get you to realign with it or to experience something it feels you need to learn. These events often do not feel like anything we would have consciously chosen or done to ourselves, but remember—from your soul's perspective—the purpose of living a physical life is to experience everything in life. At different times, that means experiencing both the good and the bad parts of life. This is a partial explanation of why sometimes bad things happen to good people or vice versa. It can mean having to be the victim to learn the other half of the lesson from another time when you were the villain. It can mean experiencing a life of perfect abundance, or it can mean being born with a mental or physical handicap.

> Importantly, the personality has free will. Life challenges may therefore be accepted or resisted. Earth is a stage on which the personality enacts or deviates from the script written long before birth. We choose how to respond— with anger and bitterness or with love and compassion. When we recognize that we planned our challenges, the choice becomes clear and much easier to make.[88]

Regardless of the experience, it is still up to us as human personalities to decide how each lesson will be received and learned or how each experience will affect our lives and those around us. Our own free will decides what we think and how we act in response to each challenge. We can choose to accept and learn from the lesson or we can resist it and go our own separate way. If we fail to learn the lesson the first time around, we will get additional opportunities to learn the same lesson—only each time, the challenge gets more intense. So it is to our advantage to learn each lesson of life as quickly as possible.

My own experience with this makes me think of how I was challenged with health issues that I felt powerless to control. I knew about the law of attraction, but my desires did not manifest for me. I could not understand why my other desires would manifest easily for me while my desire for good health remained unanswered. I later learned that there are some things that we are just meant to experience in this life. Some of these challenges are difficult to experience, and understandably we often wish against the will of our soul to manifest an easier reality for ourselves. During these times, I believe our soul's desire for us supersedes our individual free will until the experience is complete.

How do you know when the law of attraction is not working for you? You don't. Sometimes it takes the law of attraction a long time to manifest your desires and you really never know if it is working or not. My advice is to never give up on trying to manifest your desires. However, it would be wise to listen to your gut and try to feel the right path to choose in life. As Eckhart Tolle said, "Don't ask what do I want from life, but what does life want from me?" In other words: where does my soul want to guide me?"[89]

It's no fun trying to swim against the current. If the current of life is taking you in another direction, try to see if you can find a way to go with the flow and capitalize on the new opportunities it will bring. In most challenges, there is an opportunity or a lesson to be learned. It is up to us to find it and capitalize on it.

It is interesting to note that when I was dealing with my health issues, I was not able to manifest my desire of better health until I had learned the lessons my soul wanted me to learn. The more I fought this change, the more I seemed to suffer. I had to reevaluate the way I thought about my health. Even though I desired it, my good health wasn't coming to me. I decided to stop asking why all this was happening to me—and started listening to what felt right for me. I was attempting to listen to the desire of my soul. I realized that my resistance to the illness was making things worse. I needed to accept that this challenge was in my life—and then trust that my soul would eventually bring my good health to me in the way and time frame my soul wanted me to experience. I decided to stop acting like a victim and start acting like a survivor who was patiently waiting for his good health to arrive. I never stopped focusing on my original desire for good health, but I allowed it to come to me rather than me go to it. I needed to stop using action and just do nothing, which would allow the plan of my soul to unfold in my life. Doing nothing was one of the toughest things I have ever done, but looking back on it, I can see the perfection in the process. I didn't know it at the time, but the health challenges were there so that I could experience firsthand many of the lessons I would later be writing about in this book. Being completely honest, there is no way I would have consciously chosen that path myself because it involved a lot of suffering, but my soul knew it was the only way I could really know what I was going to be teaching others. Now that I have the benefit of hindsight, I agree that it was worth it. This whole experience greatly improved who I was as a person and allowed me to have much deeper meaning of life. Once I aligned with the purpose of my soul, the process became much easier, and it was like being carried by a river. It was still a challenge, but it was much more manageable.

What happens if you find yourself in a situation where you feel your desires are not manifesting? First go back and review the Nine A's to Acing the Law of Attraction Checklist to make sure you are not doing something that is keeping your desires from manifesting. Also make sure you give the law of attraction an ample amount of time to manifest. If you've checked these things and your desires are still not manifesting, then you may want to meditate on this for a while to see how this challenge feels. Ask yourself what is the right thing to do. Sometimes the thing that feels right is also the hardest thing to actually do. This could mean quitting your job, moving to a new town, getting married, getting divorced, or simply deciding not to do anything. These are only examples—I am not suggesting any of these actions for anyone else. Only you can determine what is right for you. Check to see if the answer you get feels right to you. If the answer feels right, consider following that path because resistance to the change your soul has planned for you only leads to more suffering. We are in a period of unprecedented change. Those who accept and flow with the change will not only survive but can also learn to prosper from it. Those who resist the change will cause themselves undue suffering.

You may not always have control of what happens in your life, but you do have control over how you react. Your reaction, positive or negative, works to create your future. React in a positive way and look for the lesson to be learned. As soon as you find a way to align with your soul and learn the required lessons you are meant to learn, your ability to manifest will return. Even if there are preplanned events in your life, you never completely lose your ability to manifest a new future. You are constantly creating your future with your thoughts through the law of attraction. When you are experiencing one of these preplanned events, stay focused on finding the positive parts of life and focus on the future you want to create. Sooner or later, your thoughts will manifest into a new reality. Regardless of what happens to you, you still create the future from that moment on.

## Tips for Troubleshooting the Law of Attraction

This section is a reminder of things to check for when your desires are not manifesting in your life. These items have already been listed earlier in this book, but I have found it is nice to summarize helpful info in one place so that you can troubleshoot the law of attraction when it is not working for you. The law of attraction can be tricky—and often the little things that we do, or do not do, affect how the law of attraction does or does not manifest in our life. I hope you find this information useful.

### Helpful Reminders to Manifest Your Desires:
- Review the Nine A's to Acing the Law of Attraction Checklist.
- Write down your desires and read them aloud multiple times daily.

- Become a vibrational match to your desire by seeing and feeling it as if it were already in your life.
- Find a way to laugh every day—laughter heals the soul.
- Lighten up and be easy going—your mood is reflective in your vibrational frequency.
- Think positive thoughts.
- Feel positive feelings.
- Expect and believe your desires will become a reality.
- Be patient.
- Accept your current situation.
- Make the commitment to see and feel your desired future rather than your current reality.
- Realize that your mind attracts the energy of your thoughts.
- Use your thoughts as guide to where you are heading.
- Use your feelings to tell you if your direction is desired.
- Realize that *now* is your point of power to create with your thoughts.
- When you can't think positive thoughts about your situation, stop thinking about it, and take a break to allow your mind to get off this subject. You can choose to think about any other subject that makes you feel positive emotions. An example of this might be choosing to think of pleasant memories.
- Remove resistance to remove blockages.
- Use action to create the power of momentum to catapult you to your desires.
- If you feel negatively about a subject, try changing how you think about it to change how you feel about it. Perception is reality.

## Common Manifestation Mistakes:

The following list includes common manifestation mistakes that prevent your desires from manifesting:

- Not asking or focusing on what you want.
- Not focusing on feeling positive emotions.
- Not matching both your desires and your emotions (both need to be positive).
- Asking for what you want too many times. Asking and aligning are two different vibrational frequencies. Focus on what it feels like to have your desire already in your life and you will

become a vibrational match to it. This will allow you to align with your desire and allow it to manifest in your life.

- Being fearful. Fear prevents desires from manifesting.
- Focusing on the negativity of the reality you are currently experiencing rather than the future you desire.
- Not having enough patience to stay focused on your desire long enough for it to manifest.
- Being too action-focused to allow your desire to come to you. Sometimes it takes the patience to do nothing while you wait for an opportunity to come to you.
- Not acting when opportunities arise. Waiting is good, but you need to be ready to act when opportunity knocks at your door.
- Being inconsistent with your thoughts and emotions by being hopeful and positive one minute, and then worried and fearful the next. You need to be consistent with your positive thoughts.
- Using your mind as a video recorder to simply record your life as it is happening rather than using your mind to envision and create the future you wish to be.
- Not seeing and feeling your desired future as if it was already here.
- Not believing your desires will come true.
- Not using strong enough positive emotions to manifest your desires (I want it versus I know it will come to me).

# Part 3: Your Thirty-Day Empowerment Program

This part of the book will teach you the skills you need to know to be able to work with the universal laws to empower your life by becoming the purposeful creator you were meant to be. If you follow this program precisely, within thirty days you should begin to see the results of the laws responding to your actions. This program presents the fundamentals for you to live your entire life in a way that is empowering and creative.

# Chapter 5: Planning and Evaluation of Your Life

## Journaling: Write Your Life to "Right" Your Life

This first step is not a necessary step for everyone, but it is something that I have found to be extremely helpful in my own empowerment process. Journaling has helped me through some really tough times by allowing me to sort out and vent my feelings onto paper. It also served as a device where I could track my progress. Journaling allowed me to become aware of my thoughts and emotions, which then made it easier for me to consciously, rather than subconsciously, choose the thoughts, words, and actions I wanted for myself. This made experiencing life's challenges much easier than if I had let those negative emotions force me into reacting to how I felt at those times. Let's see how you can use journaling in your life.

### Journal to De-stress

Most of us have busy lives. We go from doing one thing to the next all day long. We all build up natural stress from a variety of situations we encounter. Each day, it is important for us to find a way to de-stress our mind in one way or another. Some ways we can de-stress are by going to the gym, taking a walk, or by talking with someone. Many people are able to unwind (de-stress) over dinner by talking to their family or spouses about their day. However, there are those who do not feel comfortable talking about their private lives or deepest secrets openly with others. When that is the case, journaling is often a good alternative.

Journaling is a process that allows you to sort out your unfiltered feelings onto paper, and get into contact with your subconscious mind.

The first step in journaling is to get a notebook or journal. There are no rules to journaling. It is there for you to vent or spill out whatever you are feeling or thinking inside your head. You don't even have to ever read what you've written in previous journal entries. The act of writing *is* the purpose of journaling because getting your thoughts out onto paper is therapeutic. If you have never tried this before, it may sound absurd. Before I had ever tried to write in a journal, I thought it sounded like a dumb idea. *I already know what I am thinking in my head so why do I need to write it down in the book?* The answer, I found, was astounding.

When I first started writing in my journal, I wrote whatever I felt. I soon found out that I would write much more than what was in my conscious thoughts. It felt good to get my feelings out of my head and onto paper. In times of prolonged stress, it seemed like I would write the same things almost the same way day after day. At other times, I would read what I had written weeks earlier with no memory of writing those words. The main point is that journaling helped me sort out my feelings and make sense of the things I was experiencing on a daily basis.

I didn't feel a need to get my thoughts out of my head, but I did feel like my mind was too cluttered to make sense of everything that was happening to me. I felt like I needed to organize my thoughts and emotions. My mind was constantly trying to process the conscious and subconscious stress in my life. In my case, my mind never stopped thinking about work. Being self-employed, I thought about work virtually twenty-four hours a day, seven days a week. I was always focused on where my next business was coming from, then handling the current business I had, and then marketing to the business customers that had already closed so I could create referrals for new business. It was a never-ending cycle. Add to that a few personal challenges, and my mind was on constant overload. During these times, journaling helped me to sort out my life and my stress.

I consider myself to be a normal person who lives a life that is similar to most others. I know there are some people thinking that they are okay and that do not need to do this. The honest answer is that you do not need to do anything you do not want to do. Everything in this book is a merely a tool that can help you if you choose to take advantage of it.

I initially learned about journaling when I was going through the breakup of a relationship many years ago. During this time, I credit a lot of my recovery to my daily writing session. Before I went to bed, I would write about however I felt that day. During that time, the breakup dominated my thoughts and emotions. The breakup was part of life and something I had to go through, but enduring it was not fun. When I wrote in my journal, the pain from the hurt, sorrow, anger, and depression seemed to transfer from my soul to the pages of the journal. I know that sounds corny, but it is true. In time, I recovered from that breakup, and went on to experience other more rewarding relationships. Looking back, I see that writing in my journal helped me get through the breakup process one day at a time and one emotion at a time. Before I knew it, I woke up and realized that I was over it and ready to resume my normal life. Journaling had helped me to use the law of polarity to navigate from the negative emotions of the breakup to the positive emotions of appreciating being independent and single again.

I still write in my journal, but instead of writing only about the troubling parts in my life, I now use it write about the success as well. I set my goals in it and keep track of my successes and failures. It helps me to feel grounded and gives me a daily opportunity to get my creative thoughts out of my head and out on paper.

I hope you will use journaling to help you get your thoughts and feeling out of your head and onto paper. Try it for thirty days and see what you think. I bet you will be amazed.

Many people do not want to write in a journal because they are afraid that others will see what they have written. To mitigate that risk you could get a journal or diary with a lock, store the journal in a safe place, or use code words that only you know for the super private things in your life. Also smartphones have apps that are perfect for journaling and are secure. It would be easy to say that you also should not write something that you did not want someone to read, but the point of writing in your journal is to get out whatever is on your mind without using a filter. Decide if the risk of someone reading your journal is worth the reward of being able to vent your feelings onto paper.

Please note that if you have to censor yourself, then you are not writing from the heart, which is the whole purpose of journaling.

Also, never read another person's journal. I say this for your own emotional protection as well as for the privacy of the writer. A journal is meant to express unfiltered feelings. Not only is reading another's journal an invasion of their utmost privacy, but you may also see some things that could really hurt your feeling or those of others. We all have thoughts in our head. Most of us wisely choose to filter those thoughts before we put them into words or actions, but journaling does not do that. Journaling simply puts raw, uncensored feelings down on paper.

When writing in my journal, I often felt conflicted about what to write. I wanted to vent my negative feeling onto paper, but I also realized that we attract the energy of our focus, and writing in a journal is focusing on our feelings. I came to the realization that it is important for us to not hide from our emotions. Rather than ignoring or hiding from negative emotions, it is better to feel and deal with them, and then move on to better feeling emotions. One suggestion I figured out when journaling was to vent my actual feelings, even if they are negative, but then to always try to insert something positive afterward. I might write, "I had a horrible day today. Everything went wrong. I'm feeling really frustrated and disappointed right now." Then I would interject something good like, "The good news is that today is over and tomorrow is new day. I am looking forward to making tomorrow a better day!" When I end my journaling on a good note, I am readjusting my own energy from negative to positive. Remember that your journal is there to help you vent your feelings, but it is also an opportunity for you to reset your own vibration frequency.

## How to Journal

Now that you know about journaling, let us learn how to do it. Here is an example of my journal entry:

December 12

I feel great today! I enjoyed going out with friends last night. We went bowling. It was good to catch up with everyone. We had a lot of laughs telling many stories of us growing up together. I doesn't matter how many times I hear those stories, they still make me belly-laugh each time I hear them. We need to make an effort to get together more often.

I finally got my karate black belt diploma in the mail recently! It looks impressive! It took six years to earn the belt, and almost another year to get the diploma mailed to me, but now I finally feel my goal has been completed! Today was a great day!

Yesterday, our family was able to get together for a coffee break in the afternoon. I feel so fortunate to be part of a family is so close and supportive of each other.

On another less positive note, the neighbor's dog is still barking every morning and waking me up. I like my neighbors, but their dog's barking is driving me crazy. I am really getting tired of constantly asking them to do something about it. I know they have already done whatever they could do to stop the barking, but now I sense that they are getting annoyed with me constantly asking them to do something about it. I am not sure what to do next. I want to be neighborly, but I also want the nuisance to stop. I find this to be a great test of monitoring my emotions, thoughts, words, and actions because the constant barking is quite a test of my patience. I have maintained control of how I feel, but I would like to work toward a solution. Maybe I am focusing on the problem of the barking rather than on the solution of silence. I think I will change my thoughts from wanting the dog to stop barking to wanting the dog to be happy and me being able to enjoy the silence of nature in my backyard. Yeah, I think I was focusing on what was happening rather than what I wanted life to be. From now on, I will ignore the dog and focus on something more pleasant. I can't control the barking so why should I focus on it? (Future note: A few weeks later, after I had stopped focusing on the barking, things came together and the dog practically stopped barking altogether. The neighbors also became a little more considerate and began taking action to quiet the barking whenever they were home. Two months later, we were able to move to a new neighborhood that was very quiet and bark-free. It seems this change in thinking helped the law of attraction bring us a bark-free neighborhood.)

That is one of my journal entries. Now it's your turn.

## Journal Exercise

(Buy a journal or notebook or write in the space below.)

Open your journal to page one and write your name and date. Turn the page and put today's date and begin writing anything that is on your mind. You can write as little or as much as you want. One or two sentences are as good as one or two pages. Just start writing what you feel. The journal is like a friend that only listens. The journal is there as a venting session and to help track your progress while learning the universal laws. The more you write, the easier the words will come to you.

_____

_____

_____

_____

_____

_____

_____

_____

_____

_____

_____

_____

_____

_____

_____

_____

_____

_____

_____

_____

_____

Now that you have your journal, let's take the next step in your transformational journey, and do some self-evaluation. Before you can improve who you are, you must know who you are.

## List Your Gift: What is So Special About You?

Everyone on this planet is unique. We come in all shapes, sizes, colors, and races. Whether we know it or not, we all have at least one special gift that is unique to us. Some people are physically beautiful, some are smart, some are musically inclined, some are good with computers, and some are creative, while others are outgoing. Your gift(s) can be anything that comes easy to you or that you excel at. It can be anything that you enjoy doing or that makes you happy.

Focusing on your gift allows you to appreciate what is special about you. When you love and appreciate yourself, you are able to be happy. When you are happy, you are at a vibrational frequency that is positive. This allows you to create because you can easily align with the frequencies of your desires. Once you know what your strengths are, you can go back to them whenever you need to find happiness.

Since I enjoy being around people, I would like to think that one of my gifts is an ability to be social and relate to people. I feel that I am happiest in that kind of environment. Yet for many years I had a job that didn't allow me to deal with people as much as I would have liked. Much of my work was done in an office behind closed doors. I was able to do this job for many years, but eventually I realized I wasn't happy. In the end, my work habits made me become almost antisocial and physically ill. I realized I needed to make the changes to do what made me feel good. I took some time to analyze my life, and I realized that I was not maximizing my given gifts of being around and in front of people. I then made the necessary changes that allowed me to maximize this gift and become happy again.

I hope you will do the same. All that matters is that you are happy with life. If you are happy with where your life is now, you don't need to make any adjustments. However, if you are not happy or would like a better life, start by focusing on the gifts you already have. It could be a clear road to your happiness.

### List Your Gifts/Strengths

Here is an example of what I filled out for My Gifts/Strengths.

1. I thrive and am happiest when I am around people in a social environment.

2. I have great self-confidence. I believe in myself.
3. I have the ability to finish tasks that I start.
4. I am very creative.
5. I have a skill for understanding finances.
6. I believe in the power of the mind to create. This makes me a conscious creator of my own reality.

I could list more things about myself, but I think this is sufficient for you to get the idea of how to do this exercise.

Now it is your turn. Please turn to a new page in your journal and label it as My Gifts/Strengths. Then write down any and all of your gifts that you have. (If you don't have a journal, you can write below.) You can list as few as one gift, or as many as you would like. This exercise is meant to show you how special you are so feel free to list as many as you'd like.

1. _____

2. _____

3. _____

4. _____

5. _____

6. _____

7. _____

8. _____

9. _____

10. _____

I hope you are able to appreciate who you are right now. Feeling good about yourself is necessary before you can create a better future. We are vibrational beings; how we feel affects our vibrational frequency. When we are happy, we are vibrating at a frequency that allows us to be able to create deliberately.

# My Positive Page

In your journal, list all the things in your life that make you happy. The reason why you want to create a "My Positive Page" is so that you can have a happy-thought resource readily available any time you are stressed, upset, or feeling out of vibrational alignment with who you want to be. As we've already learned, when you are happy, you are aligned with what you want to create.

Some of my favorite things that make me happy:

- Quality time with my family
- The smile on my son's face
- Quite time alone
- The sound of rain
- Meditation
- Sunshine
- Being near any body of water (pool, lake, river, ocean)
- Being in nature
- Martial arts
- Golf
- Vacations
- Investing
- Self-improvement
- Watching comedy movies
- The color blue
- Pleasant memories
- Future dreams

As you can see in the last two examples, I listed pleasant memories and future dreams. You can be more specific in your own example to list specific memories. Anything that allows you to feel love or happiness is fair game. You see, the mind cannot tell the difference between the past, present, and future. If you feel the warm happy memories of a time when you were growing up, those memories will affect how you feel right now. If you dream of a better life, those feelings will affect how you feel right now. That is what you are looking to achieve with this exercise. You are creating a tool that will help you feel good in the present moment—regardless of any negative situations you may be experiencing. When you're happy, you're aligned with what you desire. When you're aligned with what you desire, you are able to create what you want. It's that simple.

Please list this in your journal or in the space below under the heading of "My Positive Page." List as few or as many as you would like, but make sure there is something that makes you happy. If you can think of anything from the past that makes you happy, then dream of the wonderful future you wish to create.

1. _____

2. _____

3. _____

4. _____

5. _____

6. _____

7. _____

8. _____

9. _____

10. _____

# Balance Wheel

A balance wheel is a tool that you can use to sort out what is important to you and then make sure that those things get enough attention so they can grow and thrive.

Let's take the example of a successful businessman who has all the signs of success. He has the big house on a hill, nice cars, and seems to be overflowing with money, but when you look closer at his life you can see there is a lot of unhappiness. He is going through a divorce, and he rarely gets to see his kids because he works so much. He doesn't have time for the important things in his life because he has put so much focus and effort into being successful at work. He has succeeded in his career at the cost of failing the other things in life that he valued. He is out of balance and probably doesn't even realize it.

The first step of your balance wheel is to list everything that is important in your life right now. An example of my balance wheel is this: Family, Career, Finances/Investing, Spiritual Growth, Self-Improvement, Health and Fitness, and Happiness/Fun. Each of these areas is very important to me. I would feel out of balance if I were successful in one area but lagging in other areas. That is why it is called a balance wheel. When all aspects of your life are in balance, the wheel rotates perfectly. Conversely, if one spoke is too big and the others are too small, the wheel rotates out of balance until the whole wheel breaks down completely.

The next step is to put each important part of your life as a spoke in the balance wheels. Here is how mine looks.

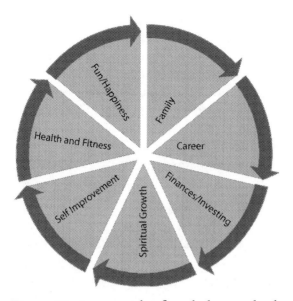

**Figure 15: An example of my balance wheel.**

Notice how all the important areas are even and balanced? Now you try it. You can open your journal and draw a big circle and list a spoke for each important part of your life like I did. You can also draw the balance wheel in the space listed on the next page. You simply need to fill in the spokes. You can use more or less than the seven categories that I used in my example.

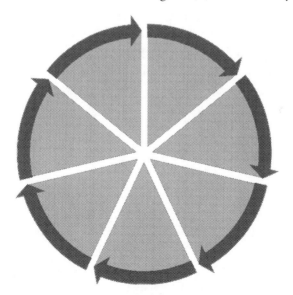

**Figure 16: Blank balance wheel to fill out.**

Once you have filled in your balance wheel, make sure you give each area enough attention to allow it to grow and flourish. Look at your balance wheel often and make sure that all areas of your wheel are growing. If one area is growing but the other areas are not, you should ask yourself why this is happening and make the necessary corrections. We know from the law of rhythm that when our lives are out of balance, the universe will eventually make the necessary changes to correct these imbalances. These changes are usually not pleasant. They could be a divorce, bankruptcy, health issues, or other undesired changes. It is always better to live a balanced life so that we can avoid nature's corrections and continue to create the type of life we want.

## Planning and Evaluation of Your Life Summary

In this chapter, you learned to journal, you found your gift/strengths, you created your "My Positive Page," and you created your balance wheel. This chapter is meant for you to learn how to express your feelings through journaling and also to appreciate what is special about you. Everyone has gifts—I hope you know yours now. Use the positive page any time you are feeling down or need an emotional boost. It's there to help you take an emotional vacation from a negative reality. When you return to focusing on reality, you will be in a better place (vibrational frequency) to handle it in a way that is more beneficial to you. Finally, use your balance wheel to ensure that the important areas of your life get enough attention to allow them to grow. When all of these tools are used together, you are able to establish a base of stability that you can revisit any time you need to find balance or when you feel you need a mental or emotional lift.

# Chapter 6: Eleven Steps to Becoming the Ultimate You!

Regardless of whether you are just learning about this information or you are already well on your way to mastering the universal laws, this eleven-step process will help you to become the best you can be by developing special skills that will allow you to maximize your use of the universal laws.

## Step 1.  Develop Your Intuition.

One of the best things you can do for yourself is to develop your gut instinct or intuition. Your intuition is your silent guide that never lets you down. Intuition is defined as being able to sense something without knowing exactly how you are sensing it. It involves feeling the energy of a person, place, or thing.

As we know from studying the law of attraction, our feelings are our guide or indicator of the vibrational frequency we are experiencing and of our own vibrational alignment. When we feel good, we are aligned and headed toward something that we desire. When we feel uneasy or bad, it is a sign that we could be headed toward something that is not good for us. This is our intuition.

Where does our intuition come from? Could our intuition come from a source other than our mind? Many believe our intuition is either our subconscious or superconscious mind (higher self) communicating with us. Regardless of the source of this input, it is hard to deny the fact that our intuition, once developed, is able to tell us the truth about whatever we are focusing on.

Einstein said, "The intuitive mind is a sacred gift and the rational mind is a faithful servant. We have created a society that honors the servant and has forgotten the gift."[90] Society, for the most part, has lost its ability to rely on its intuition and relies solely on logic to make decisions. The problem is that logic doesn't give us feedback on our focus.

Our intuition, on the other hand, gives us feedback based on our focus. Throughout this book, you've learned that every thought, feeling, word, or action emits a certain vibrational frequency. At a subconscious level, we all have within us the ability to perceive the frequencies of everything we experience. If we can learn to use this special perceptive ability, we can begin to make more informed decisions. Our intuition can be felt in various parts of our bodies, such as the heart, stomach, or solar plexus. Regardless of where you feel it, intuition usually comes in the form of thoughts or feelings that make you stop and consider if what you are feeling is good or bad for you. Let's take a look at a few examples of intuition in life.

## Relationship Intuition

Many years ago, I had a girlfriend. Our relationship had come to a point where she wanted to get married. She was great and we had a lot of good times together, but I still had my reservations. One day, I remember asking myself if she was marriage material. The response I got was an experience that was so strong that I can still clearly remember it today. When I asked myself whether she was the one for me, I heard a silent scream of no. I was stunned by that response. I knew deep down that she wasn't the right one for me, but I really didn't expect my body to answer my question. I didn't actually hear the response—it was a thought that popped into my consciousness. Rather than receiving it in my head, it popped into my heart or stomach area. The feeling of heaviness felt wrong. That is probably why I still remember it so strongly. Needless to say, I paid attention to this strong intuitive response and ended the relationship shortly thereafter. Years later, we were still friends, but I could clearly see how different we were. I felt reassured that I had made the right choice. That was the beginning of my developing and listening to my intuition.

Intuition is a natural ability that everyone has, but few people ever take the time to develop it. Women have a reputation for being more adept at developing this gift. We have all heard about women's intuition, but I believe men are just as capable of developing this sense. By listening to our intuition and by making better choices, we can all experience more of the joy in life and less of the struggles.

## Messages of Truth

We can all develop our intuition. We just need to take the time to listen to our gut instinct and decide how it *feels* to us.

Our gut instinct is the feeling in our stomach area that gives us an emotional indicator of the situation we are experiencing. It tells us if what we are focused on feels right. Many people believe that our intuition is a connection with our higher self (the superconscious mind), which is an ultimately wiser part of ourselves that is connected to everything and everyone. Others believe that our guardian angels are able to communicate to us through our intuition. Regardless of the source of our intuition, once we learn to listen to it, we can be sure that it will never lie to us. The only question is whether you are listening to what it is telling you.

## Our Sixth Sense

Most people make decisions based on logic rather than how they feel about something. Once you begin to develop your intuition, you will learn that your intuition provides input that is consistently dependable. It is always your choice to listen to the feelings it gives you. We often don't pay attention to our feelings because we choose to focus on logic rather than how we feel inside—or because we are so busy we can't hear or feel our intuition silently communicating to us.

Have you ever met someone who seemed nice enough based on their outward appearance, but when you met them, they gave you a sudden chill down your spine? You got a bad feeling about them, but had no reason for feeling that way. That was your intuition picking up on the other person's negative energy.

## Combat Awareness

Soldiers routinely talk about how intuition saved their lives in combat. Many soldiers have reported having a weird feeling about something just seconds before something bad was going to happen. Often these soldiers were able to listen to their intuition to avoid these situations while other times they chose to ignore their internal warning only to regret it later. Sometimes the danger was a bomb, sometimes it was a lurking sniper, and sometimes it was an ambush. My brother is a Marine. While deployed in Iraq, Ed saw a lot of combat. He feels that his intuition saved him from death on multiple occasions. He would often drive by a deserted alley, and the hair on the back of his neck would stand up just before the bullets started raining down on his vehicle. Luckily, he returned home safely, but his stories give credibility to the existence of senses that most people don't use every day. Ed said that most of the soldiers in combat developed this sense because they were so highly focused on their surroundings at all times. They had to be this way because anything or anyone could be a threat at any time. I believe this heightened state of awareness helped these soldiers hone their ability to sense the feel or vibration of the surrounding environment.

## Hunches

Police officers and detectives are another group that often develop their intuition or gut instinct. Through years of trial and error, many police officers learn to look beyond the facts and use hunches to zero in on a suspect. A hunch is defined as a strong intuitive feeling concerning especially a future event or result.[91] An example of when a hunch might be used is when the suspect may appear to be innocent but the detective feels something is not right. How many times have we watched a movie where the detective says, "I know his facts check out, but there is just something not right about that guy"? The murder suspect later turns out to be the killer, which validates the detective's initial intuition or hunch. Of course, proving the validity of a hunch in a court of law involves finding sufficient evidence to get a conviction, but hunches can be very helpful in narrowing down a large group of suspects.

## Natural Instincts

Animals are also naturally gifted with intuition. Have you ever met a dog that loves just about everyone but doesn't like certain people? Dogs and other animals pick up on energy that humans often do not. Animals read the energy of the people they meet. They can tell who is there to love them, who is scared of them, and who would like to cause them harm. As humans, we often don't develop this skill because we are fooled by the illusion of a smiling face or logical words that may contradict our feelings.

Intuition does not allow you to see what is going to happen in the future, but it can tell you if you are going toward the energy of something that is not good for you. If you feel good about something, then it is probably good for you. If you feel bad about something, then it is probably not good for you. It's that simple. Intuition is about learning to read the energy of a person or situation.

When making decisions, it is best to evaluate the logical and the emotional intuitive response. This allows you to use your logical mind and your intuitive feelings to make a decision. If the logic answer and the intuitive answer conflict, the intuitive answer is the one that is best for you because your intuition gives you feedback on what is best for you; logic does not.

---

## How to Develop Your Intuition

1. **Focus on whatever you want to evaluate.**
2. **What does the logic say to you?**
3. **How does that thing feel to you?**
4. **Conclusion: What do you feel is right for you?**

---

The logic is what your mind says. The feeling is what your heart says. It is a good idea to find a balance between using your logic and intuition to make decisions. Think with your mind, but make decisions with your gut. Evaluate things with your logical mind, but make decisions based on how that information feels because your logical mind can be fooled, but your intuition will never lie to you.

All you have to do to learn how to use your intuition is to retrain your mind to accept another form of input when making decision. Don't worry if at first you can't feel any response from your intuition. If you keep listening, in time you will develop this skill. Another way of building this skill is to evaluate how you felt *after* an event. The past is usually clear when we look back on it. If you look back on an event, you will probably remember how you felt before making a decision. Remember how you felt and see if your intuition was correct. If it was correct, learn to trust it more the next time you get the same feeling.

## My Intuition Exercise

In your journal, turn to another page and write "My Intuition." You can also write it here on this page.

Let's follow the three steps listed above. Here is an example.

| | |
|---|---|
| Focus: | Should I take the new job? |
| Logic: | Pays more and I need the money. |
| Feeling: | Uneasy; not excited; something doesn't feel right. |

Conclusion:    Consider passing on the job offer. Trust that your intuition is a warning that this job is not right for you for one reason or another.

Note that it is important to be able to differentiate between being nervous about change and having actual intuitive feelings. If you can't tell the difference, make a decision and evaluate the results later. Looking back on the results, you will know if your feelings were your intuition or just nerves. Learning to use your intuition is a matter of trial and error until you are able to know its feeling and trust its reliable input.

Write "My Intuition Exercise" in your journal or in the space below. Remember to ignore the logic and pay attention to the feeling. Then later go back and review.

| Focus: |
| --- |
| Feeling: |
| Logic: |
| Conclusion: |

I hope this exercise helps you to develop your intuition. Be patient—it takes time to learn to hear or feel what it is telling you. It also takes time to learn to trust your intuition. If you do learn to make decisions based on how you feel instead of what you think, you will live a happier, more stress-free life.

## Step 2. Be the Most Positive Person You Know.

Optimism is looking for the positive aspects in everything. Optimism uses the law of relativity to allow you to control how you view the events in your life. When you look for the positive things in life, you will notice that life seems to feel good. When you are optimistic, you perceive events differently than you used to perceive them. You will find that many things that used to bother you no longer do.

When events happen, you have the choice to either view them as they are or to look for the positive in them. When you look for the positive in life, you seek out the energy that feels best to you. Through the law of attraction, your focus on the positive things in life attracts more positive energy to you. When you stay positive, you stay in control of your emotions. When you are in control of your emotions, you are in control of how you feel and the energy you attract to yourself.

If you're waiting in line at a fast food restaurant and someone cuts in front of you, you have two choices; you can get upset about it, or you can decide not to let it bother you. If you let it bother you, you are allowing someone else's actions to affect how you feel. If you decide not to get upset, you are choosing to stay in control of your own emotions, and therefore are choosing to not allow someone else to affect how you feel. How you react to any given situation determines how that event will affect your reality. Everything is relative to point of view or outlook.

People who are optimistic are often criticized by society as being wishful thinkers or who are not seeing reality as it is. The ironic part is that society is right. Optimistic people are not focused on reality as it currently is, but rather on creating the reality as they choose to see it. The law of relativity states that our reality is relative (dependent) on how you choose to see it. Some people consciously choose to create lives that are positive. They understand that they have a choice in how they perceive the world. They have the choice to see the negative parts or the positive parts of life. By choosing to be positive, they choose to bring that energy to themselves.

The difference between a positive person and someone who is negative is that a positive person realizes that there is a benefit to being positive. A positive person enjoys a better life because they attract positive energy and avoid allowing outside influences to affect how they feel.

## The Thirty-Day Positivity Challenge

How would you like to become the most positive person you know? You can be that person, but it takes practice. I would like to challenge you to take the next thirty days to focus on being positive in all aspects of your life. Each night, write in your journal the situations where you chose to be positive. Writing in your journal will help you stay focused on this goal and will also help you to build positive momentum. If you are consistently positive with this exercise for the next thirty days, I promise you will see a huge difference in yourself. Not only will you see a difference, but everyone else will notice a difference in you too. Positive people have an energy about them that attracts others to them. People will want the same happiness and positive energy in their lives that you have in yours. Start being positive today and watch how it changes your life for the better.

In your journal or in the space below, write down some of the events of your day where you changed how you viewed an event and saw something positive where others may have seen something negative. List the event and how you handled the event.

Here are some examples:

## Event:

I got a flat tire today.

## Positivity:

I ended up feeling a sense of accomplishment changing the tire by myself.

## Event:

I feel sick today.

## Positivity:

Maybe my body is just telling me that I need to take a break today, and to focus on relaxing and getting better. I am thankful for the opportunity to improve my health.

## Event:

Today a customer complimented the great job I did for him. The great thing is that my boss overheard the compliment.

## Positivity:

It feels great to get rewarded for doing a great job!

List an event that happened to you today followed with something positive that you noticed about that experience.

## Event:

_____

_____

_____

## Positivity:

_____

_____

_____

**Event:**

_____

_____

_____

**Positivity:**

_____

_____

_____

**Event:**

_____

_____

_____

**Positivity:**

_____

_____

_____

Practice positivity in your life—and you will begin to see positive changes all around you.

# Step 3.  You are Responsible for Your Own Happiness.

Everyone, at one point or another, experiences unhappiness. It is part of our journey through life to experience rewarding and challenging times. Challenges in life give us an opportunity to grow by desiring to create new and better realities for ourselves. It is up to us to find ways around these challenges to find our own happiness. Those who are consistently happy have found a secret that allows them to feel consistently good. What separates happy people from the rest of the world is that they have taken responsibility for their own happiness.

Taking responsibility for your happiness means that you rely solely on yourself for your own happiness. Most people rely on the actions, reactions, or approval of others to make them happy. Growing up, we are programmed to think this way. As infants, we look to our parents for happiness, love, and our basic needs. As we grow up, we look to our parents for approval for just about everything we do. We can feel extreme unhappiness if we don't receive love or approval from our parents or loved ones. In the teenage years, many adolescents become independent of their parents, but then often replace their need for their parents' approval with the approval from their peers. When you were in high school, it didn't matter if you were in a school play, the school band, or even the star football player, how others reacted to you affected how you felt about yourself, right?

By the time we became adults, most of us are programmed to look to others for our own happiness. The problem with this model is that our happiness is in the control of someone else. We are looking for the approval or acceptance of others for the happiness we seek inside ourselves.

## Sally: A Lesson in Finding Happiness

Let us look at the case of Sally. Growing up, she did not feel loved by her father and was always looking for his acceptance. When she became an adult, she never was never able to find true love because she consistently dated men who treated her just as her father had. Subconsciously, she chose men that were just like her father because she still longed for her father's acceptance. Eventually, Sally read a book like this one and realized that if she wanted to find happiness, it would have to be without her father's acceptance. She decided to look within herself to find her own sense of self-worth and happiness. When Sally finally made this conscious change in her beliefs, she was able to change her habits, which allowed her to stop dating men who withheld love from her. She soon started dating men who appreciated her as a wonderfully loving and unique person. Sally finally realized that she had been placing her happiness in control of people who were not willing or able to give it back to her. Sally decided to use this newfound positive momentum to make the necessary change to take control of her own life.

Today Sally focuses on herself and appreciates how unique she is and all the creative things she does. By appreciating herself, Sally is now self-reliant for her own happiness. She still likes it when she is appreciated by others, but she no longer *relies* on their appreciation for her happiness.

## Client Dispute: Finding Happiness in Conflict.

Your happiness is not limited to the acceptance of others. What happens when we have conflicts with others, and they do not behave the way we would like them to behave? How does that make us feel?

For almost twenty years, I was a mortgage broker in Northern California. I always prided myself on treating my clients as I would like to be treated if I were applying for a home loan. I worked hard to provide each person with the best interest rates and loan products available. I also used my experience to prevent any stressful situations during those loan transactions. Throughout these loan transactions, I made sure to communicate with each client regularly to prevent any misunderstandings. Occasionally, there were costs during the transaction that needed to be paid up front by the client. During one of my transactions, I contacted the client to let them know about an appraisal and a special report the lender was requiring to be ordered on the property, and that both of these costs needed to be paid up front by them. The client agreed and told me to order the reports. I informed the client that, as part of my customer service to him, I was willing to pay those costs up front, which totaled $750, until the loan was closed. Once the loan was closed, I would be reimbursed from their loan proceeds through escrow. I also had the client agree via email that if for any reason the loan did not go through, he would agree to reimburse me. Since I worked on commission, I only got paid if the loan closed. If the loan didn't close—not only would I not get paid—I would personally be stuck with a $750 bill from the appraiser.

A week or two later, we got back the report that showed the house did not meet the lender's lending guidelines. This meant the lender would not lend on the property. When I informed the client of this news he became angry and said he was not going to pay me back for the appraisal and the report. He said that I should have known the report was going to come back with those findings. I could see that he was upset because he had agreed to spend money, and now it was going to be for nothing because he couldn't buy the house. So now he had turned his anger on me, and was refusing to pay the $750 bill that he had agreed to pay earlier. His refusal to pay the bill really bothered me. I thought that I had done everything right. I had communicated to him about the cost, and had him agree both verbally and in email that he would reimburse me the costs regardless of the outcome of the report. During the next few weeks, we debated in an attempt to settle the dispute. He was upset and felt that I had not done my due diligence before spending his money. I told him I totally understood how he felt, but assured him that I had no way of knowing what the report would state until we saw it. The whole reason why we needed the report was to confirm if the property met the requirements of the lender. In an effort to appeal to the humanity of the client, I showed him that my profit on his loan was only going to be $500 and, not only was I not going to be paid, but I was also now going to be stuck with a $750 bill. The client said that the loss was my business, and that I shouldn't be fronting cost for my buyers. He was right, but this made me feel angry that my generosity and customer service were being taken advantage of. The situation made me feel awful. Aside for its ability to earn a good living, the reason why I had gotten into the home loan business was because it allowed me to help people. I experienced a deep sense of gratification when I was able to help someone get a new home, or refinance them out of debt and save them enough money to put toward their retirement. I loved helping people get what they wanted.

Playing bill collector with this client was not making me feel like I wanted to feel. After a few weeks of feeling bad about this situation, it hit me! I was allowing my client's actions to control how I felt. I needed to take responsibility for my own happiness. I took some time to reflect on why I felt that way. I realized that I expected others to show me the same level of integrity that I showed them. When my client didn't react the same way I would have reacted, I became angry and resentful that they didn't do what they had promised to do. I realized that my belief had put my happiness in the control of someone else. I thought, *You may not have control over what happens to you, but you always have control over how you react.*

I realized that my belief was not working for me any longer. I decided to change it so that I would always be the only one responsible for my own happiness. From that point forward, I took responsibility for my own actions. In the instance of this client, even though we had an agreement for him to reimburse me, I realized that I should not have paid that money for him unless I was willing to accept that loss in the event he chose not to pay. That was my fault. If I was really worried about the money, I should have collected it from him up front. I accepted this fact. My happiness did not care who was right or who was wrong. It did not care about getting the money. My happiness, in this instance, was about avoiding conflict.

I took responsibility for allowing myself to be in this situation. I contacted the client and informed him that I was forgiving him of all the debt he owed me. I don't know how that news made him feel, but I can tell you it felt like the world was lifted from my shoulders. By taking responsibility for my own actions, and no longer looking to him for my happiness, I was able to free myself from the negative energy around me. I also decided that I would learn from the experience. My father used to say, "When you lose, don't lose the lesson." The lesson for me was learning not to put myself in situations where others hold my happiness. I then made it a rule to have my future clients pay for any upfront costs. Yes, it decreased my customer service a little bit, but it allowed me to prevent similar unpleasant situations.

I am glad that I finally realized that I am responsible for my own happiness. Sometimes we get caught up in living life and forget that our happiness is always ours to control. If you are not as happy as you would like to be, take a few moments to review why you feel that way. Evaluate whether your current beliefs on that subject are working for you. If they aren't, then change your beliefs, and your actions will then change to meet your new beliefs. If your actions place your happiness in your control, your happiness is assured—as long as you do whatever it takes to make you happy.

# Step 4. Putting Your Ego on a Leash

Although most of us know we have an ego, the majority of us don't realize how it affects our lives. We remember learning about the ego in school, but since the ego is part of us, we forget that it is there and usually just assume it *is* who we are. The ego is a part of us, but it is also a separate consciousness within us. This separate consciousness is constantly battling for control of who we are and how we act. As we discussed earlier, Carl Jung defined the human consciousness as the ego, the personal unconscious, and a collective unconscious.

The ego is the part of us that strives to be different or separate from the world. It is the opposite of the law of oneness, which states we are all made of the same energy. The ego is self-centered, insecure, and doesn't care about anything other than itself. It wants to control your personality because it needs your attention. It tries to do this by making you feel you need it to survive. When your ego becomes inflated, so do your problems.

The ego is not all bad though. It does create our individuality. It is the part of us that shines apart from the rest of the crowd. It is our competitiveness and uniqueness. We all need our ego to a certain extent. No one wants to be exactly like everyone else. That would be boring. This is where the law of gender comes into play. The law of gender teaches that everything has two sides. Finding the right mix between altruism (oneness) and individuality (ego) is what gives us balance in our lives.

Your ego is a positive thing when it is building your confidence and showing you that you are unique and special. The ego is a negative thing when it gets out of control and starts running your life by making you feel that you are better than others or that you are the only thing that matters. Egotism is defined as an exaggerated sense of self-importance or conceit.[92] Confidence believes you can do something. Humility is the art of not being arrogant. When managing our ego, it becomes a matter of finding balance between confidence and humility.

Growing up, I remember watching a cartoon that portrayed a man with an angel on his shoulder telling him what to do in his right ear, and a devil on the other shoulder trying to tell him what to do in his left ear. The man knows the angel is telling him the right thing to do, but the devil is whispering something morally wrong but more appealing in his other ear. He knows the devil is deceitful and that he will regret following his advice, but the man wants to do what the devil is suggesting because it feels more self-gratifying at that moment. In this instance, the ego is the devil that is whispering into his ear. Does that mean the ego is evil? No, not necessarily, it just means the ego is self-serving. It wants to be the center of your attention and will say whatever it needs for you to focus on it rather than anything else.

The problem with being overly self-centered is that our thoughts, words, and actions are being used only for our benefit rather than for the benefit of others as well. When we think we are better than others, we begin to develop negative emotions about others who we feel are beneath or different than us. With an inflated ego, we usually develop feelings toward others that are not positive. Those feelings are our indicator that we are not thinking thoughts that are good for us because when we feel we are better or worse than others, we are causing separation between ourselves and the world. Do you remember in earlier chapters we discussed how energy is circular? When we send out negative thoughts, emotions, words, or actions to others, we are actually sending it to ourselves. The law of cause and effect states that energy is like a boomerang; it always comes back to you.

Our egos can be good or bad for us, depending on how much we let them run our lives. It is up to us to keep our ego under control. Keep your ego on a leash to find the balance between confidence and humility.

When I first learned about the power of the ego, I was intrigued. I decided to do an experiment where I mentally put my ego on a leash as if I was taking a dog for a walk. This mental leash allowed me to maintain control of my ego. Basically, I became an observer of my thoughts. What I found was amazing. The ego really did appear to be sending me thoughts that were often contradictory to how I felt. I knew the ego was part of me, but it also appeared to be something separate apart from the thoughts of my brain. I was able to confirm this when I did some simple meditation exercises. I focused on doing nothing while observing my thoughts. I made sure not thing think any new thoughts. I simply sat as a bystander watching the activity of my mind. Guess what? Even thought I wasn't trying to think of anything, thoughts came pouring into my head. If I wasn't thinking these thoughts, where were they coming from? Were these thoughts coming from my ego? Were they coming from my subconscious? Where they coming from the superconscious? I saw firsthand that our consciousness is more complicated than our brain. This gives some credibility to the existence of the three minds theory of Jung and the Hawaiian Huna belief system. This little mind experiment allowed me to believe that it was possible for the ego to be part of who I was while still being a separate part of my consciousness. How else could I explain the thoughts that were not originated by my conscious brain? And no, in case you are wondering, I'm not schizophrenic. I'm just like most of you. Feel free to do the same experiments. See the meditation section in *Step 8. Schedule in Some Alone Time* for a guided example of how to do this exercise.

I learned that by being in control of my ego, I was able to control what I thought, felt, said, and did. Instead of reacting to life in an instinctual and emotional manner, I choose how I want to react. This change has allowed me to be in control of the energy I sent out.

The ego is crafty in that it hides in our consciousness and plants self-serving thoughts that we often believe to be our own. If we do not evaluate how we feel about these thoughts before we act on them, we can allow our ego to get us into negative situations that could have been avoided. As we have learned throughout this book, our thoughts, words, and actions create the reality we experience. It's the choices we make that determine the life we live. Each person is responsible for their own reality. Thinking before you act really allows you to keep the ego in check. A safe way to evaluate your thoughts is to also observe how they feel. Are these feelings consistent with your beliefs and morals? If they are, you know your actions will be in alignment with your true values. If your thoughts don't feel right, you should choose not to act on them or evaluate them further to see why you feel the way you do. Your feelings are an emotional indicator that tells you if your thoughts are in alignment with your values.

When you learn to put your ego on a leash, you are able to maintain control of your thoughts, feelings, words, and actions. When making decisions, it is wise to remember that the ego is only worried about itself—and has no problem putting you into negative situations as long as it gets your attention. Of course, the choice is always yours to decide if you want to listen to your ego, but that is okay—as long as you remember that the choices you make determine the life you live.

# Step 5. Forgiveness is Freeing Yourself

*"Forgiveness is almost a selfish act because of its immense benefits to the one who forgives."*
-Lawana Blackwell, *The Dowry of Miss Lydia Clark,* 1999

Forgiveness is often difficult to give because of unsettled emotions that we hold on to. Regardless of what has happened—we must take responsibility for how we feel. When someone does something that makes you feel negative emotions, you may feel that you have a right to feel the way you do. After all, their actions have caused you to feel negatively about them or yourself. It is okay to feel emotions as part of the events that happen in our lives, but it gets complicated when we hold on to negative emotions for long periods of time after these events.

Holding on to negative emotions from the actions of others is like injecting poison into your body. These negative emotions sit inside of you and fester. If you leave them inside long enough, they can fester in to unwanted physical manifestations, such as negative life events and even disease. Remember that the energy you focus on is the energy you attract to yourself. When you are feeling negative emotion toward someone else, this is your emotional indicator that you are actually attracting that same negative energy.

Most of us get upset and angry from time to time. Many times we feel we have every right to feel angry. The reality is that it doesn't matter if we have a right to feel the way we do. The only thing that should matter is how we feel at that moment. Do you like the way you feel when you think about this subject? Does holding a grudge make you feel better or worse? We often unknowingly cause ourselves harm when we hold negative emotions inside, like anger or resentment, for others who we feel have done something wrong to us. Often our attempt at being mad is to get revenge or have the other person feel the same pain they caused us, but when we hold negative energy for someone else, we also hold it for ourselves. So the next time you get angry with someone, you should ask yourself, "Do I really want to do that to myself?" A healthier way to deal with emotions is to feel and express them as they happen but to also let them go soon afterward.

## Act Like a Child When It Comes to Emotions

Ideally it is best to have a point of view that allows you to accept life as it happens and avoid extreme emotions (the law of relativity). This grounded viewpoint allows you to stay balanced emotionally. However, this type of positive thinking takes practice. For most people, it is not always possible or even preferred to avoid experiencing emotions when they happen. As we have already discussed, it is not a good idea to hold in negative emotions. When you experience these situations, it is better to express these emotions rather than holding them in. In these situations, you may find it helpful to act like a child does. A child cries when they get hurt, but a few minutes later, they are on to something else. They don't hold grudges or internalize anger. They simply let the emotions out as they happen and then forget about it. They experience life as it happens and then move on to the next experience. For the most part, children travel light; they don't carry emotional baggage. Be like a child and you will be happier.

Forgiveness is about realizing that everyone makes mistakes, and that each mistake is a potential learning experience. If we are wise, we will learn from our mistakes. Forgiveness is a great way to help someone learn from their mistake, while allowing our vibrational frequency to stay at the level we desire.

It is best to forgive people and then let go of the negative energy. If the other person's actions were enough to make you lose respect for them or love for them, then you can choose to not allow them to be a part of your life. When you forgive someone, you are freeing yourself from the energy of their actions. You are freeing yourself from how you felt about them. You are releasing yourself from the emotions you experienced with them in the past. My parents used to teach my brothers and I growing up that it is never too late to right a wrong and it's never too late to forgive.

If you find it difficult to go from hate or anger to forgiveness, go back to the chapter on the law of polarity to help you move from a negative emotion to a more positive one.

## Linda: Forgiveness of Abuse

Linda was sexually abused as a child by her stepfather. All her life, she has carried around this anger for what happened to her. It has affected her self-confidence, her relationships, and her happiness. Linda focused all of this anger on her stepfather, and cursed him for ruining her life. She was so unhappy that she contemplated suicide many times. Then Linda met a great guy and they eventually got married. Linda trusted Mark and shared her childhood experiences. Mark helped Linda understand that her forgiveness of her stepfather's actions was her ticket to emotional freedom. Linda had been holding on to the unwanted focus of those negative times in her life. She was unaware that her focus on those events allowed the law of attraction to keep bringing more of that same negative energy back into her life. She had not been able escape the endless negative circle. Mark helped Linda understand that although her stepfather had done those things to her, it was actually Linda who allowed those memories to stay active in her own vibration frequency. When Linda made a conscious effort to let go of those negative feelings by forgiving her stepfather, she was able to break out and away from the negative cycle that she had been trapped in for so many years. When she forgave her stepfather, she was not condoning what he had done, or suggesting that she herself had done anything wrong, but instead her forgiveness allowed her to declare, "I no longer allow this negativity to have any power over me. I couldn't control what happened to me in the past, but I can control how I live the rest of my life. I choose to set my stepfather free from my anger and resentment, and I choose to set myself free from those same emotions." She imagined that she was talking to her stepfather and said, "I love myself too much to hate you any longer." By forgiving her stepfather, she was able to set herself free from the negative energy of fear and anger that had held her prisoner for so many years.

Forgiveness is not about the other person; it is about you. Forgiveness is about releasing the poisonous feelings inside so that you can heal and go on with your life. It takes strength to let go of the hate, anger, or hurt—but you will be helping yourself to grow and prosper. It was the Buddha that correctly illustrates this point with the saying, "You will not be punished for your anger, you will be punished by your anger."

# Family Forgiveness

Years ago, I saw a sad story on TV about a family where the father had killed the mother. The father went to jail for life. Over the years, the young children went on to grow up angry and bitter toward their father because they felt that he had taken their mother away from them and cheated them out of out of their normal childhood experiences.

It was apparent that this event had greatly hindered the emotional growth of these kids. These children, now young adults, all discussed the anger and hatred they had for their father. Even though they were angry, you could also see deep down that they really just wanted to be loved, and were bitter because they had been robbed of that opportunity. I wished that each of them would somehow find a way to a counselor that could show them that forgiveness is the only way to free and heal themselves from the pain. They didn't have to forgive their father for their father's sake. They needed to forgive their father for their own sake. Through the law of perpetual transmutation of energy, the higher vibration of forgiveness will transmute the lower vibrations of anger and hate into higher vibrational emotions like love, forgiveness, and acceptance. This won't happen overnight, but in time they will see that their only way to happiness is through forgiveness. In changing the vibration of their thoughts from lower negative vibrations of anger and hate to higher more positive vibrations like love and forgiveness, they can heal themselves and bring peace into their lives.

If they don't find a way to forgive, they will be destined to carry those negative feelings around for the rest of their lives. This can lead to a variety of physical and emotional problems.

Forgiving is not easy. It takes a lot of strength. Most people cannot go from rage, anger, hurt, and fear to immediately feeling love and forgiveness.

They may not be able to make the massive jump in emotions from hate to forgiveness, but they can use the law of polarity to choose the next best emotion to slowly climb the ladder of emotions from where they are to where they want to be.

*"The weak can never forgive. Forgiveness is the attribute of the strong."*
*—Mahatma Gandhi (1869–1948)*

# Step 6. Be Selfish to Help Others

You may be wondering how being selfish will help you attract positive energy or be able to help others. In order to help anyone else, you must first make sure you are abundant and happy. How can you fully help someone else when you need help yourself? The more positive energy you have, the more you have to give others. Part of giving to others is giving to yourself.

It's like when you board an airplane and the flight attendant informs the passengers that in the unlikely event of a cabin depressurization to place the oxygen mask on yourself *before* you place it on your children. That is because you need to be make sure you can function in order to help the children.

Life is the same way—you need to make sure that you are at vibrational frequency that is in alignment with your desires before you help others. When you are aligned with your desires, you become an empowered creator capable of helping others and affecting everything and everyone you experience.

What good are you to the person you are trying to help when your energy is not uplifting and positive? You may be giving acts of kindness or quality time, but you could be giving so much more if you were happy and complete inside while you were giving to others. It's all about balance. Love is circular; to give love you must first have it. When you give to yourself, it shows that you love yourself and care about your own well-being. When you give to others but don't give to yourself, you are diminishing your own energy and the energy you give to others because you are out of balance. If you care about others, make sure to also give to yourself—when you are happy and fulfilled, you become more empowered to help others.

I don't suggest that you become too selfish and only give to yourself. That could make you out of balance even more than just giving to others.

Find an even medium where you can give to yourself and others, and you will find the happiness in your life that you deserve.

# Step 7. Help Others to Help Yourself

We need to help ourselves before we can help others so we can be at our best when we are helping them. As we discussed, giving to yourself is necessary, but so is giving to others. It's all about finding a balance between giving and receiving.

Through the law of compensation, we know the energy we give out comes back to us ten times stronger. Since energy is circular in nature, it always comes back to us. When we give to others, it is like giving to ourselves because the act of giving is attracting more positive energy that will come back to us. Love is circular; to get love you must first give it.

If you have been lucky enough to experience good financial fortune, it is always a good idea to share some of it with others less fortunate than you. Not only is it the good thing to do, it is also the smart thing to do. When you appreciate the good fortune you have experienced and you give back to others, you keep the positive energy flowing back to you. Where energy is concerned, giving is the surest way to continue getting. So help others to help yourself. When you give, it doesn't have to be money, it can be anything that comes from your heart. You could spend time with someone who is lonely; you could bring food to the hungry; or you could help someone up who has fallen down. Any act of kindness keeps the good will coming.

I invite you to play a game of generosity. For the next month, I invite you to look for ways you can help others. Try to do at least three good deeds a day. There is no need to plan out things you will do for others, as it often works better for you to just react to the situations you see. Examples of this might be helping an elderly lady open the door at the store; it could be bringing a meal from the store to a homeless person on the corner; it could be giving a smile to someone who is having a bad day; or it could be spending time with your family instead of watching the football game. Anything where you are doing something for someone or something is fair game. Do this for a month and I promise you will feel amazing!

When I do this exercise, I like to look to help any and all living things in need. If I see a spider in the house, I trap it in a cup and take it outside rather than killing it, or if a bee is trapped in the pool, I will splash it out so that it can survive. Any living thing that I see in need, I try to help it if I can. Remember the law of oneness says that we are all made of the same energy. That means we are all related. Now don't get me wrong—I don't go out of my way to do these things because that would take up all of my time, but if it happens right in front of me, I am happy to take a second to show love and charity to another living thing. Sometimes on my morning walks, I see earthworms that have traveled too far out onto the sidewalk and are in danger of dying from sun exposure. I usually stop to save the ones that are in front of my path by picking them up and returning them to the lawn. I was once asked why I bothered saving a few worms when there are so many that needed saving. They said that saving a few worms wouldn't make a difference. My reply was that it probably made a difference to the worms I helped.

I take the time to help others because it always makes me feel good. It feels best when no one knows of my good deeds. Random acts of kindness are some of the best ways of giving to others. If you are giving solely so that you will get praise or appreciation for your kindness, you are not really giving from the heart—you are giving to inflate your ego. Try to give unconditionally from the heart and you will be pleased with the way you feel. Generosity is an act that displays your soul. Others may not see your act, but the recipient of your generosity will appreciate it. That is all that really matters. You are being observed much more than you know; so, in reality, no good deed ever goes unnoticed.

## Exercise: Three Random Acts of Kindness a Day

Write down three things you did today to help others in your journal or on this page. Do this every day for a month. List your good deeds for today.

My good deeds today:

1. _____

2. _____

3. _____

Keep doing this exercise every day for a month and watch how your life changes for the better before your eyes.

# Step 8. Schedule in Some Alone Time

*"It's good for the soul when there's not a soul in sight."*
*—Kenny Chesney (with Dave Matthews), "I'm Alive."*

In today's busy world, we are often running from one thing to the next. Sometimes it can seem like there are not enough hours in the day to get everything done. I have found that—no matter how busy I am—it is important to spend some quality time by myself each day. This is important because most of us spend the majority of our time completing tasks. An example of this would be getting up in the morning to brush your teeth, going to the bathroom, then to the gym, then back home to eat breakfast, and get ready for work, then off to work, work all day, and then finally come home to cook dinner, then maybe watch some TV, and finally go to bed. If you have kids then you can multiply these tasks times two or more. My point is that we are often so engaged in life that we forget to take time to analyze our lives or to reflect on some of the deeper meanings of life.

Spending alone time is just what it sounds like. It is you spending time with no one else around. The purpose of alone time is to find a calm and quiet place that is free from interruptions and be by yourself. Spending time with yourself allows you to stop thinking for a while. You will find that you will be able to unwind and de-stress during this time as well as review and analyze your life. This time allows you to make sense of your life and enjoy it more. If you are not happy, this time will help you understand why you feel this way and what changes are necessary.

When you stop actively using your mind to think, you allow your vibrational frequency to change. Like changing the station on a radio dial, this rest in mental activity allows a deeper part of you (your higher self) to emerge or align. When you are quiet with yourself, you are able to align and listen to your subconscious and superconscious minds—which have access to infinite wisdom. Both of these minds speak to you through your intuition. When you quiet your mind, you are able to sense your intuition better because you are then aligned with it. This is the same thing that happens when people meditate.

Your vibrational frequency is different when you are thinking than when you are listening. When you are listening can you hear your intuition. It is important to have some alone time to stop and listen to your intuition. When your thoughts are turned off and your mind quiets down, your intuition becomes clearer to you.

## Free Wisdom

When the mind is listening, it can tap into the frequency of the superconscious mind or the higher self. When we connect to this part of ourselves, we begin to know things without knowing how we know them. This is a way to acquire wisdom without learning it through experiences. I call this "unearned wisdom." There becomes a feeling of knowing the truth without knowing how you know what you know, but you know that it *feels* right to you. This feeling of truth will help you solve any issues or questions in your own life. All you have to do is ask a question silently and evaluate the thoughts that come into your head. The answer to your question will be in the thought that feels right to you. It may take time to develop this ability, but it can be developed by anyone who takes the time to practice listening.

Even if you are not interested in meditation, intuition, or wisdom, you can still take time to recharge your mental battery and de-stress. Life can get busy and we can get unbalanced because we do whatever needs to be done during the day. When we take time out, we are recharging our batteries and rebalancing our energy. Make sure to take some alone time to recharge mentally and you will be more refreshed and more productive the next day.

## The Story of the Two Lumberjacks

**Figure 17: The Story of the Two Lumberjacks**

Two lumberjacks were having a contest to see who could cut down the most wood during the day. Early in the day, the lumberjacks were about even in their race. As the day progressed, the second lumberjack noticed that the first lumberjack was taking frequent breaks. The second lumberjack was sure he was winning the contest with his constant effort. At the end of the day as they tallied the amount of wood, it became apparent the first lumberjack had cut down more. The second lumberjack asked the first lumberjack how it was possible to cut down more wood when he was constantly taking short breaks. The second lumberjack said, "When I was taking breaks, I was sharpening my ax."

Just like the first lumberjack, when you take little breaks, you are able to sharpen your mental ax so that you can be more effective.

Alone time is best if you can find a safe place in your home or somewhere nearby where you can reflect for five to thirty minutes each day and enjoy being with yourself. It may feel awkward at first and you will probably be restless, but you will appreciate this time and crave the silence and peace that it brings.

When I get up, I go out on my deck and sit in a chair and look at the vegetation on the hillside. I don't try to do anything. My goal is to just be there and to feel what it feels like to be alive in that moment. I have found a great sense of peace when I do this and the answers to life's questions and challenges have come to me intuitively through thoughts that feel right to me. I get a clearer understanding of whatever is on my mind. I also use this time to think about my life, and what I want to do with it, or why I am here. I can't say why, but I find it very therapeutic to enjoy silence. I also enjoy the sound of running water, rain, or a relaxing CD.

If you want to analyze and think about your life, then do it—but don't think about tasks or things you have to do. You have all day to do that. Spend your special time wisely.

Some people have said that they don't have time or that there isn't any quiet place in their house. If something is important to you, you will find a way to make it happen. That may mean getting up earlier than everyone else and having a cup of coffee by yourself. If it is noisy in your house, go to the local park and sit by a tree, or take a lunch by yourself and sit in the car while you reflect. If you are a parent and can't leave the kids, go into the bathroom and lock the door and give yourself five minutes of time to yourself—or wait until they take their nap. We all need time to recharge our mental batteries, but most of us never realize that is something we need or can do.

## Meditation

Meditation is the art of quieting the mind to receive wisdom from higher intelligence. I have learned to appreciate the silence so much that I eventually started doing meditation. I have found meditation to be a very important and yet simple tool in learning how to control the mind. It has taught me how to be aware of my thoughts and how to control what I wish to think about. Most people would be amazed to discover how little control they actually have over what they think about on a daily basis. It has been said that the average person can only focus on one subject for about eight seconds. You don't believe me? Close your eyes and see how long you can stay focused on the image of a blue truck before you lose focus or your mind starts throwing distracting thoughts at you. It would be very good if you can stay focused on that thought for a minute. Even a minute is not very long considering that focus is a key ingredient to using the law of attraction. I have used meditation to strengthen my mind to allow it to focus longer on the things I desire. This helps me manifest things in my life easier—you can learn to do this too.

Even sitting by yourself enjoying the beauty of the roses in your garden is a basic type of meditation. When you literally stop to smell the roses, you are giving yourself a chance to just be and relax. To me, meditation is about doing nothing but listening.

Spending alone time can help you to ground and center yourself. This is when you stop thinking about what you want to achieve—or what you are doing—and start focusing on yourself at this very moment in time. Einstein commented that most Americans were so focused on "becoming" that they rarely took time to just "be." This unfortunately is still true today. Most of us are so busy earning a living and building a life that we forget to enjoy the moment and the beauty around us. We live in a world of delayed gratification rather than enjoying each moment for whatever it is. We need to ground or center ourselves so we can stay balanced. Too much thinking without listening is not good for us.

We are just starting to learn to harness the incredible capabilities of our own minds—meditation is an amazing tool that lets us do that. The more we meditate, the more we develop our own mind. Meditation allows us to awaken latent faculties that most people don't realize they even have.

Even though meditation is also used as a tool in Eastern religions, I have not found meditation to be religious at all. If anything, meditation leads to an eventual spiritual unfolding (awareness) of the being that you already are, regardless of whether you believe in religions or not.

## Learn to Control Your Mind through Meditation

There are many forms of meditation. Some have rules and some don't. Some focus on objects or words while others do not. There is no right or wrong way to meditate. I think the best way is the way that has few—or no—rules. Below is an example of what I do for simple meditation.

Step 1. **Sit.** Find a place where you can sit uninterrupted for 5–20 minutes. You can sit on a pillow in the lotus position (Buddha position). I usually prefer a chair with my feet on the floor. Keep your back as straight as possible.

Step 2. **Breathe.** In a relaxed manner, breathe in deeply through your nose in a slow, controlled pace and then breathe out in the same controlled manner through either your nose or mouth. I try to breathe in for 4 seconds, pause for a second, and then breathe out for four seconds. Continue this breathing. In time, you will not have to focus on the deep breathing, and it will become automatic. The extra oxygen that you get from breathing deeply brings additional energy into your body. Also attempt to breathe from your stomach rather than your chest. If you see your stomach rise and fall, you are doing it correctly.

Step 3. **Close your eyes and focus on nothing.** This is the art of un-thinking or mental listening. (This will be quite an effort at first.) As distracting thoughts come into your head (and they will), just acknowledge them and let them go. Do not add any additional thought to them. If you find that you have lost your focus or let a thought take over, just refocus on nothing and start over. In time, you will be able to concentrate for longer periods—and it will be easier. Focusing on nothing takes a lot of concentration at first because you are spending a lot of mental energy trying not to focus on any of the many thoughts that pop into your head. Don't worry—before long you will begin to control the thoughts that come into your head.

That's it. There's nothing more to it. Just relax and listen. The trick to successfully controlling your mind is to become an observer in your own mind. Watch thoughts come and watch them go. Meditation will allow you to gain control over your mental and emotional minds. Your mind is both a transmitter and a receiver. When you are thinking, you are transmitting information—and when you are meditating, you are receiving information. Most people can only consciously do one of these activities at a time. That means that you need to stop thinking so that you can receive input from your higher self and the universe. This is the main point of meditation.

What you experience while meditating is individual to you. Most people simply get greater clarity in their life. Don't expect to have psychic encounters or see visions. Although those things are entirely possible, they are unlikely for a beginner. Expect nothing but intuition and you won't be disappointed.

## What If I Get Scared While Meditating?

This section is for people, like me, who have an overactive imagination. Growing up, my imagination was a great tool for creativity, but it also sometimes made me fearful of the unknown. I always wondered what lurked around the corner. As a kid, I remember swimming in pools and imagining that I could see sharks moving in and out of the shadows below. This understandably led to a fear of sharks until I faced those fears and made them go away.

I feel that the consciousness of the mind is the next great frontier for mankind to discover. When I first started doing meditation, I felt a little uneasy about the unknown environment I was entering. I wondered what I would experience. Were there other nonphysical entities out there? Would they have any control over me? Could they do me harm? What were the rules of this environment? Were there new sharks lurking in the shadows of the corners of my mind?

My first few times meditating, I was fearful of what I would experience, but thankfully I experienced nothing but the blankness of my mind. These uneventful experiences helped allow me to relax. However, there were times when my imagination would kick into gear and I would feel fearful and tense. Once I started learning about the universal laws, I discovered that the law of perpetual transmutation of energy can be used to transmute all types of energy. I figured out a way to use it to my advantage while I was meditating.

Whenever I became scared, I noticed that my heart would beat faster, my hands would get sweaty, and my body would tense up. The lower vibration of fear had changed the physical state of my body. Through trial and error, I learned that I could control the fear and the vibrational frequency of my body by choosing thoughts that were of a higher frequency. Love is said to be the highest frequency of all, so whenever I became scared I would say, "I am love. Only loving things can stand in my presence," over and over again until I felt my body transform from stiff and scared to relaxed and confident. I was able to use the law of perpetual transmutation of energy to raise my vibrational frequency from the lower vibrational frequency of fear to the higher vibrational frequency of love. When I did that, any negative energy, real or imagined, had to either raise its vibration to love or flee and leave me alone.

*The Light Shall Set You Free* said, "Dark forces have no power over you unless you give the power to them."[93] The thoughts and feelings you choose for yourself determine the vibrational frequency with which you align and attract. If you choose higher vibrational thoughts like love and compassion, you will attract only that type of energy. Imagine if we could have learned this information when we were little and we were scared of the boogeyman under the bed. This empowering breakthrough really helped me control the fears of my mind and it can help you too. Once I learned this, I never again became scared while meditating.

If you believe in angels—and you don't feel confident in your own abilities to protect yourself from your own fears—you can always call on Archangel Michael to help you anytime you need him. He will protect you from anything. All you need to do is ask for his help.

Now that you know how to protect yourself, you can meditate in confidence knowing that you are always able to be safe.

# Step 9. Learn to Live Life in the Middle

Living life in the middle means avoiding extremes and enjoying a balanced life. You should be able to enjoy life and sample all it has to offer, but you should also beware whenever you start to do anything in excess. When life is lived to extremes, the law of rhythm (nature) will seek to make corrections to restore balance.

In recent memory, we have seen nature restore balance many times. First we saw the dotcom bubble stock market crash restore balance to the stock market after many years of oversized stock gains. Only a few years later, we saw the real estate boom and bust. It seems that nature is always correcting itself to restore balance.

## *An Eyewitness to Financial Insanity*

As a mortgage broker, I saw the real estate boom and bust firsthand. After the dotcom bubble burst in 2000, investors moved their money from stocks and bonds to real estate. That influx of cash into the real estate market coupled with low mortgage interest rates and low home prices caused the real estate boom to begin. As the boom gained momentum, people became emotional about getting in on the craze of homeownership. No one wanted to miss out on the amazing amount of money there was to be made during that time in real estate. It seemed like real estate was all that anyone ever talked about.

Then, adding fuel to the fire, banks started issuing negative amortization loan programs that treated homes like credit cards. Homeowners would only have to pay a minimal mortgage interest payment each month and the remaining majority of the actual payment would get added to their loan balance each month. This caused the loan balances to go up each month rather than down. Homeowners didn't seem to care about this because, at the time, they were making so much money from their home values going up each month that it didn't matter to them if their loan balance was also increasing slightly each month.

Next the banks also came out with stated loans that allowed people to state their income without any verification by the lender. These became known as "liar loans" because the inflated income stated by the buyers allowed buyers to buy houses for much more of a sales price than they would have normally qualified if they had stated their actual income. I also noticed that credit no longer seemed to be an issue to the banks. People with low credit scores were still getting almost as good a loan as people with excellent credit. Just about anyone who wanted to get a house could get one. I remember thinking that the whole real estate boom was pure madness. It baffled me to think that the government could allow the banks to issue these programs to the public. I often wondered what was going to happen when this boom was over. I knew there would be a heavy price to pay, but I had no idea it would cause a credit crisis that would bring our financial system within inches of collapsing. Had the Federal Reserve not stepped in when it did, America—the way we knew it—might not be here today.

The real estate boom ended in 2007, and the Great Recession began in 2008. Nature had come back to restore balance in the market. The unfortunate part was that the Great Recession affected the entire country, rather than just the people who defaulted on their mortgages. As of the writing of this book, the real estate market, at least in California, has not recovered from the bust, but I know eventually balance will be restored because that is the way nature works. Warren Buffett said, "Unfortunately, the hangover from [the market bubble] may prove to be proportional to the binge."[94]

When you live a balanced life, you can avoid nature's corrections. If our country had made more balanced choices, we probably wouldn't be experiencing these challenging economic times.

Life on an individual level is no different. If you live life to extremes long enough, the law of rhythm will eventually pay you a visit. Think about people who smoke for thirty years, or business executives who work at an unending work pace for years at a time. What about the married couple that lives under constant stress of a bad marriage? What about people who don't take care of their bodies by constantly overindulging in junk food or not getting enough sleep or exercise? All of these people are putting undue stress on their bodies, and have a larger chance of nature correcting the imbalances in their lives. The correction can be the flu, a divorce, a disease, a heart attack, a mental breakdown, or anything else that gets us to change our ways. Be proactive to make positive changes to ensure balance. Just do a little bit each day to stay balanced and you will stand a better chance of keeping the law of rhythm from paying you a personal visit.

The great thing about being human is that we can choose whatever we do or don't want to do. Now that you know about the law of rhythm, you know that every action has a reaction. Every imbalance, if maintained long enough, will eventually be rebalanced in one way or another.

# Step 10. You Are Who You Hang Around

*"You are who you associate with. Look around at your five*
*closest friends and that's who you are. If you don't want*
*to be that person, you know what you gotta do."*
—Will Smith

The world is full of all different kinds of people. People can be rich or poor, nice or mean, happy or sad, ambitious or lethargic, law-abiding or mischievous, or any other combination of emotions and actions. A person may not have control of their environment or where they lived while they were growing up, but once they are an adult, they usually have a choice about these things.

How you choose to live and who you associate with is entirely up to you. However, you should check to see if the people you associate with share your same interests, or are supportive of your aspirations. If they don't support you or share your desires, their energy is not the same as yours. Often people who do not share your dreams will try to discourage you from achieving your goals. They may say things like, "You can't do it" or "Why bother trying—it's just a waste of time." If you let them, people like this can derail your dreams.

Another reason to distance yourself from people who don't share your dreams is that their actions can influence you. If you are a good person, but hang around people who are attracting negative energy, their energy will come to you as well. Guilt by association means that if you hang around a group of people, and someone in that group does something wrong, you are often seen as guilty—even if you didn't do anything yourself.

Fortunately, the opposite effect happens when you associate with like-minded people who share your goals. When someone does something positive and you're associated with the group, you are often seen as a part of that action. Also, like-minded people share the same positive energy with each other. Just being in the presence of each other helps to build more positive energy than could be created by just one person. This is an example of the Power of The Master Mind from the book *Think and Grow Rich,* which teaches the power of multiple brains focused on the same subject.[95]

If you are a student and your goal is to go to Stanford University, then you should do whatever you can to get around other people who also want to go to Stanford or other prestigious colleges. When you do this, you will notice that your thinking begins to elevate to the level of other people who have the same desires. Your energy rises to match theirs. In the past, you may have been okay with getting B's on your report card, but once you started associating with other people who also wanted to go to similar colleges, you will probably decide to raise your own standards to accept nothing short of A's when you see that everyone else who is trying to get into these colleges has excellent grades.

This mindset helps you transform yourself and apply the law of action to your life to do things that complement your goals. It is easier to do this when you are surrounded by others who share the same desires.

If your desires and goals are constantly getting squashed and not becoming a reality, check to see if other people are helping you or hindering you. If they are not helping you, you may want to consider distancing yourself from them and choose to be around people who share your desires.

# Step 11. Replace Judgment with Compassion

We've all—at one time or another—watched and judged someone else who has acted in a way that we felt was inappropriate. It might be a bully who was picking on someone smaller; an angry customer making a scene; a homeless person asking for money on the corner; or an overweight person ordering a large amount of food at a fast food restaurant.

It seems to be human nature for us to judge the actions of others based on how we feel they should act. We often do this without even knowing the factors in that person's life that might be making them act the way they are acting. An angry person might have had a really bad day, or gotten fired from his job, or she may have just found out that day that she has terminal cancer. If we knew those facts about that person, we would probably be more compassionate and understanding about that person's actions.

Unfortunately, most people make assumptions about people while they judge them. They might assume that the only reason why someone is overweight is because of their own neglect and gluttonous eating habits, when that person might have a metabolic problem that prevents her from being thin regardless of how little she eats or how much exercise she gets. The reality is that most times we simply don't know the facts about the person we are judging. Even if we do know all the facts, does that give us the right to judge someone? What business is it of ours what someone else is doing? Haven't we all made mistakes? Our mistakes allow us to learn and grow. After all, we all create our own reality.

The law of cause and effect is a self-regulating law in that it will ensure that positive actions attract more positive energy and negative actions attract more negative energy. Each person creates their own reality with the thoughts, words, and actions that they choose. They don't need our judgment to make them conform; their own actions will create a reality that will mirror the energy they give out. It is up to them to decide if they want to change their future reality by changing how they think and act.

Ironically the most important reason not to judge others is for our own benefit. When we judge others, we are lowering our own vibrational frequency by thinking negative thoughts and that, in turn, attracts more negative energy to us. Think about that for a minute. When we judge others, we are observing a perceived negative action of another, and then choosing to respond with our own negative thoughts that affect the energy we attract to ourselves. Do we really want to attract negative energy to ourselves?

It is better to respond with compassionate thoughts. We don't have to understand or condone the actions of another, but when we respond with thoughts of compassion, we send healing energy to that person. Through the law of compensation, we attract that same energy to ourselves. A good way to find compassion is to ask yourself how you would feel if you were that person in that situation and others were judging you. Would you want to be judged?

## Energy Comes Back Around

Recently I watched a children's cartoon called *Astro Boy*. The robot boy, Astro Boy, has a unique type of positive blue energy that is very special and powerful. One day he came across a broken down "dead" robot named

Zog, and decided to be compassionate and use some of his energy to bring Zog back to life. The two robots became friends. Later, Astro Boy had to use all of his positive blue energy to defeat the negative red energy of the villain robot. This left both Astro Boy and the villain as "dead" robots. Then Zog shared some of his positive blue energy with Astro Boy to bring him back to life.

I liked this part of the movie because it showed the law of compensation in effect. The same energy that Astro Boy had given out eventually came back to him. Astro Boy had unknowingly saved his own life with his generosity and compassion to Zog.

Real life is no different. The energy we give out comes back to us in the events that happen in our lives. The next time you feel like judging someone, take a few seconds to replace your thoughts of judgment with thoughts of compassion. You will be helping both them and yourself.

Another great story about learning not to judge others is called "The Cookie Thief."[96]

## The Cookie Thief Story

A woman was waiting at an airport one night,
With several long hours before her flight.
She hunted for a book in the airport shop,
Bought a bag of cookies and found a place to drop.

She was engrossed in her book but happened to see,
That the man sitting beside her, as bold as could be,
Grabbed a cookie or two from the bag in between,
Which she tried to ignore, to avoid a scene.

She read, munched cookies, and watched the clock,
As the gutsy "cookie thief" diminished her stock.
She was getting more irritated as the minutes ticked by,
Thinking, "If I wasn't so nice, I would blacken his eye!"

He offered her half, as he ate the other,
She snatched it from him and thought, "Oh, brother,
This guy has some nerve and he's also *rude*,
Why, he didn't even show any gratitude!"

She had never known when she had been so galled,
And sighed with relief when her flight was called.
She gathered her belongings and headed to the gate,
Refusing to look back at the "thieving ingrate."

She boarded the plane, and sank in her seat,
Then she sought her book, which was almost complete.
As she reached in her baggage, she gasped with surprise.
There was her bag of cookies, in front of her eyes!

"If mine are here," she moaned in despair,
"Then others were *his*, and he tried to share!"
Too late to apologize, she realized with grief,
That *she* was the rude one, the ingrate, the thief.
By Valerie Cox[97]

Another story illustrates how compassion can affect someone you don't even know.

## Compassion to a Kid Named Kyle

When I was a freshman in high school, I saw a kid from my class was walking home from school. His name was Kyle. It looked like he was carrying all of his books. I thought, "Why would anyone bring home all his books on a Friday? He must really be a nerd." I had quite a weekend planned (parties and a football game with my friends tomorrow afternoon), so I shrugged my shoulders and went on. As I was walking, I saw a bunch of kids running toward him. They ran at him, knocking all his books out of his arms, and tripping him so he landed in the dirt. His glasses went flying, and I saw them land in the grass about ten feet from him. He looked up and I saw this terrible sadness in his eyes. My heart went out to him. So, I jogged over to him as he crawled around looking for his glasses, and I saw a tear in his eye. As I handed him his glasses, I said, "Those guys are jerks. They really should get lives." He looked at me and said, "Hey thanks!"

There was a big smile on his face. It was one of those smiles that showed real gratitude. I helped him pick up his books, and asked him where he lived. As it turned out, he lived near me, so I asked him why I had never seen him before. He said he had gone to private school before. I would have never hung out with a private school kid before. We talked all the way home, and I carried some of his books. He turned out to be a pretty cool kid. I asked him if he wanted to play a little football with my friends. He said yes. We hung out all weekend and the more I got to know Kyle, the more I liked him, and my friends thought the same of him. Monday morning came, and there was Kyle with the huge stack of books again. I stopped him and said, "Boy, you are gonna really build some serious muscles with this pile of books everyday!" He just laughed and handed me half the books.

Over the next four years, Kyle and I became best friends. When we were seniors, we began to think about college. Kyle decided on Georgetown and I was going to Duke. I knew that we would always be friends, that the miles would never be a problem. He was going to be a doctor and I was going for business on a football scholarship. Kyle was valedictorian of our class. I teased him all the time about being a nerd. He had to prepare a speech for graduation. I was so glad it wasn't me having to get up there and speak. On graduation day, I saw Kyle.

He looked great. He was one of those guys that really found himself during high school. He filled out and actually looked good in glasses. He had more dates than I had and all the girls loved him. Boy, sometimes I was jealous! Today was one of those days. I could see that he was nervous about his speech. So, I smacked him on the back and said, "Hey, big guy, you'll be great!" He looked at me with one of those looks (the really grateful one) and smiled. "Thanks," he said. As he started his speech, he cleared his throat, and said, "Graduation is a time to thank those who helped you make it through those tough years. Your parents, your teachers, your siblings, maybe a coach ... but mostly your friends ... I am here to tell all of you that being a friend to someone is the best gift you can give them. I am going to tell you a story." I just looked at my friend with disbelief as he told of the first day we met. He had planned to kill himself over the weekend. He talked of how he had cleaned out his locker so his mom wouldn't have to do it later and was carrying his stuff home. He looked hard at me and gave me a little smile.

"Thankfully, I was saved. My friend saved me from doing the unspeakable." I heard the gasp go through the crowd as this handsome, popular boy told us all about his weakest moment. I saw his mom and dad looking at me and smiling that same grateful smile. Not until that moment did I realize its depth. Never underestimate the power of your actions. With one small gesture, you can change a person's life. For better or for worse.[98]

As you can see, you never can tell the effects of a smile, a helpful hand, or compliment. It may not mean much to you, but it may mean the world to the person you give it to.

## Part 3 Summary

- *Journaling* can be used to de-stress and document your personal growth.
- Everyone has a special *gift* they are born with. Find yours to strengthen your life.
- A *positive page* can be used to stay positive when experiencing negativity.
- A *balance wheel* can be used to prioritize the important parts of your life.

Then you learned the Eleven Steps to Becoming the Ultimate You:

1. *Develop your intuition* to use higher knowledge to make decisions.
2. *Be the most positive person you know* to attract positivity to your life.
3. Take accountability for your own life as *you are responsible for your own happiness.*
4. *Putting your ego on a leash* allows you to be balanced and centered as a person.
5. *Forgiveness is freeing yourself* from the negative emotions of others.
6. *Be selfish to help others* because you must be loved before you can spread that love to others.
7. *Help others to help yourself* because the energy of giving attracts that same energy back to you.
8. *Schedule in some alone time* to sharpen your mind and allow input from the universe to be mentally received.
9. *Learn to live life in the middle* because a balanced life avoids more of nature's corrections.
10. *You are who you hang around with.* The energy of the people you associate with affects you.
11. *Replace judgment with compassion* to attract positive energy rather than negative energy.

If you can implement and follow this information for thirty days, I promise you will begin to see a total transformation in yourself and others will notice it too. This program helps you use the universal laws to your advantage. It will allow you to maximize the influence of the universal laws to empower you to create whatever it is you wish to create.

# Part 4:
# How to Use the Universal Laws in Everyday Life Situations

# Chapter 7: Change

*"The only thing constant in life is change."*
*-Francois de la Rochefoucauld (1613-1680)*

Have you noticed how much change there has been in recent years? At the time of this writing, the world seems to be in an evolutionary storm. Change is everywhere. From the year 2000 until 2010, we experienced the dot com bubble, the housing bubble, the Great Recession, and the credit crisis. At the time of this writing, unemployment is at the highest level it has been in a long time. Natural disasters, such as tsunamis, earthquakes, and hurricanes that cause massive destruction, have been occurring with increasing frequency. All of these factors contribute to the constant change in our lives. We can no longer expect the same results from life that we did in the past.

The ancient Mayan civilization predicted that a great period of change would come upon us in 2012. Many have said that this change would be caused by celestial alignment and the raising of the vibration of the planet as a whole. Whether you believe in the hype of 2012 or not, no one can deny that change is a constant part of our lives today.

Most of us would prefer not to experience change. We like to know that the structures of our lives are secure and that we can depend on the same things happening in the future that have always happened in the past. Like it or not, this time is teaching us that change is going to be the norm rather than an occasional occurrence.

The dinosaurs probably didn't want the change that happened to them either. It is interesting to note that the species that survived over time were not the ones that were the strongest or the smartest, but rather were the ones that were most able to adapt to the changing environment.

Change always presents us with two choices. The first choice is to resist the change and try to hold on to the way things were. The second choice is to accept the change and find a way to use it to our advantage.

Change is a manifestation of energy. When we resist this energy it often feels wrong—and we experience worry, anger, fear, hate, or frustration. When we proactively see and accept change, we can accept it for what it is and look for positive ways to make it work for us in our lives. We know that change is working for us when we eventually feel happiness, relief, pride, excitement, enthusiasm or positive anticipation. In every crisis, there is usually a hidden opportunity. We just have to look for it.

## Job Loss: Crisis or Opportunity?

Let's take a look at an example of change. Due to a recession, John lost his job. He had been working at his company for twenty years. Although he didn't really enjoy his job, he was good at it, and it paid the bills.

John had mixed emotions. In one sense, he was stunned that his safe, consistent job had vanished, and he no longer had a way to pay his bills. He was scared by the uncertainty of what was going to happen. After sulking for a while, he started to think about things in a more positive way. He had always wanted to start a construction business to fix up and rehabilitate houses, but had never had the guts to quit his job and go for it. He had always been worried about how he would pay his bills. His unemployment allowed him to realize that he was now in the perfect situation to follow his dream. He had been forced out of his job and no longer had to worry about making the decision to leave his old job. The choice had been made for him. John decided to follow his heart and open his own new business.

John understood the power of positive thinking and decided to accept his situation by choosing to focus on the exciting new future he was going to create. John used this opportunity to do what he had always wanted to do. It wasn't always easy, but years later, John's business was thriving. He was always talking about how much he loved his job. He loved it so much that he said it wasn't work to him. If he had another job, the job that he was doing would be his hobby. John had found a way to work with the change that affected him.

## Relationship Change

Another example of change comes from Rhonda. In the past few years, she had learned to accept change. She thought positive thoughts and noticed that change seemed to be working for her rather than against her. It was almost as if life was manifesting things around her that matched her vibrational frequency. The only thing that troubled Rhonda was that her husband of ten years had not changed in the same way—and it had made them grow apart. She loved him very much, but they no longer had much in common. This saddened her, but she realized that life is about change and if she and her husband didn't grow together, they would grow apart.

Rhonda did the right thing. Instead of trying to change her husband, she accepted her husband for the person he was, and desired their relationship to be mutually beneficial and loving again. She understood the law of compensation, so she gave her husband the love and attention that she desired herself. She knew that, in time, her actions would be noticed. The choice was then left to her husband to accept or resist these changes. If he accepted the changes, he would treat her the way he wanted to be treated, and they would again be a couple. If he resisted change and refused to alter his behavior, the relationship would deteriorate and they would go their separate ways.

Rhonda had already accepted the changes in her life. She had done all the things that she could to make the relationship better. She had to let her husband decide if he wanted to catch up with her. Rhonda realized that to be happy as a couple, both parties need to be happy—she needed to make sure that she was happy first. Then she could focus on trying to do things that would make her husband happy while maintaining her own happiness. She accepted the fact that if her husband did not match her vibration, their relationship could fail. She understood this, but decided that the reason for being in a relationship was to be happy. Fortunately, Rhonda's husband eventually chooses to embrace "the new Rhonda" and they were able to rekindle their love. Many people in this situation would have tried to save the marriage by appeasing the other person even when that meant that they would be unhappy. Rhonda fortunately didn't make that mistake.

The next time you are confronted with unexpected change, remember that it doesn't matter what change happens to you, what matters is how you happen to change.

# Chapter 8: Health

Most people feel that life happens to them. The truth is that we create our own reality. We often feel that sickness is something that is outside of our control. The reality is that we have the power to manifest sickness or wellness, depending on how we think, feel, and treat ourselves. For the most part, our health is an emotional issue that is within our control.

We are vibrational beings and when our vibrational frequency is misaligned or out-of-balance, it causes physical manifestations in our bodies that take the form of disease. The word "dis-ease" says it all. We get diseases when our bodies are not "at ease" or when we are out-of- balance in one way or another. A disease is usually the law of attraction at work. The thoughts and feelings we have felt are evident in our current health. If we are sick, it is often because we have attracted negative energy to ourselves through our thoughts, words, and actions.

A disease is a physical manifestation, an indicator of the vibrational frequency the person is emitting. A disease is the body's warning that we are out of balance in one way or another. When our bodies are exposed to abusive lifestyle choices such as drugs, stress, worry, smoking, anger, unhealthy foods or chemicals, or negative emotions for long periods of time, the result is usually the eventual manifestation of some form of a disease or ailment in the body.

> One of the basic principles of holistic health is that we cannot separate our physical health from our emotional, mental, and spiritual states of being. All levels are interconnected and a state of "dis-ease" in the body is often a reflection of conflict, tension, anxiety, or disharmony on

other levels of being as well. So when we have a physical disorder, it is inevitably a message for us to look deeply into our emotional and intuitive feeling, our thoughts and attitudes, to see what we can do to restore natural harmony and balance to our beings.[99]

Louise Hay, bestselling author and founder of Hay House, Inc., a self-help publishing company, said, "I believe we create every so-called illness in our body. The body, like everything else in life, is a mirror of our inner thoughts and beliefs. The body is always talking to us, if we will only take the time to listen. Every cell within your body responds to every single thought you think and every word you speak."[100] In *You Can Heal Your Life*, she claims that she was able to cure herself from cervical cancer through the use of holistic treatments and by releasing long-held negative emotions.[101]

Most diseases come from subconscious thoughts that we have programmed into our minds. In *The Miracle of Mind Dynamics*, Dr. Murphy lists the following examples of the mind's power to influence the body:

The subconscious mind controls all the functions of your body and is active twenty-four hours a day. It never rests; it governs all the vital functions of the body; the thoughts, feelings, and beliefs buried in the subconscious represent "subconscious thinking" or "thinking in the heart."[102]

The minute you give power to germs, external causes, or think that cancer has an intelligence and power of its own to destroy you, your affirmations of Divine perfection, wholeness, and vitality will prove fruitless.[103]

It is no use to say, "God is healing me now," if you believe deep down that cancer can kill you. You must cast out fear of all manifested states, ulcers, cancer, arthritis, etc., are externalized, manifested states, and the result of conscious or unconscious thinking. These diseases have no intelligence or power to hurt or destroy you. They are merely products of destructive thinking. To reason in this way, you can cast out your fear, and confidence and faith in your healing power of God will follow. As you change your mind, you change your body, because the body is the mind condensed.[104]

The image he held in his mind sank down into his subconscious mind, and whatever is impressed on the latter is expressed.[105]

Your surgeon may remove the block, such as the ulcer, the abnormal growth which was caused by negative thinking, but unless you change your thinking, there will be no permanent healing.[106]

Your body will follow your mental vision or image. You go where your vision is.[107]

Dr. Murphy then tells one of many stories of miraculous healings.

## The Secret of Getting Well

During a visit to San Francisco some months ago, I visited a friend in the hospital. He had a kidney infection and also a damaged heart. He said to me, "I won't be here long. I am constantly picturing myself back at my desk at my office, and also in my home with my loved ones. I am doing all the things in my mind which I would do were I whole and perfect. It is my divine right to be healthy, and my vision is always on being well."

This man was in the hospital only ten days, even though he was told he would have to be there about six weeks. His medical doctor pronounced him perfect, saying to him, "You had an intense desire to get well, and Nature responded." You must want to be well with all your heart and soul, then you will be made well and stay well, also.[108]

*The Miracle of Mind Dynamics* is one of many books that show the power of the mind to influence the body. Much of society is awakening to the reality that our minds are much more powerful than was previously considered.

Eastern medicine has long taught that sicknesses are caused by some type of imbalance within the person. It has been my experience that Eastern medicine treats the whole person, rather than just the symptoms of the illness, while Western medicine in the United States often treats only the symptoms. In my opinion, Western medicine is good at treating trauma and sickness that need immediate attention, while Eastern medicine is good at healing chronic diseases. Both of these types of medicine have their pros and cons, and both are necessary in today's world. I hope that the medicine of the future will be a marriage of these two types to ensure that the short-term and long-term needs of the patient are met.

Not all the causes of diseases can be explained, but I believe all diseases have the potential to be cured. If you want to prevent a disease, you can simply monitor your lifestyle and environment, as well as your thoughts, words, emotions, and actions. If you live a balanced life, the chances are good that you will live a healthy life.

If you are already sick, you must regain balance by removing the stressors that caused you to become sick. Once these stressors are removed, your body will rebalance itself and your immune system will be able to heal you. Your body's immune system is the best doctor you will ever find. It knows what to do to heal you.

Use the law of attraction to attract wellness into your life. Focus your mind to remove all negative thoughts about illness, and replace those thoughts with positive thoughts of perfect health. See and feel your perfect health as already in your life. Envision how wonderful you feel and how much energy you have. See all the great things you are enjoying with your perfect health. Believe that it is only a matter of time before this reality begins to manifest. Make a list of positive affirmations and say them to yourself often. This will help to reprogram your subconscious mind as well as your conscious mind. Analyze your life and attempt to remove the causing stressors. This will be helpful in allowing the healing to begin. It is often necessary for us to use action that complements our desires in order for them to manifest in our lives. In healing yourself, this action may be researching the illness you are facing and learning all of the different ways that it can be healed. Another way to use action is to agree to mentally commit yourself to doing everything in your power to get better. That can be eating right, being diligent about taking your medicine each day, exercising, or thinking positive thoughts all the time.

On the other hand, if you are currently healthy but are experiencing constant stress, worry, angry, or unhappiness, you should see that as a warning sign, and do what you can to change how you feel right now. Don't wait for the physical symptoms of a disease to show up before you change how you think and feel.

Once a disease has physically manifested, it becomes more difficult to will it away through the law of attraction. Once the disease is in your life, its unpleasant symptoms begin to dominate your attention and your focus. This leads to negative emotions and thoughts, such as worry and fear. These emotions make matters worse by attracting more of this negative energy through the law of attraction. This is a vicious negative circle that continues to feed itself until you do something to change it. In order to cure yourself, you have to choose to ignore the unpleasant symptoms of your current reality—and focus on the good feeling of the future of good health you wish to create. This is very difficult and takes a strong will, but it can be done. Once you are at that point where the disease is apparent, what other choice do you have other than focusing to save yourself through positive thought? If you continue to focus on the negativity you are experiencing, you will only make things worse by attracting more negative energy.

## From Cancer to Champion

One of my favorite examples of positive manifestation is Lance Armstrong. In *It's Not About the Bike: My Journey Back to Life,* Lance Armstrong talks about how he battled cancer.[109] In 1996, before he became the cycling legend he is today, Lance Armstrong was diagnosed with cancer. His prognosis wasn't good. The cancer had spread to his brain. What did Lance do? Instead of feeling sorry for himself, he decided to fight for his life with his willpower.

Lance stated, "I began to talk to it, engaging in an inner conversation with the cancer. I tried to be firm in my discussions." "You picked the wrong guy," I told it. "When you looked around for a body to live in, you made a big mistake when you chose mine." When talking about chemotherapy with his doctor, Lance said, "You can't kill me. Hit me with everything you've got, just dump it all on me. Whatever you give to other people, give me double. I want to make sure we get it all. Let's kill this thing."

The doctor informed Lance that too much chemotherapy could kill him and destroy his system. Nevertheless, that statement by Lance showed his determination to fight the disease with everything he had. Lance later talked about coping with chemotherapy.

> To cope with it, I imagined I was coughing out the burned-up tumors. I envisioned the chemo working on them, singeing them, and expelling them from my system. When I went to the bathroom, I endured the acid sting in my groin by telling myself that I was peeing out dead cancer cells. I suppose that's how you do it. They've got to go somewhere, don't they? I was coughing up cancer, pissing it out, getting rid of it every way I knew how.

These statements show his willingness to be an active participant in his recovery, and how he used his mind to influence the outcome. He chose to mentally fight the disease.

Amazingly, Lance's determination and willpower to live was so strong that he beat the odds and made a full recovery. Once he recovered, Lance took his willpower and applied it to his career as professional cyclist. He went on to win seven straight Tour De France championships from 1999 to 2005. He also started the Lance Armstrong Foundation to help others struggling with cancer.[110]

I love this success story. Did Lance know about the law of attraction, or did he just listen to his intuition on how to heal himself? Did his mental willpower have something to do with his recovery? I believe it did. I also believe that he intuitively understood how to use the law of attraction, and his battle with cancer taught him how to strengthen his will so that he could also use it in his cycling career.

Lance's story of using his willpower to manifest his good health certainly is inspiring and definitely worked for him, but there appears to be an even better way to use the law of attraction to heal from a disease. That way is to accept your current reality and open your heart to the reality you desire. When you remove resistance to anything, you remove the focus that keeps you attracted to that reality. This creates space within you to create something new.

The ego uses willpower to push a reality into manifesting. The heart uses the power of allowing by making a request of the universe and then allowing it to come to you in the way that is best for you. So the ego pushes things into reality; the heart allows things to be pulled to you.

## Adjusting to living from the heart

Creating from the heart is more powerful and requires less effort than creating from the ego. You do not have to bother about the details; you just need to be open to all there is, both inside and outside.

From this openness, you may now and then sense a certain pull. You may feel drawn toward certain things. This pull is actually the quiet whisper of your heart; it is your intuition. When you act from intuition, you are being pulled instead of pushing. You do not act until you sense on the inner level that it is appropriate to act.

Since you are very much used to pushing, i.e. using your will to create things, the energetic shift from ego to heart is quite challenging for you. The shift requires a tremendous "slow down." To really get in touch with the flow of your intuition, you consciously have to make an effort to "not do," to let everything be. This runs counterintuitive to much that you are taught and are used to. You are very much in the habit of basing your actions upon thought and willpower. You let your thinking determine your goals and you use your will to realize them. This is quite opposite to heart-centered creating.

When you live from the heart, you listen to your heart and then act accordingly. You do not think, you listen with an alert and open awareness to what your heart is telling you. The heart speaks through your feelings, not through your mind. The voice of the heart can best be heard when you feel quiet, relaxed and grounded.

The heart shows you the way to the most loving and joyful reality for you right now. Its whispers and suggestions are not based on rational thinking. You can recognize the voice of your heart by its lightness and the note of joy in it. The lightness is there because the heart does not impose; there are no strings attached to its suggestions. Your "heart-self" is not attached to your decisions and it loves you whatever you do.

Living from the heart does not mean you become passive or lethargic. Letting things be without labeling them right or wrong, without pushing them in one way rather than another, requires a lot of strength. It is the strength to be totally present, to face everything there is and just look at it. You may feel empty, or depressed, or nervous, but you do not try to drive these things away. All you do is surround them with your consciousness.

You do not understand the true power of your consciousness. Your consciousness is made of Light. When you hold something in your consciousness, it changes because of that. Your consciousness is a healing force, if you do not bind it by your thinking and your addiction to "doing."[111]

By using the heart to heal, rather than the ego, you can accept the disease. You can see the disease as a friend that has come to get your attention to change your destructive behavior before it is too late. Again, when you accept the disease, you have removed resistance to it. When you remove resistance to the disease, you are no longer attracting it because your focus is no longer on disease. You have noted it and are choosing to focus on creating a healthier future.

When you use your will to create, you are only giving the universe one way—your way—to manifest your desire. When you simply desire a new outcome and leave it open to how it can manifest, you allow your desire to come to you in the way that is best for you. Again, your focus is everything. What you focus on, you attract. If you focus on what it feels like to be sick, you are attracting more sickness. If you focus on what it feels like to be well, you are attracting wellness. It is important to note that Lance Armstrong did resist his disease, but his focus was on getting better and not on the negative symptoms. I believe this is why he experienced such miraculous healing.

The will and the heart work to manifest your desires, but the heart allows the way that is best for you to arise. Remember to focus on the feeling of what you want rather than the fearful feeling of what you don't want. When you focus on your perfect health, you are able to align yourself as a vibrational match to the perfect health you desire. That is what will allow your perfect health to manifest.

Here is a breakdown of what you can do to maintain health—or to be cured from disease. Note that these suggestions are to be used in conjunction with your regular doctor and are by no means meant to be a replacement. Health is a personal thing. If you are sick, consider doing research online to learn how to become well again. Then work with your doctors to find a treatment that works best for you. Listen to your intuition when making decisions. Above all, make sure to be an active participant in your recovery. As long as your focus is on getting better, you can use your *will* to fight like Lance Armstrong did, or you can use your *heart* to simply allow your good health to return to you. Using the heart to heal is arguably the better method, but both ways can work.

## Commanding Your Body into Action

A good friend, Nikki Moses of Moses Nutrition, gave me some great advice on how to use the law of attraction with health issues.[112] She said to use your mind as if you are a military general and the cells of your body are troops under your command. It is the idea that being healthy is a foregone conclusion. A general goes into battle expecting nothing less than to win and leads his troops with that certainty, which gives them certainty to their job. The troops (your cells) look to you for direction. When you show confidence in them, it gives them confidence in themselves, and gives them direction and purpose to complete the job you have given them. It's telling the troops to do their jobs and that everything is going to be okay. You are their leader—command them to get working on healing yourself. See them in your mind, like little soldiers in your body working in the parts of your body that need healing. This form of mental healing appears to be very similar to what Lance Armstrong used to heal himself.

## The Placebo Effect

The placebo effect is when a patient is healed after taking medication they were told would heal them, but in reality the medication was a fake. Since the treatment was not real, it appears the mind's *belief* in the treatment was responsible for the healing.

The placebo effect appears to support the theory that the mind actually has the ability to heal. The patient's beliefs often seem to affect the outcome of their health. If the patient believes he or she will be sick, then they will stay sick. If he or she believes they will be healed, then they often are. Doesn't this sound like a little trick to use the law of attraction?

## How to Prevent Sickness

You can prevent sickness by learning to focus on how you feel at all times. This goes for both physical feeling and emotional feelings. When you feel good, you are heading toward being healthy, but when you feel bad, you are heading toward ill health. Remember that sickness is usually caused by being out of balance in one way or another. As directed in "Thoughts are Things," use your feelings as a guide to find the direction you are headed with your life and make the appropriate changes to restore balance. I have successfully used this method many times to prevent a cold or sickness when I felt the beginning symptoms. Tell yourself that you feel fine and will be 100 percent healthy soon. Then address how you physically feel. If you are tired all the time, then you might be working too much or not getting enough rest. You may be able to remedy this by changing jobs, or by choosing to go to bed a little earlier to ensure you are getting enough rest. If you are smoker, you can begin to restore balance by stopping smoking. I know this sounds like common sense, but that is all it takes sometimes to restore balance in our lives. Find the imbalance in your life and then take measures to restore the balance.

If you are beginning to feel the effects of illness, depending on the severity of your symptoms, you can usually mentally will yourself to be well. The next time you feel yourself coming down with a cold or the flu, immediately start sending yourself positive healing thoughts. Tell yourself that you will be well and that the sick feeling you are feeling will pass. When you think this way, you are commanding the cells of your body to work toward healing you. Most times you will recover immediately—and if you do get sick, it won't be as severe as if you gave into the reality and started telling yourself that you are sick because you are feeling ill. Your cells are always listening to your thoughts and will obey whatever thoughts you give them. When you tell yourself that you are sick, you are giving your body permission to feel sick. You are attracting that energy. It's better to focus on what you want: perfect health. Add action that is complementary to your desire, which could be getting some rest, eating healthy, and avoiding all self-abusing activities like smoking and drinking alcohol.

# Alternative Healing Methods

Alternative healing is any healing method that is not usually offered at the hospital or doctor's office. Most of these methods involve using energy to rebalance the body. Here are a few alternative healing choices:

- Qigong/Tai Chi
- Acupuncture
- Reiki
- EFT (Emotional Freedom Technique)
- Chiropractic care
- Crystal Healing
- Nutritional Balancing
- Rife Machine
- Self-Controlled Energo Neuro Adaptive Regulation
- Hypnosis
- Counseling
- Natural Spring Water with Customized Labels
- Diet
- Exercise
- Thinking Thoughts of Wellness

Qigong and Tai Chi involve using Qi to balance the body's energy systems. Qigong means "energy work." Tai Chi is similar to Qigong. Both of these methods are used for achieving and maintaining energy balance within the body to promote good health. I am a certified Qigong instructor, and can attest that this energy is real.

Acupuncture is the art of using needles to stimulate invisible energy points called meridians that run along the body. The purpose of acupuncture is to remove energy blockages in the body to heal the patient by restoring the flow of energy throughout the body. This often restores wellness in the patient. This treatment works under the premise that when energy is blocked, diseases form—and when energy flows freely, health is restored.

Reiki is another form of energy healing where a healer works with a patient using unseen energy from their hands.

EMF is a psychological acupressure technique that involves using simple affirmations and tapping routine on specific acupressure points along the body to remove emotional blocks that are creating physical problems.[113]

Chiropractic care is often important in energy balancing because energy runs along your spine. If your spine is out of alignment, it can affect the flow of energy throughout your body.

Crystal healing is the practice of using crystals to rebalance the body's energy. The practitioner places crystals on different parts of the body, often corresponding to the chakras, or places crystals around the body in an attempt to construct an energy grid, which is believed to surround the client with healing energy. The healing is supposed to remove blockages in the aura or the body's electromagnetic field.

Nutritional Balancing using hair mineral analysis is a healing method that tests various mineral and toxic metal levels in a sample of hair in order to identify nutritional and mineral imbalances that cause overall illness. This health program often consists of mineral and vitamin supplements, diet recommendations, near-infrared saunas, and coffee enemas to be used in conjunction with each other. Mineral and vitamin supplements are used to rebalance the body chemistry over a period of time to improve or restore health.[114]

The Rife Machine claims to use the principle of vibratory resonance to destroy bacteria, viruses, and diseases such as cancer within the patient's body.

Self-Controlled Energo Neuro Adaptive Regulation was developed for the Russian space program to overcome the unique problems of space travel. SCENAR uses biofeedback by stimulating the nervous system. It is able to teach the body to heal itself. Tests conducted in Russia have shown SCENAR proves to be effective in 80 percent of cases.[115]

Hypnosis may be helpful if your subconscious mind is creating havoc in your life. Hypnosis involves being put into a relaxed state, much like meditation, where suggestions to the subconscious are easily made.

Counseling can also be very helpful if you have emotional issues that are affecting your life. Much like a journal, a counselor is there to help you to express and make sense of your emotional challenges. Counseling is important because stored negative emotions are the cause of many illnesses. If those negative emotions are removed, good health usually returns.

Water is one of the simplest treatments you can use. Your body is made mostly of water and this water is very receptive to the thoughts, words and actions you feed it. It's best to drink three quarts a day of natural spring water. Take this a step further by getting some masking tape and writing loving and healing words on your water container and everything else around you. Write words like love, appreciation, wellness, perfect health, energy, success, happiness, or whatever else you want to experience in your life.

Diet is a no-brainer. What you eat is used to build the cells of your body. If you eat poor quality building materials, your body will eventually breakdown. If you are serious about your health, you need to feed your body healthy foods so that you give it good energy to make new healthy cells. Eat balanced meals in moderate proportions.

Moderate exercise and weight training helps to keep your entire body active, healthy, and strong. If you have any health issues that need to be addressed, make sure to get the approval of your doctor before starting a new exercise program.

Thinking thoughts of wellness is very important to your health. You are what you think. If you are not well, start thinking and feeling thoughts of wellness. In time, if you believe in yourself, your good health should return.

## Rife Machine: Treatment of the Future from the Past?

Many alternative treatments involved techniques or instruments that rebalance the body's energy field.

In the 1920s and 1930s, Dr. Royal R. Rife discovered that every living thing was associated with a specific energy level that he termed its mortal oscillatory rate, or MOR. He then created an instrument called the Rife beam ray (Rife Machine), which could deliver a matching electromagnetic frequency. By using the principle of vibratory resonance, Rife could tune the ray to the precise MOR and destroy the bacteria within the patient's body. He also found it could destroy cancerous tissue.[116] Unfortunately mainstream medicine refused to accept Rife's findings and his work was never accepted by mainstream medicine.[117] Even though he never achieved commercial success, Rife Machines are still available and are used by some alternative doctors and healers.

I feel this technique fits in especially well with the energy premise of this book and deserves further investigation to see if its claims are valid. Since we are vibrational beings, it seems reasonable that devices that use vibrational frequency realignment would be part of the evolution of medicine for mankind.

During the writing of this book, our dog Carlos developed an open malignant tumor on his nose the size of a golf ball. We decided to try to the Rife Machine on him in an attempt to heal him. We were told it was alright to use on animals and that it could take up to three months to see a remission of the cancer. The first month we saw no positive change in the size of the tumor. After about 5 weeks, amazingly the tumor reduced in size about 50% and went from being ball shaped to being concaved! Then for the next few weeks the cancer did not change in size. A week later the cancer came back with a vengeance and almost immediately grew to be as big as it was when we started using the Rife Machine. When I inquired, the vendor, who sold me the machine, told me that one of the side effects of the Rife Machine is that it often shrinks tumors so rapidly that the dead cancer cells can overload the lymph nodes, liver, and immune system of the body allowing the cancer to return. Since Carlos' lymph nodes were swollen to the size of quarters, I am inclined to believe this is what happened to him. We were instructed that we could try reprogramming the Rife Machine with another cancer frequency to start the treatment again from another angle, but at this time, Carlos, who was thirteen years old, was beginning to show signs of suffering from the cancer. So after considering our options, we decided to forgo any additional attempts to cure him with the Rife Machine and humanely chose to put him down.

Carlos was a dear family member and a best friend. The law of oneness says that everything is energy and that this energy cannot be created or destroyed but it can change form. So when someone dies they just change their form. Even though Carlos is no longer in his physical form, we believe he is still in our presence watching over us.

I suspect that if we had more time, and if Carlos was younger, we could have made minor adjustments to his treatments—using different frequencies, and adjusting the time spent on the machine—to find a solution that cured the cancer. Of course, that is just my opinion. If it were me on the machine, I would have tried using coffee enemas and near infrared saunas in a effort to help detoxify my liver and immune system from the waste products caused by the Rife Machine killing the disease.

With regards to the Rife Machine, our experience with Carlos' illness was inconclusive because the cancer was disappearing for a while, but ultimately the cancer came back to win this battle. The Rife Machine we bought cost about $400 and was ordered online through an Internet search for Rife Machines. So if you or so someone you know is looking for an alternative method to heal from a disease, the Rife Machine might warrant your investigation.

As you can see there are many alternative medicine treatments that work with energy to rebalance and heal the body. It is up to you to look into them to see if they have any value to you.

## Disclaimer:

*Please note that the information listed in this chapter is only meant to help you in your search for knowledge. It is not a recommendation to start or stop any current or future medical programs. I am not a doctor, and my opinions are solely based on what I have experienced with my own research and challenges.*

# How to Heal from Sickness

Do you want to know how to heal from an illness? Use the law of attraction. The easiest way is to use the Focus, Feel, and Expect Process of focusing on your desire and then feeling how it feels to have it in your life now. For those who desire a detailed checklist, here is an example of how to use the Nine A's to Acing the Law of Attraction Checklist for obtaining good health.

1. **Accept your current health situation.** You are where you are and there's nothing you can do about that, but you can start working on your future health by accepting your current health situation. Also stop worrying and focusing about what is happening to you or why it is happening to you. You are probably not feeling well and you are probably scared. This is understandable, but you must realize that worrying only brings more negative energy. You must become strong enough to make the mental link that your thoughts are powerful and they can help you if you can focus on positive feelings of feeling better. Next, stop talking about your sickness. This just keeps the sickness vibration activated within you. Tell others not to talk to you about your sickness.

2. **Ask for what you want.** If you want perfect health, visualize your perfect wellness. Say your desire aloud and write it down. You might write something like, "I am perfectly healthy and strong. Every day, I am getting better and better."

3. **Align with your desires**. Think, feel, say, and do things that support your goal of perfect health. This is necessary to reprogram your subconscious mind to communicate to your superconscious mind the things you desire. Say your affirmations aloud or to yourself multiple times each day. Set your alarm to go off when you get up, at lunch, at three o'clock, and before you go to bed to remind you to consciously think of and feel your wellness. Post pictures of yourself when you were healthy, or put up pictures of someone you want to look like when you do become healthy. Tell yourself out loud that you are well and that you feel well regardless of how much pain you are in. If it is too much of a mental jump for you to go from feelings of fear and being worried to feeling of wellness and happiness, use the law of polarity to ease into it. When I was in a situation where it was too big of a mental jump to feel good, I told myself, "I accept that I am suffering right now, but I have felt better before, and I believe that I can and will feel better again soon. I know if I keep thinking thoughts of wellness and good feelings of what it is going to feel like when I am well again, my body will eventually heal itself. I have faith in myself and the law of attraction. I can do this. I will be patient knowing it will come." I would say this to myself over and over again until I felt better emotionally. This helped me ease from fear to hope and faith. Once I started feeling better, I was able to focus on appreciating the real feeling of good health because my thoughts had brought me to a better feeling place vibrationally. This helped to build momentum and continue my healing. Also use your mind, like Lance did, to command your body to heal itself.

4. **Avoid negative thoughts and feelings**. Even though you might be suffering, it is important not to focus on the negative reality that you are experiencing. Fear, anger, and worry are a few of the negative emotions that are common when we are not feeling well, or have an illness. It is important to remember that we attract what we focus on—it is important to ignore the negativity in our present reality and instead

focus on the reality we wish to create. Use the law of polarity to traverse from negative emotions to more positive ones.

5. **Acknowledge what you are willing to give.** The law of action says that when you work toward your desires, you give the law of attraction something to manifest through. What do you plan to give to make your desire of good health come true? Here is an example of what I might give. I desire perfect health. In return for my good health, I am willing to constantly focus on my good health—regardless of how I feel. I vow to do my best to ignore my current unpleasant reality and focus on the reality I choose to create in the near future. I will wait for my good health to manifest in my life. I will commit myself mentally and physically in every way that supports my goal of getting better. I will eat the proper foods and be diligent about following my daily healing regiment so that I will give myself every opportunity to heal. I will get plenty of rest, and I will distance myself from any and all thoughts and actions that do not support my goal of perfect health. These are the things that I vow to give to allow my desires to manifest.

6. **Allow yourself to be open-minded.** Become open to any way that you can feel better. Your good health may come to you in the form of a miracle cure, it might be a new medicine, it might be a holistic cure, a spiritual cure, or you mind may heal your body. Be open to getting better in any positive way that is presented to you. When you are open-minded, you give the law of attraction more ways to manifest in your life.

7. **Agree to be patient and persistent.** Being patient is very difficult because most people want results right away. It is important to stay focused and determined on your goal of getting better—no matter how long it takes for your health to return. Your single-minded and constant positive focus is needed for you to get better. If you are constantly moving between positive thoughts and fearful thoughts, it is unlikely that your desire of good health will manifest because you cannot stay focused on your desire for good health long enough for it to manifest in your life.

8. **Act when opportunity arises.** It is up to you to act when opportunities arise. You can be an active participant in your recovery by being aware of your illness by learning about it and all the possible cures. The Internet is an amazing tool that allows you to learn just about anything. Go to a search engine and type in whatever subject you have an interest in learning about. It will give you a wealth of information. Just be sure that when you learn about the illness you continue to focus on your good health and not the fact that you have an illness. Sometimes learning about a disease can be frightening and that can lead to fearful thinking. Decide that you have the ability to control your fearful thoughts long enough to empower yourself to take positive action that can positively affect your healing. You can also do other actions that help you reach your goal of becoming healthy. You might choose to eat right, drink pure water, watch funny movies, go for daily walks, or think positive thoughts. Just make sure your actions and thoughts always match your goal of perfect health.

9. **Appreciate when your desires manifest.** Appreciating your manifested good health will help attract more healing energy and allow your good health to thrive.

Use this process to create your future reality. In the spaces below or in your journal, fill in each step of the process.

Step 1. **Accept your current situation.**

_____

_____

_____

Step 2. **Ask for what you want.**

_____

_____

_____

Step 3. **Align with positivity.**

_____

_____

_____

Step 4. **Avoid negative thoughts and feelings.**

_____

_____

_____

Step 5. **Acknowledge what you are willing to give.**

_____

_____

_____

Step 6. **Allow yourself to be open-minded.**

_____

_____

_____

Step 7. **Agree to be patient and persistent.**

_____

_____

_____

Step 8. **Act when opportunities arise.**

_____

_____

_____

Step 9.  **Appreciate when your desire manifests.**

_____

_____

_____

# Chapter 9: Money

*If you want to be wealthy, you've got to think wealthy.*

Do you desire money? Do you desire to be rich? Most people do. We either need money for survival or comfort in our daily lives, or we desire money for the feelings of fulfillment and success.

The reason why most people never become rich is because they don't think about money the right way. They often are overloaded with bills and have a lot of debt. This debt makes them think that they do not have enough money. This leads to fear and worry because their focus is on the lack of money rather than the abundance of money.

Money can be earned through hard work alone, but a crystal clear focus of desire is usually needed to acquire wealth. Remember that we are vibrational beings. Our thoughts attract similar thoughts. If we want money, we must think of it in a positive way. We must see money as a welcomed friend and attract it with our positive thoughts. We must choose to accept and ignore our current reality of not having enough—and dream, envision, and feel what it feels like to have all the money we desire right now. Going from being worried to being hopeful is not easy. It takes constant monitoring of your feelings to make sure you are thinking positively about money.

Dusty Baker, the professional baseball player and manager, said, "Like my old coach, Luke Appling, said here, he told me if you're going to be lucky, you've got to think lucky."[118] The same principle applies to money. If you want to be wealthy, you have to think wealthy. As we have discussed throughout this book, your thoughts have the power to attract the type of energy to make this desire a reality. If you can think about money in a positive way that feels good, you will attract it. The law of attraction will bring it to you. I know this because I have used it myself.

## Who Wants to Be a Millionaire?

When I got out of college in 1990, I was in my early twenties. I didn't know what I was going to do for a living, but I knew I wanted to make money. I told everyone that would listen that I was going to make $100,000 a year, and that I would someday be a millionaire. Secretly, I set my goal of becoming a millionaire by the time I was thirty-five. During the early 1990s, earning $100,000 was an admirable accomplishment. I kept this vision in my head twenty-four hours a day, seven days a week. I had not yet learned about the law of attraction, but I was unconsciously using it.

I initially took a salaried sales job, but I soon realized that if I was to achieve my goals, I was going to need more freedom with my earning potential. This led me to find a new job as a mortgage broker. The job was 100 percent commission. I didn't get a regular paycheck—I was paid a percentage of each home loan I closed. This pay structure, if I was successful, would allow me an opportunity to earn more than if I was on salary. The down side to commissioned income is that if I didn't bring in any business, I wouldn't get paid at all. I was determined to be successful so I took the gamble. The feeling of knowing that my success was up to me excited me. I enjoyed being in control of my own destiny.

My mind constantly envisioned what it would feel like to have the money I desired. I knew I was going to be successful, but I didn't know how long it would take. Each day as I went to work, I reviewed my clear vision of success. Becoming successful was all I ever thought about. Whenever I experienced setbacks or crises at work, I saw them as obstacles to my goal that I merely had to move around rather than seeing them as dead-end roadblocks to my success. I never allowed these obstacles to move my focus off my goal.

Unknowingly, I also applied the law of action to my desires by doing everything I could to complement my goal of being successful. Each day, I would go by all the local Realtor offices to see if there were any new prospective homebuyers who needed mortgage financing. My consistent work ethic and positive attitude allowed me to create momentum to build my business over time. I was focused and patient. I knew the money would come if I stayed persistent and dedicated.

I had set a goal to make $100,000 by my fourth year in the business. My plan was to make $25,000 the first year, $50,000 the second year, $75,000 the third year, and $100,000 my fourth year.

Reality turned out to be a little different. The first year, I only made a few thousand dollars. Most of that was my fault because I made a lot of costly mistakes by mispricing deals where there wasn't enough profit left for me. Luckily, I had enough money saved to get through that first year. The second year, I made $45,000, which was almost the amount of my goal of making $50,000. The third year, I made $65,000, which was just short of the $75,000 I planned to make. During the fourth year, I was looking forward to achieving my $100,000 income goal, but the housing market slumped due to higher interest rates. Being on commission, I was vulnerable to the ups and downs of the market. Due to this slump, I was only able to make $25,000 that year. The slump continued into my fifth year, but I was able to double my efforts to allow myself to make $55,000. During my sixth year, the market recovered and helped me achieve my goal of earning $100,000. It felt wonderful to realize my goal. I had initially given myself four years to reach my goal, but I was okay with it taking six years.

I never lost sight of my income goal. I saw bad years as nothing more than a time delay in reaching my goal. Never did I believe that I wouldn't succeed. Once I broke the $100,000 barrier, my job seemed to get easier and I was able to make more each year. My career had taken off and I had gained momentum. Success had bred more success. During the good times, I tried to save and invest as much money as I could so that I could achieve my second goal of becoming a millionaire by the age of thirty-five.

My first goal of making $100,000 was complete, but as my thirty-fifth birthday came and went, I was still not a millionaire. You would think this would discourage me, but it only made me want it more. I redoubled my focus and efforts at work.

Two years later at the age of thirty-seven, my goal of becoming a millionaire became a reality. The feeling of success and accomplishment was amazing. I remember thinking that dreams really do come true!

Since I was very humble and private about the value of my assets, most people never knew of my accomplishment—but I knew about it, and that was all that mattered. It had taken me fourteen years to accomplish my goal. My patience, persistence, and action had allowed me to use the law of attraction to manifest this desire into a reality.

**Figure 18: During the mid 1990s as a mortgage broker,
I may have been losing my hair, but I was gaining
momentum toward achieving my goals.**

Skeptics may say that I achieved my goal by simply working hard rather than using the law of attraction. My rebuttal is that I desired to become a millionaire; I applied the law of attraction and the law of action; and my desire eventually became a reality. That is proof enough for me. Once my desire manifests, what does it matter how it manifested? Why would I question how it came to me? Why mess with a formula that works?

Looking back, I see that I made a mistake. Instead of focusing on financial abundance that would support me for the rest of my life, I simply desired to have a net worth of one million dollars. It never dawned on me to be more specific about what I wanted. The law of attraction brought me exactly what I desired and nothing more. I was soon to discover what that meant.

Ironically, almost as soon as I reached the million dollar mark, the real estate bubble collapsed, followed by the credit crisis, and then the stock market collapse. Like many other people, much of my assets were tied up in real estate and the stock market; my net worth plummeted.

It would have been easy to be discouraged by the loss of something that I had worked so hard to achieve, but I chose to see this adjustment as a temporary setback and an opportunity to set even better goals. Knowing that I had already been a millionaire once gave me confidence that I could do it again. Anyone can do this. All we need to do is use the law of attraction with the right frame of mind and be willing to act when necessary.

I developed a new desire that included a vision of financial independence that allowed me to have sufficient assets to enjoy all that life has to offer. This financial abundance would also allow me to have the resources to help others. Not only do I enjoy helping others—I also understand that giving is part of receiving. The law of compensation says that you get back whatever you give out.

One of the ways I wanted to give back to society was by sharing the empowering information I had learned about the universal laws. I decided to set a goal of writing a book about these laws so that others could learn what I have learned and experience what I have experienced. You are reading that book now. I was able to use the law of attraction to manifest this desire into a reality. It wasn't always easy, but I stayed focused and persistent, and my desire to become a self-help author became a reality.

Hard work and patience are often required to create your dreams, but one characteristic is more important that the others. That characteristic is your focus. Focus on being abundant and you will attract opportunities that will allow you to become abundant. What do you want to create in your future?

Do you want to be rich? Use the law of attraction. The easiest way is to use the Focus, Feel, and Expect Process of focusing on your desire and then feeling how it feels to have it in your life now. For those who desire a detailed checklist, here is an example of how to use the Nine A's to Acing the Law of Attraction Checklist for obtaining wealth.

## How to Become Rich

Use the Nine A's to Acing the Law of Attraction Checklist. Here's an example of how I would use this process if I was struggling financially but wished to become rich.

1. **Accept your current situation.** Even though I currently have money troubles, I realize that this is a temporary situation. I believe that I can change my future by thinking positive thoughts and doing actions that complement my desires.
2. **Ask for what you want.** I desire to have a net worth of $10 million before I retire in twenty years.
3. **Align with positivity.** I think positive thoughts about money. I feel the joy and security that it brings me to have this

money in my life. I can do and have whatever I desire. It is a certainty in my mind that I will achieve my goal of becoming wealthy.

4. **Avoid negative thoughts and feelings.** I understand that negativity sends mixed messages to my subconscious mind. I will monitor my thoughts and feelings to make sure I am programming my subconscious mind with the necessary commands that allow my dreams to become a reality.

5. **Acknowledge what you are willing to give.** I am willing to work hard to make my desires a reality. I am also willing to save my money and invest it so that I can give the law of attraction more ways to manifest my desires.

6. **Allow yourself to be open-minded.** I agree to be open to different ways that this money can come to me. I will be thankful if I win the lottery, but I am also willing to do whatever it takes to be successful as long as it doesn't conflict with my integrity and ethics.

7. **Agree to be patient and persistent.** I agree to stay focused on my goals and to be patient for it to arrive. I promise to stay patient and persistent for as long as it takes for my desire to manifest in my life.

8. **Act when opportunities arise.** I vow to act when opportunities present themselves to me. I will be an opportunist!

9. **Appreciate when you desire manifests.** I will appreciate my desire coming to me by giving thanks and sharing some of this money with less fortunate people through charities or acts of kindness. This is not only the kind thing to do, but it will also ensure that this wonderful energy will continue to be abundant in my life.

Use this process to create your future reality. In the spaces below or in your journal, fill in each step of the process.

Step 1. **Accept your current situation.**

_____

_____

_____

Step 2. **Ask for what you want.**

_____

_____

_____

Step 3. **Align with positivity.**

_____

_____

_____

Step 4. **Avoid negative thoughts and feelings.**

_____

_____

_____

Step 5. **Acknowledge what you are willing to give.**

_____

_____

_____

Step 6. **Allow yourself to be open-minded.**

_____

_____

_____

Step 7. **Agree to be patient and persistent.**

_____

_____

_____

Step 8. **Act when opportunities arise.**

_____

_____

_____

Step 9. **Appreciate when your desire manifests.**

_____

_____

_____

# Chapter 10: Conflict

Whenever there is a difference of opinion, you have an opportunity for a conflict. A conflict is when two or more people are in opposition to each other. Humanity has a long history of conflict. It often seems that we don't like it when others are different. Think of Jesus being crucified for preaching something that the governments at that time saw as different and threatening. Think about the Crusades and the Spanish Inquisition where the Church tried to force others through war and torture into believing the way it wanted them to believe. Think about the countless wars that have occurred since the beginning of time. The Middle East is a perfect example of a place that is ravaged by constant conflict. On a more personal level, think of the number of arguments that you had—or even a fistfight or two. It often seems like conflict is a part of who we are.

Some amount of conflict is inevitable during life. It is part of our life experience; however, the effect of conflict and how intense it gets is almost always up to us. The law of relativity states that everything in our life is relative to our point of view, and the law of perpetual transmutation of energy states that higher energies will consume and transmute lower energies, or the lower energies will have to flee. This means we have a choice in how we respond to any conflict. Our actions or reactions can cause or prevent a conflict. Since a conflict requires at least two parties, if we choose not to participate, there is no conflict for us. If we have a positive outlook, we are often able to ignore the negative actions of others and stay unaffected. On the other hand, if we have a negative outlook and get angry or upset at the negative actions of others, we are helping to escalate that conflict in our life. If we choose higher emotions like compassion, love, and understanding, we can transmute or deflect the negative energy of others.

It's always best to try to avoid conflict whenever possible—but sometimes that can be difficult.

# Three Choices to Change Any Negative Situation:
*Permanent positive change can't be forced—*
*it must come from within.*

When conflict happens, there are three choices. The first choice is to try to change the other party's behavior. This is always an uphill battle and is not recommended because you may be able to change the other party's behavior, but unless it is something they want to do themselves it will be short lived or they will eventually resent being made to change. It's best to accept people for how they are because they will never be content unless they are happy. If they are not acting in a way that is beneficial to you, you can try to make them aware that their behavior is not something that is helping your relationship. It is then up to them to decide if they want to change their behavior. Forcing them to behave the way you want them to behave only makes them more resistant. The wise decision is to do positive things for them to entice them to decide for themselves to change their negative behavior. Permanent positive change can't be forced—it must come as choice from within.

The second choice is to change yourself. You can do this by changing how you think and feel about whatever the other person is or is not doing. You can accept the behavior from this person and focus on their negative qualities or you can focus on their positive qualities. You can choose to change your own actions in an effort to change your response. You can try to ignore their actions or think of them in a way that is more positive.

The third choice is to leave the situation. If you have tried unsuccessfully to change the behavior of the other person or party and you have tried to change yourself, your last option is to distance yourself from the situation. This may not solve any issues, but it will allow you to get away from energy that is not positive for you.

## Three Choices to Change Any Negative Situation

1. Change the other person's behavior.
2. Change how you think and feel.
3. Leave the situation.

Remember that you are in charge of your own happiness. Focus on what you have the ability to control. You have the ability to control how you think and to choose your actions. You do not have the ability to think and choose for anyone else.

These principles apply whether the conflict is between two people or if it is between two countries.

## Conflict in War

I hope that humanity will begin to learn that our thoughts and actions really do create our reality. When that time comes, government can begin to think of the wellbeing of other governments as much as their own. Only then will war be avoided. Diplomacy and win-win situations should always be exhausted before resorting to force. In fact, force should only be used in self-defense. Governments should take a page out of martial art teachings and look to find ways to settle disputes without fighting. No one really ever wins when fighting is involved because—regardless of who wins—damages are inflicted, and often negative karmic energy is accrued. In *The Art of War,* Sun Tzu said, "There has never been a protracted war from which a country has benefited."[119]

For diplomacy to work, both sides must be willing to give and change their previous ways of thinking. Being open-minded is imperative for meaningful change to occur. Sometimes by sacrificing our ego, we can save our own life or save our country. By not letting an insult or challenge affect us, we are able to maintain control of a situation—and prevent a potential conflict from turning into a real one.

Remember that you are in charge of your own happiness—no one else is responsible for that. Do whatever it takes to find happiness. When you're happy, you will attract the type of people and things to you that you desire.

# Chapter 11: Happiness

*"Happiness is an attitude. We either make ourselves miserable,*
*or happy and strong. The amount of work is the same."*
—*Francesca Reigler*

I feel that the meaning of life is to experience many different things so that we can learn and grow from those experiences. The ups and down are necessary so that we can experience all of the emotions and experiences that life has to offer. In these life challenges, we find ways to grow by desiring to create better futures for ourselves. Our primary objective throughout life is to seek out happiness. Happiness is not a place. It is a state of mind. It's an attitude. It's a perception. The law of relativity says that everything is relative to our point of view or our outlook. Our happiness is no different. Our happiness is relative to how we think.

Why is it that some people can find happiness when they seem to have nothing, but others cannot seem to find happiness when they have everything? This is because happiness is a state of mind. Happiness is about focusing your mind on the good things in your life while ignoring the negative things. What you chose to focus on is always your choice. Your happiness is also your choice.[120] "The happiest people don't have the best of everything; they just make the best of what they have."[121] Every day, each of us experiences a variety of things that can range from joyful to upsetting. It is up to us to find the good in each situation.

## Happiness Exercise

The happiness exercise is simply looking for happiness in every part of life. Many of us ignore the beautiful trees or the blooming flowers as we rush to work. We don't enjoy the rewarding taste of a good cup of coffee while we talk to a customer at work, or we don't take the time to enjoy the smile on our child's face.

The happiness exercise is being centered, grounded, or aware enough of our surroundings to be able to appreciate whatever happiness is occurring in our lives.

---

### The Happiness Exercise

Step 1. Recognize your current reality.
Step 2. Find something positive about that reality.

---

It's that simple. I will start with an example.

Step 1.     I am currently typing this page of my book.

Step 2.     I enjoy this time that I have right now where I can do what I love to do, which is writing. I enjoy the creative thoughts that go through my head about the order of how to organize this book. I also enjoy the silence around me that allows me to be completely relaxed.

Write down what you are experiencing and what you find positive about it. It may sound silly to appreciate something simple, but start to program yourself to be positive all the time. Positivity is all around you all the time. You just have to look for it.

Step 1. Recognize your current reality.

_____

_____

_____

_____

Step 2. Find something positive about that reality.

_____

_____

_____

_____

# Chapter 12: Stress

We all experience stress. There is good stress, and there is bad stress. Good stress is the stress that inspires us to rise to action. This is the stress that you may get before an athletic event or a public speaking engagement. This is your body's natural fight or flight response that allows it to instantly perform at its peak potential for short periods of time.

Negative or chronic stress is physical or emotional stress that goes on for long periods of time, eventually causing damage to the body. Stress has been defined as a physical, chemical, or emotional factor that causes bodily or mental tension and may be a factor in disease causation.[122]

You can manage your stress levels by controlling how you react to events. If you get upset at negative things, you add stress to your life. However, if you choose not to get upset at negative events, you maintain control of your feelings and avoid adding stress to your life. Stress is almost always self-induced. Someone or something may be doing something to you, but you are the one who decides how to react and how the actions of others will affect you. Remember that energy is circular, and regardless of the actions of others, you ultimately decide what type of energy you attract to yourself through the thoughts, words, and actions you choose for yourself. If you are having a tough time dealing with stress, use the law of relativity and the law of polarity to change how you see and think about the issues that are causing you stress.

# Chapter 13: Revenge

*"You will not be punished for your anger;*
*you will be punished by your anger."*
*—Buddha*

Everyone has had encounters with someone who has done something wrong to them. It seems to be a natural human response to want to retaliate and do the same thing back to the person who has wronged us. We want the person who has hurt us to feel how it feels to have that deed done to them so that they will learn not to do it in the future. The problem with this type of thinking is that when we seek justice or retribution for the actions of others, we end up choosing for ourselves the same negative energy as the person who did the wrongful act.

When you seek revenge, you are choosing to align with the negativity of someone else's wrongful deed. Remember that your thoughts, words, and actions are alive and attractive. When you think of revenge or retribution, you make those qualities active within yourself, which then attracts more of that negative energy. Is that what you really want? You will be making the other person feel your wrath—and you might even have every reason to seek revenge—but when you seek revenge, you are not just hurting the other person. The revenge you seek is actually done to yourself.

When I was younger, whenever I was wronged by someone I often felt that I had to be the one to show that person that their actions were wrong and unacceptable. Luckily, I quickly learned that whenever I meddled in others people's business, I ended of being the focus of their negative energy—and then they wanted to engage in some type of conflict with me. This added a lot of needless drama in my life. I had aligned with their energy and made their problems mine.

Today I believe in the law of attraction and the law of cause and effect. These laws are connected and state that the energy we give out is the energy we receive. I realize that if someone is doing something to me that I consider wrong, I don't need to be the one to correct their behavior. I understand that their actions, good or bad, will be coming back to them and will eventually manifest in their life. We really do create our own lives. If we are smart, we will realize that we are creating our own troubles through the thoughts, words, and actions we choose. If we don't realize this fact, we will be destined to repeat the same type of experiences until we learn to alter our behavior. In effect, we will unknowingly be creating one negative life experience after another for ourselves.

What someone else is doing is none of our business—even if their actions affect us. How we respond to their actions is our business. Our response to any given situation determines the future we will experience. We are in control of our own destiny by controlling our thoughts, emotions, words, and actions. If we let ourselves be lured into replying in anger and revenge, we are activating those types of lower vibrations within ourselves. If we choose to reply with higher emotions, such as love, forgiveness, or even indifference, we are keeping a higher vibration active within ourselves.

It can be difficult to resist responding in anger, hurt, or misery to the person who has offended you, but even if you get revenge, it will still not take away your negative feelings. You may feel better momentarily, but you will realize that seeking revenge made you feel negative inside because negative feelings or negative reactions can never change your initial feelings into better ones. Only higher feelings or emotions can do that. This is the law of perpetual transmutation of energy in effect.

# An Eye for an Eye

*"When seeking revenge, dig two graves, one for yourself."*
—Doug Horton

This is a story of how a Florida boy handled being bullied by two boys.[123] While walking home through a local park, the boy was jumped by two kids who had been bullying him for a long time. Mark had finally had enough of their harassment, and pulled out a knife and killed one of the attackers.

Before the case went to trial, the District Attorney ended up dropping the charges against Mark based on the fact that he acted in self-defense.

Amazingly, instead of the story ending there, it was just getting started. The surviving attacker, Roy, decided that if the legal system didn't punish Mark for killing his friend, then he would seek his own justice.

While driving around town, Roy spotted Mark and started chasing him. Fearing for his life, Mark drove all the way across town to his home, and then ran into his house. Roy chased Mark to his house and ran up onto Mark's property, threatening to assault him. What happens next? Yep, you guessed it; Mark comes out of the house with a gun and shoots Roy dead on his driveway.

After being held in jail awaiting trial, the charges against Mark were again dropped on the basis of self-defense. Apparently the reason for this was that Roy was on Mark's property accosting him at the time of the incident.

Regardless of how you view the legality of this story, Roy and his friend both would not have been killed if they had not chosen to bully Mark. After the first killing, Roy got a second chance with his life, but instead of celebrating that he was not the one killed, he chose to focus on seeking revenge. This kept the negative vibration active, which ultimately manifested in a way that he was killed.

I do not know what happened to Mark. He moved away as a free man, but he was extremely lucky not to spend the rest of his life in prison. Our judicial system is very fickle. I wouldn't want to have the future of my life left in the hands of a jury. It is better to find another way to settle conflicts.

In summary, we are energy and we get back whatever energy we give out through our thoughts, words, and actions. If we seek revenge, we are giving and attracting that same negative energy to ourselves. The only way to heal ourselves is to forgive those who have done us wrong. Don't forgive them for them—forgive them for you.

# Chapter 14: Success

*"The only limits in life are the ones you place on yourself."*
*—Author Unknown*

Success is individual to each person. One person's definition of success might be graduating from high school or college, while another person's definition of success might be becoming a billionaire. You can achieve your desires if you set your mind to it and use the universal laws. Decide what you want to achieve and use the Focus, Feel, and Expect Process or the Nine A's to Acing the Law of Attraction Checklist to make that a reality.

## Key Tips to Creating Success

- Set your ultimate goal as high as you can envision becoming a reality. The energy you attract is proportionate to your desire. Your success is limited only by your imagination so set your ultimate goals high.
- Set smaller goals along the way to give you tastes of success and progress on your way to achieving your main goal.
- Stay focused on achieving your goal. Write down your goals and read them aloud many times daily.
- See setbacks and obstacles as speed bumps to your goal rather than barriers.
- Decide what you are going to give to accomplish your goal.

- When you achieve momentum through success, take advantage of the opportunity to create more momentum. Fight the urge to take a break and rest, or the momentum will fade away.
- Focus on how you feel. It's not about working harder; it's about vibrationally aligning with your desires, through your thoughts, words, and actions to attract what you want into your life. If you feel good, you are aligned with your desires.
- When negativity happens, ignore it and focus on the positives of what you will create. This keeps your vibration and your goals aligned.
- When success comes, be appreciative and make sure to give back to others when opportunities arise. This keeps the goodwill coming back to you.
- Be happy. This keeps your vibration matching your goals.
- Be determined to succeed.
- Be patient to succeed.
- Be dedicated to succeed.
- Have the mindset that you already are successful, but no one knows it yet.

*"I've always been famous, you just didn't know it."*
*—Lady Gaga*

Whatever you decide to desire, just follow the law of attraction and the above tips and you will be on your way to creating your dreams.

Remember that failure is a part of success. Setbacks and obstacles are lessons for us to learn and overcome. When you have a setback, just brush it off, and refocus on your goal. This is where determination and persistence take over. If you want something enough, you can attract it into your life—if you stay focused and ignore the distractions.

When times get tough, you have the option of quitting or refocusing your attention on your goal. Those who can overcome adversity will reap the rewards of success. Adversity is a challenge to overcome. It is only an obstacle to your goal. Find a way around it and proceed with your quest.

Do you want to be successful? Use the law of attraction. The easiest way is to use the Focus, Feel, and Expect Process of focusing on your desire and then feeling how it feels to have it in your life now. If you would like to use the Nine A's to Acing the Law of Attraction Checklist, you can do that in the spaces provided below or in your journal.

Step 1. **Accept your current situation.**

_____

_____

_____

Step 2. **Ask for what you want.**

_____

_____

_____

Step 3. **Align with positivity.**

_____

_____

_____

Step 4. **Avoid negative thoughts and feelings.**

_____

_____

_____

Step 5. **Acknowledge what you are willing to give.**

_____

_____

_____

Step 6. **Allow yourself to be open-minded.**

_____

_____

_____

Step 7. **Agree to be patient and persistent.**

_____

_____

_____

Step 8. **Act when opportunities arise.**

_____

_____

_____

Step 9. **Appreciate when your desire manifests.**

_____

_____

_____

# Chapter 15: Love

*"Love knows no boundaries."*
*—Author Unknown*

Love is a part of us and something we need in our lives whether we realize it or not. Love is tied to our happiness. Most of us will do anything to find or keep love. When we are growing up, we crave the love of our parents and family members. When we get older, we seek the love of a mate. If we have children, we desire the love of our children. Above all, whether we understand it or not, we have a need to love ourselves.

Since everything in life is energy, everything is vibrational, we have the power to attract or repel love—depending on the vibrational frequency we choose for ourselves.

Do you seek love? Have to you taken the time to visualize exactly where and who you want this love to come from? Do you want the love of your parents, children, your lover, the loyal love of your pet, or to love yourself? Figure out what you desire and ask for it mentally and aloud.

If you don't have enough love in your life, you need to ask yourself why that is. Regardless of what anyone has or has not done to you or for you, it is your responsibility to find and keep love for yourself. If you desire love, and you do not have it in your life, it is a direct reflection of your vibrational frequency. You are the answer to your own question. How do you find love? You ask for it, and then you allow it happen.

Some people may say, "That can't be right, I've been asking for love for as long as I remember and it has never come to me. The more I ask for love, the further away it seems to go. I'm so tired of asking, I think I am going to give up on love." Don't worry—the solution is easier than you think. If you have asked for love and it has not come, it can only be because your focus was not aligned with your desires. For some reason, you were not allowing it in your life.

If you were asking for love, but then focusing on why it is not in your life, then you are focusing on the lack of love rather than the future of abundant love that you desire. The law of attraction is tricky—you must learn to stop using your mind to see your current reality as it is and start using it to mentally create the future you want.

As you are waiting for love to manifest, you can monitor your feelings to let yourself know if your vibrational frequency is a match to your desire of love. If you feel good and hopeful, then your vibrational frequency is aligned with your desires. The law of attraction states that your desires cannot manifest for you until you become a vibrational match to them. Currently our world population is estimated to be almost seven billion people. This means the odds are definitely in your favor that there is someone who is perfect for you waiting to meet you right now. Rather than searching the world for this person, use the law of attraction to bring them to you.

## When One Door Closes, Another One Opens

I had been with a girlfriend for years. My friends really liked her and said I should have married her, but I trusted my intuition that was telling me something was not right between us. After we broke up, some of my friends commented that I would never find anyone like her again. While that is true—each person is unique—I had other plans. I set a picture in my mind of the type of person I wanted to meet. She was lean, attractive, brunette, and had a light brown complexion. She would be loyal, smart, funny, fun, and someone who just wanted to be with me. I kept this image in my mind and thought of it many times each day. I was mentally and emotionally over the last relationship, and ready to meet someone new. I applied the law of action to my desires by focusing on myself to become the best I could be. This meant getting into shape, being happy and enthusiastic, and having a positive outlook. I didn't know it at the time, but my vibration matched my desire. Each time I went anywhere, I was excited at the prospect of who I might meet—and if that person might be the one I was searching for. In the past, the period after a breakup was miserable. I usually focused on what was missing in my life, which made things worse.

This time was different. I had learned from past experiences, and I knew that there were a lot of other people to choose from. I was certain that someone out was perfect for me; we just hadn't met yet. I had accepted that I might be single for a while, and so I became comfortable with that. I enjoyed the positive sides of that choice by enjoying my freedom to go and do whatever I wanted whenever I wanted. This acceptance of my situation changed how others saw me. They didn't see me as someone who was suffering—but rather as someone who was enjoying life. This attracted new people to me—people want to be around fun, positive people.

I was open-minded and enjoyed meeting people. I had an idea of the type of person I wanted to meet, but I wasn't going to limit myself to the specifics of my desires. If someone sparked my interest, I would see where it took me.

Two months after the break up, I went out for sushi with a group of friends for my birthday. It was crowded and everyone was having a great time. I turned my head and saw a beautiful brunette walk in the door. Boosted with a little liquid courage, I made my way to meet her through the crowd. I introduced myself, and we hit it off.

As time progressed, we began dating and found that we really enjoyed each other's company. We were a vibrational match. Years later, we married and started a family.

I didn't realize it until years later, but she was almost exactly the person I remember desiring long before I met her. I really feel that I was able to use the law of attraction to bring her into my life. I think it worked because I was never wondering where she was or when she was coming to me. I just enjoyed my life one day at a time knowing that eventually an opportunity to meet her would appear. This carefree attitude kept me from worrying or thinking negative thoughts that would have prevented my desire from coming into my life.

If you want to find love, envision what you want and stay positively focused on it until it comes to you. *The secret is to become so independent that you no longer need your desire to come to you.* You may want it, but you no longer need it. When you get to that point, you will allow your desire to come to you by removing any resistance of fear, impatience, or doubt, and replacing it with your vibrational alignment of positive anticipation.

You may ask, "What happens when I want love from a specific person, but they won't give it to me?" Unfortunately, you can only control yourself and attract people who match your vibrational frequency. You can use the law of attraction to attract cooperative components or other vibrationally matched people into your life, but you can't force someone to think, feel, or do something unless they want to do it themselves.

Love has no boundaries. It can be the love of a spouse; it can be gaining the love and respect of a family member; or it can be caring for another person or animal.

Do you want love? Use the law of attraction. The easiest way is to use the Focus, Feel, and Expect Process of focusing on your desire, and then feeling how it feels to have it right now. If you would like to use the Nine A's to Acing the Law of Attraction Checklist, you can do that in the spaces provided below or in your journal.

Step 1. **Accept your current situation.**

_____

_____

_____

Step 2. **Ask for what you want.**

_____

_____

_____

Step 3. **Align with positivity.**

_____

_____

_____

Step 4. **Avoid negative thoughts and feelings.**

_____

_____

_____

Step 5. **Acknowledge what you are willing to give.**

_____

_____

_____

Step 6. **Allow yourself to be open-minded.**

_____

_____

_____

Step 7. **Agree to be patient and persistent.**

_____

_____

_____

Step 8. **Act when opportunities arise.**

_____

_____

_____

Step 9. **Appreciate when your desire manifests.**

_____

_____

_____

# Chapter 16: Fear

*"Your power ends where you fear begins."*
*-The Path of Empowerment*

Fear is the opposite of love. It has been said that all emotions can be reduced down to just two base emotions: love and fear. If love is the concept of oneness, then fear is the concept being separated from what you want. Fear is a crippling emotion that keeps us from being able to create what we desire. Fear has many faces. Let's take a look at a few:

- Fear of dying
- Fear of flying
- Fear of success
- Fear of failure
- Fear of happiness
- Fear of not being worthy
- Fear of control
- Fear of water
- Fear of money
- Fear of love
- Fear of snakes
- Fear of spiders
- Fear of sharks

Fear can be found anywhere we look for it. Most of us have become good at putting our fear away in the closet of our minds. We do this because it is easier for us to cope with fear by simply ignoring it rather than confronting it. Ignoring this fear may make it bearable in the short run but it also means that it is still a constant companion in our lives. We do not realize how powerful we are and that we have the capacity to create miracles in our own lives. But before that is possible we must first unchain the shackles of fear in our lives. This is necessary because fear is what prevents our desires from manifesting. When you are fearful, you are focused on the negative energy of something you do not want in your life. When you are focused on this negative energy, you are not able to focus on the positive energy that you want to allow into your life. The law of attraction considers your focus on fear to be its command. So it brings more negativity to your life. This is an endless negative circle until you decide to change the pattern of energy by choosing to focus on a new positive desire rather than the fear you are experiencing.

When we experience fears most of us want to run from them, but that is exactly what we should not do. In order for us to become empowered creators of our own lives we must stop running from our fears and instead turn around and embrace them. Fear can only live in the shadows of our mind. When you shine the light of your consciousness on your fears you are bringing them out into the open to be examined. At that point, you are able to ask yourself why you are scared? Most of the times you will find that your fear is unwarranted and then choose to release that fear and create a new and more positive belief about that subject.

Have you ever worried for long periods of time about something that was going to happen only to have the event never actually happen? I think we all have. When an event that we feared doesn't happen we look back and are able to see how much energy we wasted on fear worrying about something that never happened.

In this book we have learned that the only time that is pertinent is the present moment of now. Fear is tied to thoughts of the future or the past. But the past has already happened and the future has not happened yet. When you are experiencing something in the present moment you are usually so busy dealing with that situation that there isn't much room for fear. So focusing on fear is a complete waste of energy.

I used to have a fear of flying. Any type of turbulence put me into an internal state of panic. Eventually I examined the logic behind this fear and realized that the reason I was fearful was because I dreaded being in any situation where I was not in control. Examining my feelings about this fear, I discovered that the origin of this fear went back to a negative childhood experience where I experienced great terror and fear of being out of control on a rollercoaster. This childhood fear followed me into my adult life.

I further dissected the belief I held about this fear to find a solution for it. I decided that unless I was going to become a pilot, I was not going to be in control of the plane while I was a passenger. I conceded this point and then decided to focus on controlling what I could control which was myself. I decided that my fear of control could further be reduced to a fear of dying. So to address this, I accepted that if the plane somehow crashed then I would die, but I made a conscious choice that I would not be afraid of dying anymore. I had discarded my old belief that loss of control meant fear, and replaced it with a new belief that I would only be focused on things I had control over the outcome. If I was in a situation where I was not in control—like being a passenger in an airplane—I would release all resistance and just enjoy the ride. The releasing of the fearful belief was unbelievably empowering.

The last step I used to overcome this fear was to add actions that supported this new belief by flying as much as I could. Each time I went on a plane I would notice how much the plane would bump around while it was taxiing down the runway. The plane usually bounced around more on the ground than it did during the flight. Then anytime we experienced any turbulence in the air I would just tell myself to release my fear and to let go of my need to be in control. I told myself to just ride the ride rather than resisting it. Eventually I got used to normal turbulence to the point where it no longer bothered me. Believe it or not this helped greatly and allowed me to completely overcome this fear. Now when I fly I focus on relaxing and enjoy the ride instead of the fear of what could happen.

In *Path of Empowerment*, it states "Your Power Ends Where Your Fear Begins."[124] It shares that by examining our feelings we can discover the beliefs we hold about any particular subject. Once the limiting belief is known we can use our own free will to discard the old belief and replace it with a new more empowering belief.[125]

## Overcoming Your Fears

Here are some steps for dealing with fear:
1. *Fear.* Acknowledge your fear.
2. *Old Belief.* Review the belief you hold that makes you fearful.
3. *New Belief.* Change the belief to set yourself free.
4. *Supporting Actions.* Add actions that support your new belief.

Here is how I dealt with my fear of flying:

1. *Fear:* I acknowledged that I had a fear of flying.
2. *Old Belief:* I discovered I held a belief that being out of control equaled fear.
3. *New Belief:* I discarded my old belief and replaced it with a new one that believed that it is useless to worry about the outcome of an event you cannot control.
4. *Action:* I added supporting action to this belief by flying as much as possible.

Now you try it. List your fear here:

| *Fear:* |
| --- |
| |
| *Old Belief:* |
| |
| *New Belief:* |
| |
| *Action* |
| |

If you are scared and worried, simply change how you think to change how you feel. How you think is reflective of your beliefs about whatever you are thinking about. If you have trouble changing how you think, you can always use the law of polarity to move from emotion to emotion. You can move from being fearful to being inquisitive to why you feel the way you do. Then you can move to feeling curious as to what it would feel like to leave this fear behind, and after you have faced this fear you can move on to feeling confident that you have confronted this fear. This confidence allows you to change your belief about this fear and change how you think about it. It is no longer something to be feared. It is just an event to experience.

These techniques can be used with any worries or fears you have. If you have fearful issues that are too much or too confusing for you to figure out on your own, you can always get the help of a qualified counselor to help you sort out the details. The bottom line is that in order for you to evolve, grow, and find true happiness you need to address your fears. Once you do this you will notice than many of your problems will dissolve or simply go away.

*"The only thing we have to fear is fear itself."*
*—Franklin D. Roosevelt*

# Chapter 17: Fate / Destiny

*Fate is something that happens to you, destiny is what you make of your fate.*

Fate is an event that is evitable—regardless of the actions we take. We have the free will to affect the outcome of any event, but some events make us wonder why they happened. Did we manifest them through our vibration frequency, were they events that were preplanned before this life that were meant to be some type of tests or learning experiences, or were they just random events?

It has been said that we create 50 percent of our reality through our thoughts, words, and actions, and the remaining 50 percent is co-created through outside influences from the assistance of higher beings and from the collective consciousness of everyone's thoughts and beliefs, which create the reality we experience.[126] If this statement is true, then this means that we have control over 50 percent of what happens to us and the remaining 50 percent of life's events will be out of our control to influence. The truth is that we currently do not have any way of knowing for sure how or why fate plays out in our lives. For example, what happens when a child is born sick or disabled, or when an innocent man goes to prison? Are these events karmic debts that are being repaid for actions in the past, or are they simply new situations for our soul to experience? As we discussed earlier, many of life's challenging events, especially those where the law of attraction doesn't work, may be because our soul wants us to experience different things. These experiences can be positive or negative—depending on the plan your soul has for you.

The good news is that—regardless of whether or not you created the events in your life—you always have an ability to affect the outcome of any event you experience. How you react to what happens to you determines the future of that event in your life. If you spend too much time looking back on your life wondering why this happened or why that happened, you will be making the mistake of putting your focus on the past. If your focus is on something negative, then you are attracting negative energy. Whatever has happened and whatever is happening now is a reality until you do something to change it. Trying to figure out why something has happened can be futile, but when enough time has passed, the meaning or reason for an event often becomes clearer.

Again, whatever has happened has happened. Your current reality is whatever it is. There is nothing you can do about it now. What you can do is start creating the future you desire by focusing on what you want in this present moment. The best way to handle fate is to accept your current reality and then choose how you want to react with your thoughts, emotions, words, and actions to create a new and better future for yourself.

Now is the only time you can create because the past is already gone and the future is not here yet.[127] You can create this future with your thoughts, feelings, words, and actions. Find a way to see whatever has happened to you as positive and you will empower yourself to create the future you desire.

## Did I Cause That?

As I have already listed in this book, I have had quite a few events in my life where I think fate, karma, or life's challenges paid me a visit. Many people don't like the word fate because it implies that we don't have any control over the outcome of these events. We usually don't know why these things happen, but we always have a choice in the outcome based on how we react to these events. They say everything happens for a reason. Let's look at some of the fate events that happened to me during my life and what I learned from these experiences.

Being hit by the car nearly killed me. This experience taught me patience, endurance, perseverance, optimism, acceptance, compassion, and many other great qualities. I don't know why I got hit, but I know that asking why is futile. Instead, I chose to be positive and look for the good in every experience. Had I had a negative outlook, I may have had a much more challenging life than I have had.

Fate may have paid another visit when I was diagnosed with thyroidism. It made me change the direction of my life and got me interested in the subjects that you are reading about in this book. Did my lifestyle cause this disease through the law of cause and effect, or was this disease part of a bigger plan to make me search out and find new ways to live a better life? What if the answer was yes to both of those questions?

Fate may have come to me again when I was at my karate school. I didn't understand why my back injury happened, but I can see that it led me to learn about Qi, Qigong, acupuncture, and other alternative and holistic ways to heal. These are subjects that I didn't know anything about before that injury, but they have become part of who I am. Each day I practice meditation or Qigong, and I strive to live a holistic lifestyle by taking care of and maintaining my body.

Did I do anything to create any of those events that happened in my life? I don't know. Were these fateful events that determined the direction of my life? I think they were. I believe these events were the lessons my soul had for me to accomplish during this life. Regardless of the reason why these events happened, I had a choice in how I reacted to them. I could have made each experience much worse had I had the wrong attitude or focus. I accepted my situation and started working toward the better future I desired. I was able to work through the challenges and found a way to benefit from them. I hope you will choose to accept whatever has happened to you and focus on the future that you wish to create for yourself.

In summary, fate is hard to define and harder to prove. There is not currently a way to know for sure how many of our experiences are caused by our thoughts, words, and actions, and how many are preplanned events by our soul for the purpose of learning a specific lesson. Regardless of the reason for whatever happens to us, we are the ones who control how we react. Our reactions determine the future we experience from those events. This is our destiny. So even though there may be some unplanned events in our lives (fate), we are never powerless to create the future we desire for ourselves (destiny). The secret is to accept whatever has happened to you, and then choose to create a better reality from there. Fate is something that happens to you, destiny is what you make of your fate.

*"Each man is the architect of his own fate."*
*—Appius Claudius (Roman Statesman, 300 BC)*

# Chapter 18: Death

*"We are not human beings on a spiritual journey.*
*We are spiritual beings on a human journey."*
—Pierre Teilhard de Chardin

Death is inevitable. We are all on the same path to eventually end this journey of life. The law of gender says that death is necessary for life to be fully understood. The law of gender states that there need to be two halves of something for either half to be truly experienced. In order for life to be appreciated and lived fully, death must be a part of that equation.

Even though our lives in our physical bodies will eventually end, we will never truly be dead because the law of oneness states that everything is made up of energy. Remember that energy can neither be created nor destroyed, but it can be transformed into something new. When we die, we transform into something else. Some would say we transform into pure positive energy.

It is not in the scope of this book to discuss what happens after we die, so I won't go down that path. What is in the scope of this book is showing how we can live our lives fully and how we can view death in a more positive way.

## The Death of a Loved One

When a loved one dies, family members often mourn them for long periods—sometimes for the rest of their lives. It's understandable and natural to mourn the loss of a loved one for a period of time. We all experience loss and have to go through the grieving process at some point in our lives, but when we stay sad for extended periods of time, we are causing ourselves undue sorrow. When we grieve for someone who is no longer in physical form, we are focused on the lack of them in our lives. When we focus on something that we can't or don't have, it makes us feel emotional distress. This is the law of attraction at work. We owe it to ourselves to focus on feeling better by cleaning up our vibrational frequency by focusing on more pleasant thoughts.

One of the ways to do that is to focus on the pleasant memories of the deceased loved one. In some cases, the loss of a loved one is so emotionally painful that the family doesn't talk about them any longer. This is unfortunate. It's not only okay, but it's healthy to remember the good things about the ones who are no longer with us. They would probably like for you to remember them for the positive parts of their lives. If you were dead and you were somehow watching over your family, would you prefer for your family and friends to worry and be miserable that you are gone, or would you want them to be happy and remember you for the life you lived? Most people would choose the latter. When you let the deceased person go, you allow yourself to heal and move on—and you allow the deceased person to move on.

## In the Process of Dying

Another facet of death is when a loved one is sick and in the process of dying. Family members often plead with the loved one not to leave. What the family members don't realize is that they are thinking of themselves—rather than the person who is dying—because they don't want the loved one to leave them. However, the person who is dying may be ready to end their suffering and take a journey into another part of their existence. They may be hanging on to life solely for your benefit rather than their own. When you experience someone who is suffering and on the verge of dying, think of their wishes rather than your own. Just because they won't be in their physical body any longer doesn't mean they will cease to exist. They will just exist in a different form. All you have to do is think of them—or talk to them—and they will be with you. Remember that energy is everywhere and everything. Since it cannot be destroyed, neither can we.

When it comes to our own death, we can either fear it or accept its eventual inevitability. No one knows how long they have before they die.

The trick is to appreciate your life and to live it fully, rather than wasting your time fearing death. If you are healthy and relatively young, the chances are good that you probably haven't thought about death much. However, if your health has been challenged, you may have thought about death a lot.

## Dealing with Death and Disease

While I battled thyroidism, my health felt like it was spiraling out of control. The heart palpitations and sudden jolts made me feel like I was going to drop dead at any minute. My fear level was off the charts.

Eventually, in an effort to deal with my fear, I decided to accept the worst case scenario—the possibility of my death. I felt helpless to control my health, but I did have control over how I reacted to my fear. To cope, I decided to accept that I could die at any minute. The acceptance of my death allowed me to release my fear and resistance. Don't get me wrong, I didn't give in to dying, I still had a strong desire to live. I simply gave up my focus on the fear of dying. This new mindset allowed me to start focusing on my good health and enjoying my life. As soon as I made that decision, I began to appreciate every second of my life. Sounds became clearer, colors became more beautiful, words were more meaningful, and life was sweeter! Eventually my health improved, allowing me to make a full recovery and live a normal life, but I found it ironic that I had to face the possibility of death to truly learn how to live life.

If you are faced with the fear of death, accept your current situation—the possibility of death—and then choose to focus on creating a new and improved reality of your own good health. Releasing the fear of death may be just what you need to allow the law of attraction to bring your good health to you. Regardless of the outcome, releasing fear can only be good for you. Peace comes when you move fear out of the way.

# Chapter 19: Cooperation versus Competition

*Forget your opponents; the real competition is with yourself.*

Most of us were taught to compete for what we want. We've been taught that there is only so much of whatever we desire so we need to get our share of it before someone else gets it first.

The law of compensation states that there is always enough of whatever we desire. Everything is made of energy and there is never a shortage of that. We can attract whatever we want without having to take it from another. In fact, we are often be able to attract the energy of what we want by helping someone else get what they want rather than competing with them. The law of compensation says that the more you give, the more you receive.

When you see someone in need and you take time to help him or her, you are adding to your own positive energy. Your kindness is often reciprocated by that person who is affected by that kindness. In the future, they may be in a similar situation where they are able to show that same kindness to another person. This is an example of the law of oneness and entanglement where every thought, word, and action affects the rest of the world in ways that are hard for us to fully see or understand. The energy of your act of kindness can live on indefinitely through the kind actions of others that were affected by your initial act of kindness.

One of the secrets of happiness, success, and longevity is in balancing the flow of energy in your life. If you always practice kindness, compassion, and love for yourself and others, you will find that life rewards these behaviors. This is true for competitions and life alike.

So there is never a need to compete with others. There is infinite amount of energy in the universe and this energy can manifest into whatever we desire to attract to our lives. We can excel in our lives by focusing on our own excellence rather than beating opponents or winning a competition. This applies in business, athletics, school, and all other aspects of life.

In reality, all competitions can be reduced down to a personal challenge to be our best. Forget your opponents; the real competition is with yourself. Regardless of how talented a competitor is, we can only affect our own performance. We can focus on our own excellence to manifest the absolute best performance we can give. By focusing on ourselves, we are able to take competition out of the equation and instead focus on our own personal excellence. Personal excellence is a much better attractor of positive energy than desiring our opponents to perform at a lower level. In the end, we create our own reality, success, or happiness. The actions of others are not a factor in our lives—unless we allow them to be. Since we control our own success, there is no reason why we shouldn't wish others well with their endeavors. The energy you attract with your compassion and encouragement may be just what you need to succeed.

# Closing

Now you have learned about the universal laws and how to use your mind to create the reality you desire.

I hope this information has resonated with you. Throughout this book, you have been given the tools to create the life you want. A tool is useless if it is not used—it's up to you to use this information in your life. Remember that you are responsible for yourself. If your life is not exactly the way you want it to be, start making the necessary changes to make it so. Remember that we were meant to be powerful co-creators of our own reality. Start creating the reality you want today!

As stated earlier, I recommend reading this book multiple times, and eventually using it as a reference guide to life because our minds only learn as much information as we are ready to absorb at any given time. After you have read the book once, you will have a new level of understanding. When you read it again, you will learn new things and develop an even greater level of understanding. This is how learning works.

If you have enjoyed this empowering knowledge, you can do your part to help others by telling them about this book and others like it. The more people who awaken to the reality that their thoughts create their reality, the better our world will be.

Visit me online at www.JoeRapisarda.com for updated material, my blog, manifestation life coaching, and other helpful information.

Whether you desire to be rich, happy, and successful, to find love, to be healthy, or anything else, you now have the knowledge to *Awaken Your Power* to make that reality. Remember, the only limits in life are the ones you place on yourself. And with that, I wish you happy and creative life!

# Appendix A.
# Thoughts Are Things Poem

## Thoughts are Things

Whatever you think, whatever you feel,
It doesn't matter if it's make-believe, or if it is real.
Thoughts are things that go out into the unknown
To bring you back whatever you've sown.
Positive thoughts vibrate high,
While negative thoughts vibrate low.
Just focus on your own thoughts to see how your future will go.
You see, your thoughts are a map of where you are headed,
And your feelings decide if that direction is welcome,
Or if it is dreaded.
So change how you think to change how you feel,
And watch how the universe attracts to you,
That which you have made real.

# Appendix B.
# The Universal Laws

**The Law of Oneness**

Everything is made up of the same energy source. Everything is connected. There is no separation from oneness. Anything separate from oneness is an impermanent illusion.

**The Law of Vibration**

Each thought, emotion, word, action, or thing has its own unique energy signature or vibrational frequency.

**The Law of Attraction**

This law states that like-type energy is attracted to itself. Positive energy attracts more positive energy, and negative energy attracts more negative energy. Being human, we are able to choose our own energy and the energy we want to attract through the thoughts, words, and actions we choose for ourselves.

**The Law of Action**

You can help things to manifest in your life by adding actions that complement your desires.

**The Law of Cause and Effect (Karma)**

Energy is circular and attracts itself. Our choices attract back to us the same energy we give out. "What goes around, comes around."

**The Law of Compensation**

The law of compensation says that the energy of our thoughts, words, and actions will come back to us ten times stronger in the future. This can be a positive or negative thing, depending on what we choose for ourselves and others.

**The Law of Perpetual Transmutation of Energy**

Higher vibrational frequencies will always consume and transform lower vibrational frequencies into higher ones, or the lower frequencies will be forced to leave.

**The Law of Relativity**

Our reality is relative to our point of view. We are the ones who determine how the events of our lives affect us.

**The Law of Polarity**

Everything has two poles or opposites. There are many different points of reference along the continuum from one polar-opposite to the other. These points are instrumental in making small manageable changes to move from one place or emotion to another.

**The Law of Rhythm**

This law states that everything in our existence has its own season or flow, and that nature is always seeking to find balance or equilibrium. We can minimize the re-balancing effects of this law by living a balanced life that avoids extreme thoughts, words, or actions.

**The Law of Gender**

Everything has an opposite. Light must have dark in order for us to realize that either exists. This is also called yin and yang by the Chinese. It is up to us to appreciate the need for both sides of everything in our world because we need the contrast of the two sides to understand the meaning of either side. We can use our free will to choose which sides we wish to have in our lives.

**The Law of Correspondence**

All of the universal laws correspond to each other. In reality, it is impossible to use one law by itself because they are all part of each other.

# Appendix C.
# The Focus, Feel, and Expect Process and The Nine A's to Acing the Law of Attraction Checklist

## The Focus, Feel, and Expect Process

Step 1.     *Focus* on what you desire.
Step 2.     *Feel* the good feeling of having that desire in your life.
Step 3.     *Expect* your desire to show up in your life.

## The Nine A's to Acing the Law of Attraction Checklist

Step 1.     *Accept* your current situation.
Step 2.     *Ask* for what you want.
Step 3.     *Align* with positivity.
Step 4.     *Avoid* negative thoughts and feelings.
Step 5.     *Acknowledge* what you are willing to give.
Step 6.     *Allow* yourself to be open-minded.
Step 7.     *Agree* to be patient and persistent.
Step 8.     *Act* when opportunities arise.
Step 9.     *Appreciate* when your desire manifests.

# Appendix D.
# Tips for Troubleshooting the
# Law of Attraction

## Helpful Reminders to Manifest Your Desires:

- Review the Nine A's to Acing the Law of Attraction Checklist.
- Write down your desires and read them aloud multiple times daily.
- Become a vibrational match to your desire by seeing and feeling it as if it were already in your life.
- Find a way to laugh every day—laughter heals the soul.
- Lighten up and be easy going—your mood is reflective in your vibrational frequency.
- Think positive thoughts.
- Feel positive feelings.
- Expect and believe your desires will become a reality.
- Be patient.
- Accept your current situation.
- Make the commitment to see and feel your desired future rather current reality.
- Realize that your mind attracts the energy of your thoughts.
- Use your thoughts as guide to where you are heading.
- Use your feelings to tell you if your direction is desired.
- Realize that *now* is your point of power to create with your thoughts.

- When you can't think positive thoughts about your situation, stop thinking about it, and take a break to allow your mind to get off this subject. You can choose to think about any other subject that makes you feel positive emotions. An example of this might be choosing to think of pleasant memories.
- Remove resistance to remove blockages.
- Use action to create the power of momentum to catapult you to your desires.
- If you feel negatively about a subject, try changing how you think about it to change how you feel about it. Perception is reality.

## Common Manifestation Mistakes:

The following list includes common manifestation mistakes that prevent your desires from manifesting:
- Not asking or focusing on what you want.
- Not focusing on feeling positive emotions.
- Not matching both your desires and your emotions (both need to be positive).
- Asking for what you want too many times. Asking and aligning are two different vibrational frequencies. Focus on what it feels like to have your desire already in your life and you will become a vibrational match to it. This will allow you to align with your desire and allow it to manifest in your life.
- Being fearful. Fear prevents desires from manifesting.
- Focusing on the negativity of the reality you are currently experiencing rather than the future you desire.
- Not having enough patience to stay focused on your desire long enough for it to manifest.
- Being too action-focused to allow your desire to come to you. Sometimes it takes the patience to do nothing while you wait for an opportunity to come to you.
- Not acting when opportunities arise. Waiting is good, but you need to be ready to act when opportunity knocks at your door.
- Being inconsistent with your thoughts and emotions by being hopeful and positive one minute, and then worried and fearful the next. You need to be consistent with your positive thoughts.

- Using your mind as a video recorder to simply record your life as it is happening rather than using your mind to envision and create the future you wish to be.
- Not seeing and feeling your desired future as if it was already here.
- Not believing your desires will come true.
- Not using strong enough positive emotions to manifest your desires (I want it versus I know it will come to me).

# Works Cited

Andrews, Synthia, and Colin Andrews. *2012: An Ancient Look at a Critical Time*. New York: Penguin Group, 2008.

Armstrong, Lance, and Saly Jenkins. *It's Not About The Bike: My Journey Back to Life*. New York: The Berkley Publishing Group, 2001.

Ball, Ron. *Freedom At Your Fingertips: Get Rapid Physical And Emotional Relief With The Breakthrough System of Tapping*. Fredericksburg: Inroads Publishing, 2006.

Braden, Gregg. *The Spontaneous Healing of Belief*. Carlsbad: HAY HOUSE, INC., 2008.

Canfield Jack, Hansen Mark Victor. *A 3rd Serving of Chicken Soup for the Soul: "The Cookie Thief" By Valerie Cox*. Deerfield Beach: HCI, The Life Issues Publisher, www.hcibooks.com., 1996.

*What the Bleep!? - Down the Rabbit Hole (QUANTUM Three-Disc Special Edition)*. Directed by Betsy Chasse and Mark Vicente. August 1, 2006.

Emoto, Masaru. "The Hidden Messages in Water." In *The Hidden Messages in Water*, by Masaru Emoto. Hillsboro: Beyond Words Publishing, 2001.

Gawain, Shakti. *Creative Visualization: Use the Power of Your Imagination to Create What You Want in Your Life*. Novato: Nataraj Publishing, 2002.

Greene, Brian. "The Elegant Universe: Superstrings, Hidden Diminisions, and the Quest for the Ultimate Theory." New York: W.W. Norton & Company, 1999.

Hawking, Stephen. "The Universe in a Nutshell." New York: Bantam Books, 2001.

Hay, Louise L. *You Can Heal Your Life.* Carlsbad: Hay House, Inc., 2004.

Hicks, Esther and Jerry. *Ask and It Is Given.* Carlsbad: HAY HOUSE, INC., 2004.

Hill, Napoleon. *Think and Grow Rich.* New York: Penguin Group, 2005.

Jung, C.G. *The Archetypes and the Collective Unconscious.* Princeton: Princeton University Press, 1981.

Kribbe, Pamela. *The Jeshua Channelings: Christ consciousness in a new era.* www.jeshua.net, 2008.

Marciniak, Barbara. *Path of Empowerment: Pleiadian Wisdom For A World In Chaos.* Novato: New World Library, 2004.

McKay, Dr. Noah. *Wellness At Warp Speed.* San Rafael: Mandala Publishing, 2007.

McTaggart, Lynne. *The Field: The Quest For The Secret Force of The Universe.* New York: HarperCollins Publishers Inc., 2002.

Milanovich, J. Norma, and Shirley D. McCune. *The Light Shall Set You Free.* Alburquerque: Athena Publishing, 1996.

Moring, Gary F. *The Complete Idiot's Guide to Understanding Einstein.* New York: Penguin Group (USA) Inc., 2004.

Murphy, Joseph D.D, D.R.S., Ph.D., LL.D. *The Miracle of Mind Dynamics.* Paramus: Reward Books, www.phdirect.com, 1964.

Orleane, Rebecca Smith, PHD, and Cullen Baird Smith. *Conversations With Laarkmaa: A Pleiadian View Of The New Reality.* Bloomington: AuthorHouse, 2010.

Oxford University Press. *The New English Bible.* Oxford University Press, Cambridge University Press, 1961,1970.

Peirce, Penney. In *frequency,* by Penney Peirce. Hilllsboro: Beyond Words Publishing, 2009.

Schwartz, Robert. *Your Soul's Plan: Discovering the Real Meaning of the Life You Planned Before You Were Born*. Berkeley: North Atlantic Books, 2009.

Siegel, Daniel J. *The Mindful Brain: Reflection and Attunement in the Cultivation of Well-Being*. New York: W.W. Norton & Company, 2007.

Stewart, Jeff. *E=mc2: Simple Physics Why Balloons Rise, Apples Fall, and Golf Balls Go Awry*. Pleasantville: The Reader's Digest Association, Inc., 2010.

*Navy SEALs*. Directed by Lewis Teague. July 20, 1990.

Tolle, Eckhart. *The Power of Now: A Guide to Spiritual Enlightenment*. Vancouver: Namaste Publishing, 2004.

Travis S. Taylor, Ph.D. *The Science Behind The Secret: Decoding The Law of Attraction*. New York: Baen Publishing Enterprises, 2010.

Walker, Thomas, D.C. "The Force Is with Us: The Higher Consciousness That Science Refuses to Accept." In *The Force Is with Us: The Higher Consciousness That Science Refuses to Accept*, by D.C. Thomas Walker. Wheaton: Quest Books, 2009.

Webster, Richard. *Miracles: Inviting the Extraordinary Into Your Life*. St. Paul: Llewellyn Publications, 2004.

—. *Pendulum Magic for Beginners: Power to Achieve All Goals*. Woodbury: Llewellyn, 2007.

Zukav, Gary. *The Dancing Wu Li Masters: An Overview of the New Physics*. New York: HarperCollins Publishers, 2001.

# Suggested Reading

Einstein, Albert. *The Meaning of Relativity.* Fifth Edition. Princeton: Princeton University Press, 1966. Print.

Al-Khalili, Jim. *Quantum: A Guide for the Perplexed.* New York: Weidenfeld and Nicolson, 2003. Print.

Arntz, William, Betsy Chasse, and Mark Vincente. *What the Bleep Do We Know!?* Deerfield Beach: Health Communications, Inc, 2005. Print.

Bohm, David. *The Undivided Universe: An Ontological Interpretation of Quantum Theory.* New York: Routledge, 1993. Print.

Capra, Fritjof. *The Tao of Physics: An Exploration of the Parallels between Modern Physics and Eastern Mysticism.* 5th. Boston: Shambala Publications, Inc., 2010. Print.

Chopra, Deepak, MD *Quantum Healing: Exploring the Frontiers of Mind/body Medicine.* New York: Bantam Books, 1989. Print.

Chopra, Deepak, MD *Unconditional Life: Discovering the Power to Fulfill Your Dreams.* New York: Bantam Books, 1992. Print.

Fayer, Michael D., PhD *Absolutely Small.* New York: Amacom, 2010. Print.

Freud, Sigmund. *The Ego and the Id.* New York: W.W. Norton and Company, Inc., 1960. Print.

Goswami, Amit, PhD *Physics of the Soul: The Quantum book of Living, Dying, Reincarnation, and Immortality.* Charlottesville: Hampton Roads Publishing Company, Inc., 2001. Print.

Gubser, Steven. *The Little Book of String Theory*. Princeton: Princeton University Press, 2010. Print.

Hawking, Stephen. *The Universe in a Nutshell*. New York: Bantam Books, 2001. Print.

Karges, Craig. *Ignite Your Intuition: Improve Your Memory, Make Better Decisions, Be More Creative and Achieve Your Full Potential*. Deerfield Beach: Health Communications, Inc, 1999. Print.

Lipton, Bruce H., PhD *The Biology of Belief: Unleashing the Power of Consciousness, Matter, and Miracles*. Calsbad: Hay House, Inc., 2008. Print.

Lorentz, H.A., et al. *The Principle of Relativity*. U.S.: Methuen and Company, Ltd., 1923. Print.

Moore, Pete. *E=MC²: The Great Ideas That Shaped Our World*. New York: Sterling Publishing Company, Inc., 2002. Print.

Musser, George. *The Complete Idiot's Guide to String Theory*. New York: Penguin Group, 2008. Print.

Price, Robert. *Top Secret: The Truth Behind Today's Pop Mysticisms*. New York: Prometheus Books, 2008. Print.

Riley, D.R. *Waves*. London: The Macmillan Press LTD, 1974. Print.

Sheldrake, Rupert. *The Presence of the Past: Morphic Resonance and the Habits of Nature*. New York: Random house, Inc., 1988. Print.

Slitchter, Charles, Prof. *The Principle of Magnetic Resonance*. New York: Harper and Row Publishers, 1963. Print.Stewart, Jeff. *E=MC²*. Pleasantville: Reader's Digest Association, Inc., 2010. Print.

Talbot, Michael. *The Holographic Universe*. New York: HarperCollins Publishers Inc., 1991. Print.

Wheland, George. *The Theory of Resonance: And Its Application to Organic Chemistry*. New York: John Wiley and Sons, Inc., 1945. Print.

Wolfe, David, and Nike Good. *Amazing Grace*. San Diego: Sunfood Publishing, 2008. Print.

Yogananda, Parmahansa. *Autobiography of a Yogi*. 12th ed. Los Angeles: Self-Realization Fellowship, 1994. Print.

Zimmerman Jones, Andrew, and Daniel Robbins PhD. *String Theory for Dummies*. Hoboken: Wiley Publishing, Inc., 2010. Print.

# Glossary

## Affirmations

Affirmations are emotionally charged written statements of what you desire that are read consistently day after day to help program the subconscious mind.

## Balance

Nature is about maintaining balance. When life gets unbalanced, nature will always eventually take corrective actions to restore balance.

## Balance Wheel

This is a tool that helps to itemize the important parts of your life so that each part gets enough focus and attention to thrive and grow. It promotes a balanced lifestyle.

## Change

Change is the one constant in the world. How we adapt to change depends on how we experience our reality.

## Conscious Mind

The conscious mind (middle self) is the mind we use to think with each day. It is our consciousness. It is the mind that most of us associate with who we are. The conscious mind is in charge of thinking and logic. It is the consciously awake part of you that makes conscious decisions. The conscious mind sends orders to the subconscious mind (lower self) through its thoughts and feelings.

## Conservation of Energy

This physics law states that the amount of energy in a system remains constant. This means that energy cannot be created or destroyed, but it can change forms.

## Double Slit Experiment

Sometimes called the Thomas Young experiment, this experiment shows that energy behaves both as waves of formless energy and as particles of matter. It was also shown that this energy is intelligent and is able to change how it acts based on the observation and expectation of an observer. This supports the claim of this book that our thoughts create reality.

## Ego

The ego is the conscious part of each of us that strives to stand out and be different. The ego is best served when it is kept under control so that a balance between individuality and oneness can be found.

## Emotions

Consistent emotions are your guide to what type of energy you are attracting. Positive emotions mean you are aligned with energy that supports your desires. Negative emotions mean you are aligned with energy that is probably not desired. Consistent emotions are a precursor to manifestation.

## Entanglement

Quantum entanglement, or non-locality as it is often called, happens when subatomic particles that have originally interacted with each other are able to affect each other even if they are separated by space and time. This gives support to the law of oneness, which states that everything in our existence is connected.

## Frequency

Frequency refers to the number of up-and-down cycles of oscillation that a wave completes every second. *See Vibrational Frequency.*

## The Focus, Feel, and Expect Process

This is the simplified process of using the law of attraction to manifest thoughts into reality. Focus on what you desire, feel with desire what it will feel like to have that desire in your life, and expect it to show up in your life.

## Forgiveness

Forgiveness is the act of letting go of the negative energy of the actions of another person.

## Higher Self

*See Superconscious Mind.*

## Intuition

Intuition is the ability to be able to sense something without knowing exactly how it is being sensed. It involves feeling the energy of a person, place, or thing.

## Kenpo Jiu-Jitsu Karate

Kenpo Jiu-Jitsu Karate is a martial art consisting of both stand-up and grappling self-defense techniques.

## Law of Oneness

Everything is made up of the same energy source. Everything is connected. There is no separation from oneness. Anything separate from oneness is an impermanent illusion.

## Law of Vibration

Each thought, emotion, word, action, or thing has its own unique energy signature or vibrational frequency.

## Law of Attraction

This law states that like-type energy is attracted to itself. This means that positive energy attracts more positive energy, and negative energy attracts more negative energy. Being human, we are able to choose the vibrational frequency of our own energy through our thoughts, words, and actions, which aligns us with the type of energy we attract to ourselves.

## Law of Action

You can help things to manifest in your life by adding actions that complement your desires.

## Law of Cause and Effect (Karma)

Energy is circular and attracts itself. Our choices attract back to us the same energy we give out. "What goes around, comes around."

## Law of Compensation

The law of compensation says that the energy of our thoughts, words, and actions will come back to us ten times stronger in the future. This can be a positive or negative thing, depending on whether we choose positive or negative energy for ourselves and others.

## Law of Perpetual Transmutation of Energy

Higher vibrational frequencies will always consume and transform lower vibrational frequencies into higher ones, or the lower frequencies will be forced to leave.

## Law of Relativity

Our reality is relative to our point of view. We are the ones who determine how the events of our lives affect us.

## Law of Polarity

Everything has two poles or opposites. There are many different points of reference along the continuum from one polar-opposite to the other. These points are instrumental in making small manageable changes to move from one place or emotion to another.

## Law of Rhythm

This law states that everything in our existence has its own season or flow, and that nature is always seeking to find balance or equilibrium. We can minimize the re-balancing effects of this law by living a balanced life that avoids extreme thoughts, words, or actions.

## Law of Gender

Everything has an opposite. Light must have dark in order for us to realize that either exists. This is also called yin and yang by the Chinese. It is up to us to appreciate the need for both sides of everything in our world because we need the contrast of the two sides to understand the meaning of either side. We can use our free will to choose which sides we wish to have in our lives.

## Law of Correspondence

All of the universal laws correspond to each other. In reality, it is impossible to use one law by itself because they are all part of each other.

## Lower Self

*See Subconscious Mind.*

## Meditation

Meditation is the art of quieting the mind to receive insight and wisdom from higher intelligence.

## Middle Self

*See Conscious Mind.*

## Morphic Resonance

The idea that the thoughts, words, or actions of one person are added to the universal consciousness in a morphic field that is able be absorbed and used by others with the same vibrational frequency—regardless of time or distance between the parties, or even if they know of each other.

## Nine A's to Acing the Law of Attraction Checklist

This is a step-by-step process for learning to successfully influence the law of attraction.

# Now

Now is your point of creative power. The present was created by thoughts from the past and the future is created by the thoughts of now.

# Qi (Chee)

The life force energy in all things throughout the universe.

# Resonance

Two vibrational frequencies of two or more things align and interact with each other.

# String Theory

This premise of this theory is that every atom, at its most basic level, is composed of vibrating strings that act like a DNA code that tells energy how to manifest into reality.

# Subconscious Mind

The subconscious mind (lower self) lives beneath our conscious awareness. It is in charge of physically manifesting the desires of the conscious mind. It deals with our feelings and emotions. The subconscious mind acts as an intermediary between the conscious mind and the superconscious mind by taking instructions from the conscious mind in the form of focused thoughts and feelings and relaying them to the superconscious mind to create that physical reality.

# Superconscious Mind

The superconscious mind (higher self) is also known as the universal mind, the collective unconscious, the higher self, or spiritual self. This superconscious mind is the divine part of each person. This mind has the power to manifest thoughts into reality. The subconscious mind communicates desires to the superconscious mind, which then manifests those desires into reality.

# Mass-Energy Equivalence

Einstein's famous formula $E=mc^2$ states that energy and matter are equivalent to each other. I believe that they are the same thing. This gives support to the law of oneness that states that everything in our existence is made up of the same energy.

## Time Delay

This is the period of time between when a thought is desired and when it shows up as a reality.

## Universal Laws

Laws of Nature that are energy based. These laws promote balance throughout the universe. Humans can use these laws, through their thoughts, words, and actions to become empowered creators of their own destiny.

## Vibrational Frequency (a.k.a. Vibration, or Frequency)

Each person, place, and thing has its own unique vibrational frequency that acts like a DNA code, telling energy how to manifest into formless energy or physical matter. We as humans have the ability to determine our own frequency by the thoughts, words, and actions we choose for ourselves. These frequencies then determine what energy we align with and attract to ourselves using the law of attraction.

## Wave-Particle Duality

Energy has the ability to travel as both waves of energy and particles of matter.

## Wavelength

The distance between successive peaks or successive troughs of the waves.

# Notes

## Preface

1. www.skylinedesigns.yolasite.com
2. www.wisdomandpeace.com
3. Permission for the "Thought are Things" title was given by Napoleon Hill Foundation.

## Introduction

4. http://www.merriam-webster.com/dictionary/luck

## Chapter 1

5. Milanovich and McCune, *The Light Shall Set You Free.*
6. In my initial Internet search into the universal laws, I found that some sources listed universal laws that were different than the twelve universal laws I had read about in *The Light Shall Set You Free.* I have not researched these additional laws and would suggest testing their validity by testing them out in your own life. The proof is in how they affect your life.
7. McTaggart, *The Field, XIII.*
8. Critics have argued that they have been unable to duplicate Emoto's work in the laboratory. I personally do not know if these claims are true or not, but I will say that Emoto's teachings, if correct, give us some excellent visual examples of how our thoughts affect our physical reality. Emoto also has a

unique ability to give clear and easy-to-understand definitions of vibrational frequencies and resonance.

9. Note: Throughout this book the term vibration, frequency, and vibrational frequency are all meant to have the same meaning.

10. Ibid., 376

11. Emoto, *The Hidden Messages in Water*, 39.

12. Ibid., 40.

13. Ibid., 41.

14. Ibid., 42.

15. Peirce, *Frequency*, XV.

16. Greene, *The Elegant Universe, 89.*

17. Andrews, *2012*, 106.

18. Emoto, *The Miracle of Water*, 32.

19. Ibid., 33.

20. http://www.merriam-webster.com/concise/resonance

21. Emoto, *The Miracle of Water*, 53–54.

22. The topic of time delay for manifestation will be discussed further Part 2 of this book under the section on Time Delay.

23. Moore, $E=mc^2$, 35.

24. The police officer and a newspaper article stated the car was going sixty miles per hour, but the driver, years later, disputed that by declaring that the car was traveling at a speed closer to twenty-five miles per hour.

25. Hicks, Ask and It Is Given.

26. http://en.wikipedia.org/wiki/Chronic_stress

## Chapter 2

27. McKay, *Wellness at Warp Speed*, 73.

28. Moore, $E=mc^2$, 37.

29. Mckay, *Wellness at Warp Speed, 74.*

30. For the remainder of the book when I use the term matter it is meant to be interchangeable between mass and matter.

31. McTaggart, *The Field*, 33.

32. Zukav, The Dancing Wu Li Masters, 136.

33. Critics might argue that energy and matter are equivalent, but not the same thing. I agree that matter does not always mean solid mass, but feel that, at its most basic level, all mass or matter is energy.

34. Mckay, *Wellness at Warp Speed*, 70.
35. Braden, *The Spontaneous Healing of Belief.*
36. Stewart, $E=mc^2$, 167.
37. http://en.wikipedia.org/wiki/Quantum_entanglement
38. Stewart, $E=mc^2$, *167.*
39. Ibid.
40. Ibid.
41. Taylor, *The Secret Behind The Secret*, 185.
42. http://en.wikipedia.org/wiki/Double-slit_experiment
43. If you are interested in learning more about this experiment, there is a great and simple animated cartoon by Dr. Fred Alan Wolfe as Dr. Quantum. It is from the DVD *What the Bleep!? Down the Rabbit Hole (QUANTUM Three-Disc Special Edition).* You can also find it at www.youtube.com by typing into the search box "Dr Quantum—Double Slit Experiment." This video does the explanation of this experiment justice and is more fun and easier to understand than other explanations.
44. Braden, *The Spontaneous Healing of Belief.*
45. Moring, *The Complete Idiot's Guide to Understanding Einstein*, 349–350.
46. McTaggart, *The Field*, XVI.
47. Emoto, *The Hidden Messages in Water*, 39.
48. Ibid., 40.
49. Taylor, *The Secret Behind The Secret*, 123–124.
50. *The Science Behind The Secret* states that coherence is the condensation in which particles become unified and act collectively as a single larger entity. It's a correlation between the phases of two or more waves so that interference effects may be produced between them, or a correlation between the phases of parts a single wave. The Merriam-Webster dictionary states that cohere is to hold together firmly as parts of the same mass; broadly: stick, adhere.
51. Taylor, *The Secret Behind The Secret,* 114.
52. Ibid., 108.
53. Ibid.
54. Greene, *The Elegant Universe*, 3.
55. Ibid., *15.*
56. Ibid., 15–16.

## Chapter 3

57. http://www.merriam-webster.com/dictionary/coincidence
58. Webster, *Miracles*, 59–64.
59. Moore, *E=mc²*, 187.
60. Webster, *Miracles*, 63.
61. Ibid.
62. Hill, *Think and Grow Rich*, 230.
63. Webster, *Miracles*, 63.
64. Jung, *The Archetypes and the Collective Unconscious*, 43.
65. Gawain, *Creative Visualization*, 53.
66. Hill, *Think and Grow Rich*, 14.
67. Hicks, *Ask and It Is Given*.

## Chapter 4

68. http://www.merriam-webster.com/dictionary/alchemy
69. www.merriam-webster.com/dictionary/belief
70. http://en.wikipedia.org/wiki/Faith
71. Oxford University Press, *The New English* Bible, Mark 11:23–24.
72. Ibid., Matthew 13:12.
73. Ibid., Luke 17:21.
74. Tolle, *The Power of Now*.
75. Emoto, *The Hidden Messages in Water*.
76. http://twitter.com/#!/McIloryRory/status/57467512161447937
77. Milanovich and McCune, *The Light Shall Set You Free*, 373.
78. www.drlwilson.com.
79. Teague, Navy SEALs, 1990.
80. A *kata* is series of karate moves choreographed together in succession to help the student remember the techniques.
81. A "gi" (pronounced "ghee") is a karate training uniform.
82. Pamela Kribbe is one such channel who claims to channel Jeshua (Jesus) (www.jeshua.org). Some other popular examples of channels are *Law of Attraction* teacher, Esther Hicks, who claims to channel a group of non-physical entities called "Abraham" (www.abraham-hicks.com), Jane Roberts who claimed to channel the non-physical entity "Seth," and

Doreen Virtue who claims to channel angels (http://www. angeltherapy.com ).

83. Schwartz, *Your Soul's Plan*, 21.

84. Ibid., 30.

85. Ibid., 31.

86. Ibid., 24.

87. http://www.jeshua.net

88. Ibid.

89. Ibid.

## Chapter 5

90. Moring, *The Complete Idiot's Guide to Understanding Einstein*, 286.

91. http://www.merriam-webster.com/dictionary/hunch

92. http://www.merriam-webster.com/dictionary/egotism

93. Milanovich and McCune, *The Light Shall Set You Free*, 152.

94. http://en.thinkexist.com/quotation/unfortunately-the-hangover-from-the-market-bubble/655972.html

95. Hill, *Think and Grow Rich*, 14.

96. Canfield and Hansen, *A 3rd Serving of Chicken Soup for the Soul:* "The Cookie Thief" By Valerie Cox.

97. The text being reprinted in "The Cookie Thief Story" is a paraphrase of the original.

## Chapter 7

98. This is an Internet story that was sent to me via email. The author of this version is unknown, but http://www.snopes.com/glurge/kyle.asp states that this is a changed internet version of "A Simple Gesture" written by John W. Schlatter that appears in the 1993 book, *Chicken Soup for the Soul*.

99. Gawain, *Creative Visualization*, 76.

100. Hay, *You Can Heal Your Life*, 123.

101. Ibid., 215-224.

102. Murphy, *The Miracle of Mind Dynamics*, 26.

103. Ibid., 27.

104. Ibid.

105. Ibid., 28.

106. Ibid., 29.

107. Ibid.

108. Ibid., 25.

109. Armstrong and Jenkins, *It's Not About the Bike.*

110. www.livestrong.org

111. www.jeshua.net/lightworker/jeshua8.htm

112. www.MosesNutrition.com

113. Ball, *Freedom at Your Fingertips*, 1.

114. My experience with this program was at www.drlwilson.com and www.mosesnutrition.com.

115. http://www.scenar.info/index.html

116. The Rife Machine claims to be able to destroy a number of different pathogens, including cancer.

117. Walker, *The Force is With Us*, 139.

## Chapter 9

118. http://www.baseball-almanac.com/quotes/luke_appling_quotes.shtml

## Chapter 10

119. http://www.brainyquote.com/quotes/authors/s/sun_tzu_2.html

## Chapter 11

120. An exception to this may be those who suffer from chemical imbalances, clinical depression, or mental illnesses. Medical attention can usually help those individuals.

121. http://thinkexist.com/quotation/the_happiest_of_people_don-t_necessarily_have_the/309436.html

## Chapter 12

122. http://www.merriam-webster.com/dictionary/stress

## Chapter 16

123. Some of the details of this story have been changed to protect the identity of the people involved.

124. Marciniak, *Path of Empowerment*, Novato, 115.
125. Ibid., 112.
126. Orleane and Smith, *Conversations with Laarkmaa*, Bloomington, 249.
127. Tolle, *The Power of Now*.